**ACTFL**
Language Connects

Connect with your world language community

Discover a network of support with ACTFL and connect with thousands of language educators worldwide.

Memberships start at just $45

JOIN ACTFL TODAY AND GET:

- Professional Development
- ACTFL Convention discounts
- Must-read publications
- Access to members-only teaching resources
- And much more!

 actfl.org

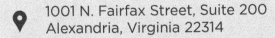 1001 N. Fairfax Street, Suite 200
Alexandria, Virginia 22314

 membership@actfl.org

 (703) 894-2900

PROFICIENCY-BASED INSTRUCTION

Input & Interaction in World Language Education

Catherine Ritz
Christina Toro

Dedication

To our children and to working mothers everywhere

ISBN: 978-1-942544-73-9
© 2022, ACTFL
1001 North Fairfax Street, Suite 200
Alexandria, VA 22314

Cover: istockphoto/RLT_Images

Acknowledgments

When schools were shut down in the spring of 2020, teachers were tasked with adapting the way they teach on a moment's notice. This forced all of us to pause and reflect on how we had been teaching and how we would have to adapt. It was an opportunity for us to go back to the basics and focus on our methodology while learning how to leverage new technology tools. It was during this time that this book came together.

We would like to thank Paul Sandrock and Howie Berman of ACTFL for their support of this project when it was still in its infancy. We are grateful for your faith in us and your guidance along the way.

We are deeply indebted to the hard work of our *Classroom Close-Up* contributors. Their work has inspired us, and we are thrilled to highlight their lessons in this book. Thank you to Borja Ruiz de Arbulo Alonso, Bárbara Barnett, Katrina Griffin, Yingmin He, Allison Litten, Sheng-Chu Lu, Victoria Pascual, Katie Quackenbush, Nicole Russo, and Ikuko Yoshida. Thank you as well to Xiaoyan Hu for contributing a lesson example, which, although not featured in this book, was an excellent example of proficiency-based instruction.

We would also like to thank the many teachers who contributed the examples of strategies or other classroom materials that are featured throughout this book: Zack Bagan, Francesca Crutchfield-Stoker, Maria DiPietro, Khadija Tlaiti, and Mike Travers. Thank you for sharing your amazing work!

We would like to especially thank our reviewers, who encouraged us on this journey and provided invaluable feedback and insights that have greatly strengthened the final version of this book: Victoria Gilbert, Mary Redmond, and Karen Tharrington.

We would also like to acknowledge that many of the images in this book came from Pixabay.com and Pexels.com, which provide a wealth of royalty-free images.

Christina would like to recognize her children—Samuel, Alex, Benjamin, and Kathleen—who motivate her to be better and to make a difference in the world; her husband, Jorge, who encourages her to chase her dreams and has taught her so much about his country of Colombia; her parents, Michael and Kathleen Berry, for their constant love, support, and inspiration; and her teachers George Watson, Linda Segal, and Robin Stuart, who were important figures in her language studies and now serve as her role models.

Catherine would like to acknowledge the unwavering support of her husband, Romain, and her children, Adrien, Emma, and Mae. She would also like to acknowledge the students in her Methods of Teaching Modern Foreign Languages course at Boston University, from whom she has learned much more than she feels she has taught. A few of her students have their amazing lessons included in these pages!

Finally, we would like to acknowledge the many professional organizations which have been sources of learning and growth for us throughout our careers as language educators, in particular the Massachusetts Foreign Language Association (MaFLA), the Northeast Conference on the Teaching of Foreign Languages (NECTFL), and, of course, ACTFL.

TABLE OF CONTENTS

CHAPTER 1

Introduction and Foundational Understandings

I n this book, our goal is to equip teachers of any language and of any level with specific, practical, and straightforward tools to bring input and interaction to life in the classroom. Teaching for proficiency is fun and engaging for both students and their teachers, and the practices that are found in proficiency-based classrooms—while they may appear daunting at first—are easily implemented with the right guidance. Whether you are an experienced teacher looking to shift your practice toward proficiency-based instruction, or a beginning teacher just starting on your teaching journey, you will find numerous resources in this book to support your teaching—coupled with sample lessons from real teachers' classrooms—that will make proficiency-based teaching a reality for you and your students.

While we believe that proficiency-based instruction leads to stronger student learning outcomes across all age groups and levels, we also feel strongly that it can help address issues of inequity and inequality in our classrooms. In many ways, the world language teaching profession is at a critical juncture. Will language learning continue to be viewed as "elite" and unattainable for the many students who have experienced the traditional grammar-driven approach or simply not had access to our courses? Or will teachers embrace proficiency-based instruction and teaching for equity, justice, and sustainability to ensure that *every student* has access to and is successful in language classrooms? Disparities in access to world language education are evident for different racial groups and genders (Baggett, 2016; Murphy & Lee, 2019; National Center for Education Statistics, 2017, qtd. in Glynn & Wassell, 2018, p. 19), and more private schools offer world language programs (particularly at the elementary level) than public schools (Pufahl & Rhodes, 2011). Students of color withdraw from language courses with more frequency than white students, and many are discouraged from even enrolling through counseling (Glynn & Wassell, 2018; Pratt, 2012). Teachers must examine their own implicit biases around who can succeed in world language learning, as well as take a close look at their curriculum. The curriculum that teachers engage students with must be culturally relevant and culturally sustaining, allowing all students to see themselves in the curriculum while also engaging with other cultures. We encourage our readers to explore *Words and Actions: Teaching Languages Through the Lens of Social Justice* (Glynn, Wesley, & Wassell, 2014) to begin the important work of reframing the curriculum to teach for social justice.

For students who are enrolled in language courses, do all learners have access to a similar quality of instruction? Morris (2005) found that teachers "reserved communicative teaching for elite students," while students in non-honors tracks experienced more teaching in English, more drill-based activities, and more worksheets (p. 236). This finding supports our own experiences as world language teachers, where we regularly observed lower expectations for non-honors classes, stemming from beliefs that "those students" just wouldn't be successful. As Morris states, "foreign language educators must act to ensure that all learners have the opportunity to actually learn a language—not merely to study one" (2005, p. 247). We couldn't agree more. Proficiency-based instruction can provide the tools teachers need to ensure that students of all levels can experience success in their classes.

Reframing the curriculum to teach for social justice provides an opportunity to make world language education relevant and engaging for all learners, while affirming and sustaining their wonderfully diverse cultural identities and backgrounds. Retooling classroom practices to teach for proficiency equips teachers with the frameworks and strategies needed to provide high-quality instruction for all learners and at all levels. Teaching for social justice and proficiency-based instruction offers huge potential for world language education that is impactful, relevant, and effective and will help language teachers unlock the incredible potential of their learners. We hope the strategies and models of instruction presented in this book can be paired with a framework of teaching for equity and inclusion so that proficiency in another language can become a reality for all learners.

Foundations of Proficiency-Based Instruction

The ACTFL Proficiency Guidelines

Teaching for proficiency starts with a clear focus on the ACTFL Proficiency Guidelines (ACTFL, 2012), with the goal of supporting students in developing their proficiency with the target language. These guidelines help teachers describe and recognize what learners *can do* with language at different major proficiency levels: Novice, Intermediate, Advanced, Superior, and Distinguished. Each of these proficiency levels except for Superior and Distinguished is broken down into three sub-levels: Low, Mid, and High. Figure 1.1 provides a graphic visualization of the proficiency levels and sub-levels. These levels can help you be more precise in understanding what students can do with language as they progress through your program. While a deep dive into the ACTFL Proficiency Guidelines is beyond the scope of this book, we invite you to dig into some of the resources included in the *Level Up Your Learning* section at the end of this chapter for more information, and to consult Appendix A, which includes the can-do descriptors for each proficiency level from the NCSSFL-ACTFL Can-Do Statements (ACTFL, 2017). We want to highlight that teaching for proficiency focuses first and foremost on what learners *can do* with language, not simply what learners *know about* language. Teaching for proficiency means that grammar is a tool for communication, not the primary focus or goal of instruction.

The World-Readiness Standards for Learning Languages

Teaching for proficiency also asks you to build your curriculum and focus your instruction on the World-Readiness Standards for Learning Languages (National Standards Collaborative Board, 2015), which center around the 5 Cs: Communication, Cultures, Connections, Comparisons, and Communities (Figure 1.2). The World-Readiness Standards for Learning Languages guide curriculum and instruction.

While each of the 50 states in the United States directs the standards or curriculum frameworks for education within the state, a majority of states have either adopted or adapted the World-Readiness Standards (Phillips & Abbott, 2011). Table 1.1 provides a summary of each of the 5 C goal areas and standards.

The 5 C goal areas are designed to be interconnected, not focused on in isolation. Your curriculum and instruction, therefore, should ask students to communicate while investigating

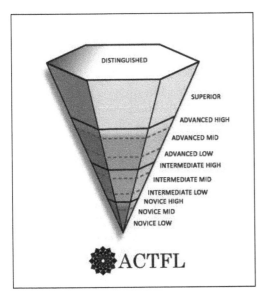

FIGURE 1.1.
The ACTFL Proficiency Guidelines

FIGURE 1.2.
The World-Readiness Standards for Learning Languages

TABLE 1.1. SUMMARY OF THE WORLD-READINESS STANDARDS FOR LEARNING LANGUAGES	
Goal Area	**Standards**
Communication: Communicate effectively in more than one language in order to function in a variety of situations and for multiple purposes.	• Interpersonal Communication • Interpretive Communication • Presentational Communication
Cultures: Interact with cultural competence and understanding.	• Relating Cultural Practices to Perspectives • Relating Cultural Products to Perspectives
Connections: Connect with other disciplines and acquire information and diverse perspectives in order to use the language to function in academic and career-related situations.	• Making Connections • Acquiring Information and Diverse Perspectives
Comparisons: Develop insight into the nature of language and culture in order to interact with cultural competence.	• Language Comparisons • Cultural Comparisons
Communities: Communicate and interact with cultural competence in order to participate in multilingual communities at home and around the world.	• School and Global Communities • Lifelong Learning

cultures, making comparisons, connecting to other content areas, and engaging with local and global target-language communities. As you will see in this book, the *Classroom Close-Up* examples included at the end of each chapter do not focus on only one C at a time. Communication in the target language is the bedrock of instruction, but students communicate about culture, making comparisons and connections to other disciplines while they engage with target-language communities. The 5 Cs are interwoven in proficiency-based instruction.

Proficiency vs. Performance

In proficiency-based instruction, the focus on developing students' proficiency means engaging them in *performance* in the classroom. Proficiency levels indicate what students can do outside of the classroom when engaging with native speakers in unrehearsed, authentic contexts. Performance levels, on the other hand, indicate what students can do with support and appropriate scaffolds with learned and rehearsed material connected to their classroom learning. As you might imagine, students can perform at a higher level than their proficiency level. So you might have a class where you are targeting Novice High *proficiency* and expecting Intermediate-level *performances*. As learners build their performance levels across different topics and themes, their proficiency level advances as well. Performance is most often thought of when discussing performance assessments, but any classroom task that engages students in the three modes of communication (interpretive, interpersonal, and presentational) can be considered a performance if it attempts to replicate a real-world task. (We will explore communicative tasks in depth in Chapter 5.) For more information on performance assessment, we refer you to *The Keys to Assessing Language Performance: A Teacher's Manual for Measuring Student Progress* (Sandrock, 2010).

The Core Practices for World Language Learning

The World-Readiness Standards for Learning Languages (National Standards Collaborative Board, 2015) help teachers understand *what they teach* and the ACTFL Proficiency Guidelines (ACTFL, 2012) help them understand *what their learners can do* with language and how they can progress through language programs. But how do teachers go about the task of actually teaching in a proficiency-based classroom? While certainly not an exhaustive list of teaching practices, the Core Practices for World Language Learning (ACTFL, n.d-a.) outline six specific practices that make up the heart of teaching for proficiency: facilitating target-language comprehensibility, guiding learners through interpreting authentic resources, designing oral interpersonal communication tasks, planning with a backward design model, teaching grammar as a concept and using it in context, and providing appropriate oral feedback. The Core Practices are shown in Figure 1.3.

CORE PRACTICES
For World Language Learning

Facilitate Target Language Comprehensibility
Students and teachers speak, listen, read, write, view, and create in the target language 90% or more during classroom time: comprehensible input, contexts, and interactions.

Guide Learners through Interpreting Authentic Resources
Present interactive reading and listening comprehension tasks using authentic cultural texts with appropriate scaffolding while promoting interpretation.

Design Oral Interpersonal Communication Tasks
Teachers design and carry out interpersonal communication tasks for pairs, small groups, and whole class instruction.

Plan with Backward Design Model
Instructors identify desired results THEN determine acceptable evidence THEN plan learning experiences and instruction.

Teach Grammar as Concept and Use in Context
Teach grammar as concept and use in context. Students focus on meaning BEFORE form.

ACTFL
AMERICAN COUNCIL ON THE
TEACHING OF FOREIGN LANGUAGES
Visit www.actfl.org/virtuallearning

Provide Appropriate Oral Feedback
Oral corrective feedback is a tool for mediating learning and language development.

FIGURE 1.3.
The Core Practices for World Language Learning

As you review these six core practices, you may notice that all but one of them involve input and interaction, the focus of this book. Target-language comprehensibility, using authentic resources, and teaching grammar as a concept all rely heavily on providing *input* in your instruction. Designing oral interpersonal tasks and providing oral feedback both involve *interaction*, either between teacher and student or student to student. Planning with the backward design model is a framework for unit and lesson design, which you will encounter in the *Classroom Close-Up* sections that are included in each chapter. In this book, you will find frameworks and strategies that will support you in putting many of the core practices into practice in your own classrooms.

Writing Communicative Student Learning Outcomes

We would like to highlight one additional concept that is essential when teaching for proficiency: writing communicative student learning outcomes. Writing learning outcomes is part of the backward design model, but in a world language classroom that is proficiency based, it is worth looking closely at a simple yet effective format for writing learning outcomes that will keep your focus on communication and support proficiency development:

I can + language function + context (+ proficiency level information).

"I can" keeps the focus on the learner and what the learner is able to do with the language. The language function identifies the communicative task (describe, identify, explain, ask and answer questions, debate, express my opinion, and so on). The context says what students are communicating about: family, friends, school, and so on. Proficiency level information may also be included to emphasize the type of language that is expected (using simple sentences and some detail, asking simple questions, and so on) (Sauer, 2016; Ritz, 2021). Here are a few examples:

Secondary-Level Lesson Learning Target:
I can

+ ask and answer questions (language functions)

+ about hunger and food waste in France. (context)

Elementary-Level Lesson Learning Target:
I can

+ find out and list (language functions)

+ favorite recess games here and in Mexico. (context)

Secondary-Level Unit Performance Target:
I can

+ identify, interact, and present information
(language function in each of the three modes)

+ on what makes a dish unique (context)

+ using simple sentences and questions with some detail.
(proficiency level information) (Ritz, 2021, p. 73, 76)

You will see this structure for writing communicative student learning outcomes used in all of the *Classroom Close-Ups* throughout this book.

The Interaction Approach in Second Language Acquisition

The importance that proficiency-based instruction places on input and interaction grew out of decades of research in second language acquisition. In this section, we will briefly highlight some of the major areas of research that underpin the classroom practices discussed in this book.

Input

A groundbreaking model that has greatly influenced the field, Stephen Krashen's (1985) Monitor Model—including its Input Hypothesis—was revolutionary in reconceptualizing second language acquisition. The Input Hypothesis "claims that humans acquire language in only one way—by understanding messages, or by receiving 'comprehensible input'" (p. 2). Krashen defined comprehensible input as $i + 1$, with i being learners' "current level" and $+1$ being learners' "next level" (p. 2). The role of world language teachers, therefore, is to use the target language with their students at a level that is slightly above their current level. Forty years later, providing input in the language classroom continues to be viewed as vital for language learning and acquisition: "In all approaches to second language acquisition, input is an essential component for learning in that it provides the crucial evidence from which learners can form linguistic hypotheses" (Gass & Mackey, 2015, p. 180). The importance and necessity of comprehensible input for learners led directly to the ACTFL (2010) Position Statement on the Use of the Target-Language in the Classroom, which will be discussed more fully in Chapter 2. This position statement established a 90%+ target-language use standard in the world language classroom. That world language teachers should provide learners with significant quantities of comprehensible input is well established and without debate. However, research shows that only 36% of K-12 world language teachers use the target language for at least 75% of classroom time (Pufahl & Rhodes, 2011, p. 266).

Despite the unanimous consensus on the importance of input, Krashen's Input Hypothesis remains highly controversial for a number of reasons, one of which is its stance that "speaking is a result of acquisition and not its cause" (Krashen, 1985, p. 2). In other words, from Krashen's perspective, speaking is not a part of language acquisition, but is instead *evidence* of language acquisition. Many researchers and teachers (including us) disagree on this point, and some have gone so far as to call this a "second language acquisition myth" (Brown & Larson-Hall, 2012).

Output

Among those who disagreed with Krashen's stance was Merrill Swain, who had been teaching in French immersion programs in Canada and observed the lack of progress among her students when *only* comprehensible input was provided (Gass & Mackey, 2015). Input alone allows learners to "succeed in comprehending L2 texts, while only partly processing them" (Mitchell, Myles, & Marsden, 2019, p. 59). Learners focus primarily on *semantics* (e.g., meaning) to make sense of what they read or listen to, and not on syntax (word order) or morphology (the way words are formed) (Mitchell, Myles, & Marsden, 2019, p. 59). Swain saw a role for output—pushing learners to focus on how they were constructing sentences and forming words—that was an important part of second language acquisition, and not simply the *result* of acquisition, as Krashen contended.

In Swain's Output Hypothesis, output is viewed as having three clear functions that support language acquisition:

1. A "noticing/triggering" function, or what might be referred to as a consciousness-raising role

2. A hypothesis-testing function

3. A metalinguistic function, or what might be referred to as its "reflective" role (Swain, 1985, qtd. in Mitchell, Myles, & Marsden, p. 223)

Essentially, when students create output (speak or write) as part of the learning process, they become aware of what they know how to say and do not know how to say in the language, realizing that there are "gaps" in their language that they would otherwise not have noticed; they are able to test what they know about the language; and they may engage in reflection on their language use, as happens when learners ask for vocabulary words they need to communicate or ask to check if what they said was comprehensible. Other researchers would also point out that producing output helps learners use it more fluently (what is called automaticity) (Gass & Mackey, 2015) as well as receive feedback on their language use (Gass, 2013), which we will discuss more below.

While there are indeed "limits on the effects of output (learner production) on language acquisition" (VanPatten & Williams, 2015, p. 11), which may lead some to believe it is unimportant in our classrooms, we agree with the sentiment that "[w]e do not need research to tell us that *using* a language is beneficial for learning it" (Mitchell, Myles, & Marsden, 2019, p. 209, emphasis added).

Interaction

Along with Merrill Swain, researcher Michael Long (1996, qtd. in Lightbown & Spada, 2013) disagreed that input alone was sufficient for second language acquisition. His pioneering work focused on the importance of interaction, outlined in his Interaction Hypothesis. When learners interact (either with a native speaker or with another language learner), they

- Check for understanding;

- Negotiate for meaning, making both input and output comprehensible; and

- Receive positive and negative feedback on their language use. (Lightbown & Spada, 2013)

Like producing output, engaging in interaction is a powerful language learning opportunity because learners are able to check if what they are saying makes sense (i.e., check for understanding). When there is a breakdown in communication (either the learner says something that is incomprehensible, or the learner hears something they do not understand), learners engage in negotiation for meaning. They ask clarification questions—*Sorry, what do you mean?*—that require their speaking partner to rephrase what was said so that it becomes comprehensible. Or they are asked clarification questions by their speaking partner that help them realize where they have gaps in their knowledge and are pushed to rephrase what they have said (if they can) in order to make their output comprehensible. Furthermore, learners receive feedback on their language use, which can either be positive or negative. Positive feedback does not mean that the learner is told, "good job!" by the speaking partner. Rather, this means that the learner has communicated successfully. This should not be overlooked! For a learner who is nervous about using the target language, realizing that they understand what the other person is saying and that the other person understands them is quite a confidence booster. For a thorough discussion of providing oral corrective feedback (or negative feedback; the sixth ACTFL Core Practice, discussed above), we refer you to Chapter 6 of *Enacting the Work of Language Instruction: High-Leverage Teaching Practices* (Glisan & Donato, 2017).

The Interaction Approach

The Input Hypothesis (Krashen, 1985), the Output Hypothesis (Swain, 1985), and the Interaction Hypothesis (Long, 1996) are subsumed into what researchers now refer to as the Interaction Approach (Gass & Mackey, 2015). Input remains an essential and necessary component of language acquisition; output pushes learners to use syntax (word order), morphology (the way words are formed), and vocabulary while developing more automatic and fluent language use and becoming aware of gaps in their knowledge; interaction allows learners to obtain needed feedback on their language use when they engage in negotiation for meaning. Without question, "it is commonly accepted in the [second language acquisition] literature that there is a robust connection between interaction and learning" (Gass & Mackey, 2015, p. 181). We couldn't agree more! There are clear and strong connections between the Interaction Approach and our teaching practices, which will be explored throughout this book.

Overview of This Book

The Chapters

In Chapter 2, we look closely at how you can provide input through teacher target-language use. We start by identifying when English is appropriate to use in the classroom, which helps clarify the 90%+ expectation. We then dig into numerous specific strategies to ensure that your teacher target-language use is comprehensible to your students.

In Chapter 3, we shift our focus to providing input through the use of authentic resources, materials made by and for native speakers of the target language. We start by discussing how learners process what they read or hear, which will help you understand how to carefully select authentic resources that are appropriate for learners' proficiency level. We then walk through the Interactive Model for Interpretive Communication, which provides specific steps and strategies for effectively using authentic resources in your classes.

Chapter 4 explores how to use input to support a focus on form in the world language classroom. We use an "input first" approach to teaching grammar as a concept and in context, drawing from research in input processing and input processing instruction. We then explore how to embed a focus on form using an authentic resource within the Interactive Model for Interpretive Communication, discussed in Chapter 3.

In Chapter 5, we shift the focus to supporting learner interactions, beginning with a close look at how teacher talk impacts the communicative focus of lessons. We look at numerous strategies to help establish student target-language use as a norm in classes. We also explore the important distinctions between drills, activities, and tasks and discuss how they can support or hinder student interaction. Finally, we discuss a number of interactive strategies that can be used in any language classroom to engage students in interpersonal communication.

In Chapter 6, we continue to discuss interaction in classrooms, with a particular focus on supporting all learners. We walk through the Gradual Release of Responsibility (GRR) Model, with specific examples on how it can be applied in a world language classroom. We also look at a range of scaffolds that support learners when they engage in interpretive tasks and how to tier interpretive tasks so that they meet the readiness levels of different learners.

Chapter 7 explores how students can develop intercultural communicative competence (ICC), learn about social justice issues, and engage in social and emotional learning while keeping a strong focus on input and interaction. We define ICC and look at what learners can do to demonstrate it at different proficiency levels. We also connect the practices outlined in this book to teaching for social justice.

In Chapter 8, we conclude by focusing on moving students from input to interaction. We look at how to develop a learning sequence that carefully and intentionally moves from a heavy focus on input toward a heavy focus on student interaction through interpersonal tasks.

The Extra Features
Classroom Close-Ups

At the end of every chapter, you will find two *Classroom Close-Ups*. These lessons were shared by world language teachers across a range of languages, age groups, and proficiency levels. The lessons incorporate many of the models and specific practices discussed in each chapter, and are designed to provide clear examples of how those practices can be applied successfully in a world language classroom. One of the two lesson samples also includes adaptations for remote or hybrid teaching.

Tech Zoom

In each chapter, you will find a *Tech Zoom* section that identifies specific strategies and technology tools that will help you leverage technology effectively for in-person instruction, as well as implement the models and practices discussed in the chapter for remote or hybrid teaching environments.

Level Up Your Learning

Each chapter includes a list of suggested further reading or additional resources that will support you in exploring the focus of the chapter more deeply.

Reflection: Single-Point Rubrics

Each chapter includes a single-point rubric that will allow you to self-assess your teaching practice in relation to the models and strategies discussed in that chapter. You will also have space to set goals for yourself so that you can take action to move your teaching practice forward.

Reflection and Next Steps

In this chapter, we have discussed some foundational understandings in world language education that are essential in proficiency-based instruction. We began with a look at the ACTFL Proficiency Guidelines (2012) and the World-Readiness Standards for Learning Languages (National Standards Collaborative Board, 2015). The Proficiency Guidelines help us understand what students can do with language as they develop their language proficiency, and the World-Readiness Standards help us understand what we need to focus on in our instruction, building curriculum, assessments, and daily lessons around the 5 Cs: Communication, Cultures, Connections, Comparisons, and Communities. We also looked at an overview of the ACTFL (n.d) Core Practices, which focus heavily on input and interaction, and many of which will be elaborated on in this book.

We then moved to a look at the research base for our focus on input and interaction, discussing Krashen's (1985) Input Hypothesis, Swain's (1985) Output Hypothesis, and Long's (1996) Interaction Hypothesis, which are part of what is currently referred to as the Interaction Approach in second language acquisition. The importance of input, output, and interaction grew from a strong research base that has significant importance for classroom practice. Before moving on, take a look at some of the *Level Up Your Learning* resources, where you can delve more deeply into some of the topics discussed in this chapter.

Level Up Your Learning

- **ACTFL. (2012). ACTFL proficiency guidelines. http://www.actfl.org/sites/default/files/pdfs/public/ACTFLProficiencyGuidelines2012_FINAL.pdf**
You can access the full ACTFL Proficiency Guidelines at no cost online. We want to draw your attention to the language-specific samples that you will find there as well. ACTFL provides speaking, writing, reading, and listening samples in over 10 languages. For every sample, you will find an explanation of why it is rated at a particular proficiency level.

- **ACTFL. (n.d-b)** *Guiding principles for language learning.* **https://www.actfl.org/resources/guiding-principles-language-learning**
To learn more about the ACTFL Core Practices, check this page on the ACTFL website, where you will find background on why the Core Practices are important, what exactly they are, and how to implement them in your classes.

- **Glynn, C., Wesley, P., & Wassell, B. (2014).** *Words and actions: Teaching languages through the lens of social justice* **(2nd ed.). ACTFL.**
Proficiency-based instruction goes hand in hand with teaching for social justice, and we encourage our readers to explore this important text. You will find a clear explanation of teaching for social justice, along with simple steps to develop or adapt your own social justice curricular units and make social justice a part of your daily lessons.

- **National Standards Collaborative Board. (2015).** *World-Readiness Standards for Learning Languages* **(4th ed.). https://www.actfl.org/resources/world-readiness-standards-learning-languages**
The World-Readiness Standards for Learning Languages is an indispensable resource to guide your curriculum and instruction.

- **VanPatten, B., & Williams, J. (Eds.). (2015).** *Theories in second language acquisition: An introduction* **(2nd ed.). Taylor & Francis.**
If you are interested in learning more about second language acquisition research in general, and the Interaction Approach in particular, this book will give you a solid understanding of the field in a format that is accessible for non-researchers.

Chapter 1 References

ACTFL. (n.d) *Guiding principles for language learning.* https://www.actfl.org/resources/guiding-principles-language-learning

ACTFL. (2010). Position statement on the use of the target language in the classroom. https://www.actfl.org/advocacy/actfl-position-statements/use-the-target-language-the-classroom

ACTFL. (2012). ACTFL proficiency guidelines 2012. http://www.actfl.org/sites/default/files/pdfs/public/ACTFLProficiencyGuidelines2012_FINAL.pdf

ACTFL. (2017). NCSSFL-ACTFL can-do statements. https://www.actfl.org/resources/ncssfl-actfl-can-do-statements

Baggett, H. C. (2016). Student enrollment in world languages: *L'égalité des chances? Foreign Language Annals, 49*(1), 162–179. https://doi.org/10.1111/flan.12173

Brown, S., & Larson-Hall, J. (2012). *Second language acquisition myths: Applying second language research to classroom teaching.* University of Michigan Press.

Gass, S. M. (2013). *Second language acquisition: An introductory course* (4th ed.). Routledge.

Gass, S. M., & Mackey, A. (2015). Input, interaction, and output in second language acquisition. In B. VanPatten & J. Williams (Eds.), *Theories in second language acquisition* (pp. 181–206). Routledge.

Glisan, E. W., & Donato, R. (2017). *Enacting the work of language instruction: High-leverage teaching practices.* ACTFL.

Glynn, C., & Wassell, B. (2018). Who gets to play? Issues of access and social justice in world language study in the U.S. *College of Education Faculty Scholarship, 11,* 18–32. https://rdw.rowan.edu/education_facpub

Glynn, C., Wesley, P., & Wassell, B. (2014). *Words and actions: Teaching languages through the lens of social justice* (2nd ed.). ACTFL.

Krashen, S. (1985). *The input hypothesis.* Longman.

Lightbown, P. M., & Spada, N. (2013). *How languages are learned* (4th ed.). Oxford University Press.

Long, M. (1996). The role of the linguistic environment in second language acquisition. In W. C. Ritchie & T. K. Bhatia (Eds.), *Handbook of second language acquisition* (pp. 413–468). Academic Press.

Mitchell, R., Myles, F., & Marsden, E. (2019). *Second language learning theories* (4th ed.). Routledge.

Morris, M. (2005). Two sides of the communicative coin: Honors and nonhonors French and Spanish classes in a midwestern high school. *Foreign Language Annals, 38*(2), 236–248. https://doi.org/10.1111/j.1944-9720.2005.tb02488.x

Murphy, D., & Lee, S. Y. (2019). The gender and race or ethnicity of majors in languages and literatures other than English in the United States, 2010–14. ADFL *Bulletin, 45*(2), 43–92. https://doi.org/10.1632/adfl.45.2.43.

National Standards Collaborative Board. (2015). *World-Readiness Standards for Learning Languages* (4th ed.). National Standards Collaborative Board.

Phillips, J., & Abbott, M. (2011). *A decade of foreign language standards: Impact, influence, and future directions.* Retrieved from https://www.actfl.org/sites/default/files/publications/standards/NationalStandards2011.pdf

Pratt, C. (2012). Are African-American high school students less motivated to learn Spanish than other ethnic groups? *Hispania, 95*(1), 116–134. https://www.jstor.com/stable/41440366

Pufahl, I., & Rhodes, N. C. (2011). Foreign language instruction in U.S. schools: Results of a national survey of elementary and secondary schools. *Foreign Language Annals, 44*(2), 258–288. https://doi.org/10.1111/j.1944-9720.2011.01130.x

Ritz, C. (2021). *Leading your world language program: Strategies for design and supervision, even if you don't speak the language!* New York: Routledge.

Sandrock, P. (2010). *The keys to assessing language performance: A teacher's manual for measuring student progress.* Alexandria, VA: ACTFL.

Sauer, T. (2016, July). *Putting the learner center stage: Developing performance objectives and learning targets*. Workshop presented at the Massachusetts Foreign Language Association Proficiency Academy.

Swain, M. (1985). Communicative competence: Some roles of comprehensible input and comprehensible output in its development. In S. Gass & C. Madden (Eds.), *Input in second language acquisition* (pp. 235–253). Boston: Newbury House.

VanPatten, B., & Williams, J. (Eds.). (2015). *Theories in second language acquisition: An introduction* (2nd ed.). New York: Taylor and Francis.

CHAPTER 2

Providing Input:
Teacher Target-Language Use

O ne of the main ways that your students will receive input and experience the target-language is through you...their teacher! You are your learners' main source of target-language input through your instruction and daily interactions. Depending on the age group you are working with, your instructional time may range from only 20 minutes every few days to 60-minute periods every day of the week. Whatever time you have with students, it won't come close to an "ideal" language learning environment, where students are immersed in the language 24/7. Knowing that you have limited time means that every second must count. Your learners need to hear and interact with the target language as much as possible. ACTFL recommends that 90% or more of class time be devoted to target-language use, starting on the very first day of class (ACTFL, 2010).

Why should such a high percentage of your class time be in the target language? Simply put, your learners need a *lot* of language input. Second language acquisition is "slow and piecemeal," and the "only way" learners develop their internal language system is "through exposure to input" (VanPatten, 2017, p. 50 and 59). Whatever you may believe about how languages are acquired, there is a consensus among second language acquisition researchers that input is "essential" and forms a "basis" for learners to understand patterns in language and form hypotheses about how language works (Gass & Mackey, 2015, p. 182). Teachers must maximize their limited instructional time and understand that an important part of their role is to provide target-language input to their students. Although teachers rightly want to have a student-centered focus in their classes, they should also recognize the centrality of "teacher talk" in providing input, and not minimize its crucial role in language development (Ellis & Shintani, 2014).

But just speaking in the target language isn't enough. As you know, language needs to be *comprehensible* for your learners; they need to be able to make meaning of what you are saying. First, what you say to your students should be meaningful. When you speak, you want to actually communicate something to your learners, not just have them repeat what you are saying for the sake of practice. Second, you need to modify how you speak to adapt to their proficiency level, or slightly above—what Krashen calls the "*i + 1*" with *i* being the learner's "current level" and *+ 1* being the "next level" (1985, p. 2). Modifying how you speak and using a number of strategies to support comprehension—which we will explore deeply in this chapter—will help ensure you are providing comprehensible input for your students. While it can feel like an insurmountable challenge to achieve 90%+ target-language use with Novice level learners on the first day of class, the numerous strategies we present here will help make it easy and fun!

Please keep in mind, however, that there is also a place for English in second language learning. Should you be translating key words into English or asking your students to translate? Should you use English to save time when going over directions? Or maybe just reserve English for teaching grammar rules? No, no, and no! Learners use English (their L1) for many reasons (Ellis & Shintani, 2014), but with the limited instructional time in world language education, you need to proceed with caution. The L1 should only be used in instruction when it supports language acquisition without undermining the primary goal of providing significant quantities of comprehensible input. You may also want to use English to make personal connections with your students, fearing that if you do not, you will not get to know them well. While this fear is completely understandable, you can get to know your students just as well *in the target language*. They will experience you as a speaker of the target-language and build their relationship with you through that language. While doing this may feel overwhelming at first, you will be able to build strong relationships with your students in the target-language and their language proficiency will be stronger as a result of your efforts.

So, how can you maximize teacher talk to provide that crucial target-language input for your learners? What strategies can you use to ensure that your language is comprehensible for the proficiency level of your learners? And how can you purposefully use English in a way that maximizes target-language use while supporting second language acquisition? In this chapter, we tackle each of these important questions so that you are able to use English appropriately and teach in the target language 90% or more of instructional time with all learners, for all languages, and for all levels...even on day one!

90-10 Breakdown: Target Language vs. English, Defined

Have you ever taught a class and then looked back and wondered: Did I hit 90% today? How much English did I use? Maybe you looked at your watch and estimated that over the 55-minute class, you used English a few times here and there. You estimate that *perhaps* you hit the 90% target; or maybe you used English more than you had wanted to and were closer to 60%. Using the target language and English shouldn't be a haphazard guessing game. Both your target-language use and your English use should be planned and purposeful. But without clear guidelines on *when* to use either language, you can be left deciding to switch into English on the fly and guesstimating your time in the target language.

The use of the L1 in world language classrooms is a complex and oftentimes controversial issue (De La Campa & Nassaji, 2009; Ellis & Shintani, 2014). World language teachers may use the L1 for various reasons, such as explaining the meaning of vocabulary words, addressing discipline issues, building relationships with students, explaining grammar rules or directions for activities, and so on (Ellis & Shintani, 2014). While the use of the L1 may at times feel natural and necessary, the world language education context makes its regular use highly problematic (Ellis, 2012). Recall that you have limited instructional time with students, and hence limited time to provide crucial language input. Research shows that, nationally, only 36% of secondary level world language teachers report using the target language for the majority of class time (Pufahl & Rhodes, 2011). This is cause for concern! Regular use of the L1 undoubtedly undermines second language learning when it takes away from opportunities for input and interaction in that language (Ellis, 2012).

You can make purposeful use of the L1 to support second language learning without taking away from instructional time. One of the ways that students use their native language is as a "cognitive tool" to support metacognition and processing of their learning (Ellis & Shintani, 2014). The L1 is used by students in what is called "private" or "inner speech," where they speak quietly to themselves as they think about what they are doing or want to say (Ellis & Shintani, 2014, p. 242). Teachers can therefore use the native language strategically to help learners reflect on and process their learning. English can be used to articulate learning goals, to ask students to self-reflect, to provide written feedback to learners, and for assessment prompts. If students are at a more advanced proficiency level, they may not need the support of their native language in the same way as lower-level learners. With the use of English being reserved for *processing* learning, the target language is freed up for anything and everything related to content. Put another way, English can be used to help students think about *how* they are learning. The target language, on the other hand, is used exclusively for *what* they are learning. Table 2.1 summarizes the appropriate uses of English and the target language.

TABLE 2.1. APPROPRIATE USE OF THE TARGET LANGUAGE VS. ENGLISH

Appropriate Use of English (if needed)	Appropriate Use of the Target Language
Student learning outcomes	• Any and all content!
Reflecting on student learning outcomes	• Daily routines (morning meetings, reviewing the agenda, class jobs and handing out materials, etc.)
Student goal-setting	
Student reflection on goals	
Performance assessment prompts	• Classroom instructions
Assessment questions	
Written feedback to students	
Class emergencies	

Making Teacher Input Comprehensible

Having established parameters for using English purposefully to support language development, we will now focus on how to succeed in using the target language 90% or more of instructional time. ACTFL established the 90%+ standard through its position statement on target-language use. Box 2.1 provides the position statement in full.

BOX 2.1. THE ACTFL POSITION STATEMENT ON TARGET-LANGUAGE USE

Research indicates that effective language instruction must provide significant levels of meaningful communication* and interactive feedback in the target language in order for students to develop language and cultural proficiency. The pivotal role of target-language interaction in language learning is emphasized in the *K-16 Standards for Foreign Language Learning in the 21st Century*. ACTFL therefore recommends that language educators and their students use the target language as exclusively as possible (90% plus) at all levels of instruction during instructional time and, when feasible, beyond the classroom. In classrooms that feature maximum target-language use, instructors use a variety of strategies to facilitate comprehension and support meaning making. For example, they:

1. provide comprehensible input that is directed toward communicative goals;

2. make meaning clear through body language, gestures, and visual support;

3. conduct comprehension checks to ensure understanding;

4. negotiate meaning with students and encourage negotiation among students;

5. elicit talk that increases in fluency, accuracy, and complexity over time;

6. encourage self-expression and spontaneous use of language;

7. teach students strategies for requesting clarification and assistance when faced with comprehension difficulties; and

8. offer feedback to assist and improve students' ability to interact orally in the target language.

*Communication for a classical language refers to an emphasis on reading ability and for American Sign Language (ASL) to signed communicative ability.

Source: ACTFL, 2010

The target language should be used for any and all content: *what* students are learning. But, of course, when you use the target language, you have to be sure your students *understand* you. While it can feel daunting to expect that beginning language students will be able to understand the language—particularly on the first day of classes—there are some simple strategies teachers of any language can employ to ensure success.

FIGURE 2.1.
Body Language to Represent Confusion or Not Knowing

FIGURE 2.2.
Body Language to Represent Money or Paying

Figure 2.3.
Body Language to Represent Surprise or Disbelief

Strategy #1: Start Early, Start Strong

Establishing target-language use as the norm in your classes is something that needs to happen early on. The very first day of class sets the tone for the year. Many teachers may feel they should "build up" to 90% by starting the year at 50-50, moving to 75-25 mid-year, and then reaching 90% later on. While this may feel like a logical approach, students will form habits, thinking that English use in the classroom is normal and accepted—then they will *fight you* as you try to increase target-language use. Make your life easier by starting with 100% target-language use from day one, level one!

Strategy #2: Consider the Proficiency Level

Wanting to start strong does not mean you speak in the target language as if you are chatting with a native speaker. You want to use language that is *comprehensible* to students while still pushing them beyond their current proficiency level. You will speak differently in a class of Novices than a class of Intermediate or Advanced students.

To adjust your speech to the proficiency level of your students, there are some specific modifications you can make:

- Slow down.

- Articulate more clearly.

- Pause! Give your learners time to catch up.

- Use simple vocabulary and less slang.

- Repeat yourself.

- Elaborate! Yes, you should *say more* to give students more to "hold on to" as they figure out what you are saying.

Strategy #3: Cognates

While not all languages have many cognates with English, if yours does, take advantage of them. Particularly with early Novices, the strategic use of cognates—words that are almost mirror images in the two languages—is particularly useful. Be careful, though. Cognates are more comprehensible to learners when they are *written*. Students may not understand the word when they hear it spoken *(hôpital? ospedale? hospital?)*, but will likely catch on when they see the word written down.

Strategy #4: Routines

Build structure into your lessons so that students know what to expect. Include opening greeting activities and a structure for transitions between activities, handing in assignments, managing other logistical classroom needs, and conducting a closing activity. For younger learners, this strategy may include using illustrations or icons to indicate repeated activities, as well as replicating the types of routines students encounter in their regular classrooms. The more students engage in these routines, the more comfortable they become understanding and processing the language being used.

Strategy #5: Body Language & Gestures

When in doubt, act it out! Body language is a normal and natural part of human language and is essential in a language classroom to support comprehension. Pointing, gesturing, using your facial expressions, and dramatic reenactments all can be helpful for your students. Many teachers use strategies from Total Physical Response (TPR) in which they make up a gesture to go along with a vocabulary word or expression (Ray & Seely, 1999). Although these gestures are helpful to support student comprehension, TPR gestures can be somewhat arbitrary since they are made up by teachers. If you plan to use a number of gestures to support meaning, you may want to consider using gestures from the sign language of the target culture instead. This is a meaningful way to integrate culture and expand students' global awareness, while also making language comprehensible. Figures 2.1, 2.2, and 2.3 show simple ways that body language can be used to communicate meaning.

Strategy #6: Visuals

Most teachers today have access to computers and projectors that enable them to integrate any number of images pulled from the Internet and projected in their classroom. When planning a lesson, anticipating key vocabulary words and locating images from the Internet that can be easily pasted into a slideshow as part of the lesson will help ensure comprehensibility. Finding images that "define" a key word is a strategy best used with concrete words and in Novice/Intermediate-Low classes, and occasionally students may interpret an image as having a different meaning than you intended. However, using images and visual support at all levels is an essential strategy to support comprehension. While some images can represent simple words, such as *breakfast* (Figure 2.4), others can be used to support more complex concepts such as *friendship or childhood* (Figure 2.5).

Another instance in which visuals are crucial is when there is a word that is difficult to explain without one. For instance, students in a Spanish class may know that a *sombrero* is a hat, but they may not understand the word *vueltiao* without a visual (Figure 2.6), since it is a type of hat that is particular to the Colombian culture. Additionally, there might not be any context clues for the students to draw upon. With a picture, the students will observe that a *sombrero vueltiao* is a wide-brim hat that is made of straw with alternating colors of beige and black.

Finally, another easy way to add visuals is through emojis, bitmojis, or small icons. Students use them all the time, so this can be a fun way to engage them. Figure 2.7 shows how you can embed emojis into text to support meaning.

Strategy #7: Circumlocution

If students don't seem to understand one key word, resist the temptation to just translate it quickly into English. In addition to the other strategies listed here, try circumlocution—literally *talking around* a word without using it. If students don't know the word for dog, for example, you explain that it has four legs, is man's best friend, barks, and likes to play catch. This is also an important strategy for students to learn to use when they don't know a word. Rather than letting students blurt out the word in English, get them comfortable with circumlocution so that they try using the target language to explain the word they don't know.

FIGURE 2.4.
An Image Used to Demonstrate the Meaning of "Breakfast"

FIGURE 2.5.
An Image Used to Demonstrate the Meaning of "Friendship" or "Childhood"

FIGURE 2.6.
Image Used to Explain a *Sombrero Vueltiao*

Pregunta a tu compañero🖐

¿Te gusta jugar a los videojuegos 🎮?

Sí me gusta 👍   No, no me gusta 👎

FIGURE 2.7.
Using Emojis with Text
Translation:
Ask your partner.
Do you like to play video games?
Yes I like to. / No, I do not like to.

Strategy #8: Modeling

Don't just tell students what to do, *show* them! If, for example, you are giving directions for a class activity, ask a student to act out the task with you before the class gets to work. If you want students to write a short paragraph, give them a model of what you are looking for before they begin. Seeing an example of what you want them to do—in addition to hearing your directions and seeing them written down—reinforces expectations without the need for translation into English. Teachers of younger learners may, for example, want students to complete a craft project and could develop instructions that integrate images with clear steps and a chart and model the directions for students before they begin. This type of careful planning will enable you to remain in the target language while making it comprehensible for your learners. Modeling is an important component of the Gradual Release of Responsibility (GRR) model, which we will be discussing in Chapter 6.

Strategy #9: Circling with Questions

Another great TPR strategy that can support comprehension for your students is a carefully structured sequence of questions, called circling (Bex, n.d.). If you notice confusion on the part of learners when you say something, you may want to pause and use one or more question types to help draw attention and clarify the word or expression that is causing confusion. The question types include yes/no, either/or, and open-ended questions. While there is an order to the questions, you may choose to use only one or two of the types rather than the entire sequence. Table 2.2 outlines the question types and possible student responses.

TABLE 2.2. CIRCLING QUESTION SEQUENCE

Steps	Example
Initial Statement: The teacher makes an initial statement on the topic.	Teacher: "The sky is blue."
Yes/No Question #1: The teacher asks a question about the initial statement that prompts a *no* response.	Teacher: "Is the sky yellow?" Students: "No" or "No, the sky is blue." Teacher: "Right, the sky is blue."
Yes/No Question #2: The teacher asks a question about the initial statement that prompts a yes response.	Teacher: "Is the sky blue?" Students: "Yes" or "Yes, the sky is blue." Teacher: "Right, the sky is blue."
Either/Or Question: The teacher asks a question about the initial statement that provides two possible responses.	Teacher: "Is the sky blue or yellow?" Students: "Blue" or "The sky is blue." Teacher: "Right, the sky is blue."
Open-Ended Question: The teacher asks an open-ended question that solicits the right answer.	Teacher: "What color is the sky?" Students: "The sky is blue." Teacher: "Right, the sky is blue."

Strategy #10: Checking for Understanding

To maintain target-language use, you need to be regularly checking to see if students understand throughout each and every class. This needs to be more than just asking students if they understand! Here are a few ideas for checking for understanding:

- Thumbs-up/Thumbs-down
- Five-finger rating
- Mini-white board responses
- Stop signs on desks (red = Stop, I need help!; yellow = Slow down!; green = Good to go!)
- Show-me-you-got-it ideas:
  - Ranking, matching, voting, putting items in order, different movements to indicate a choice, and so on.
- Exit tickets

BOX 2.2. WHY CAN'T I JUST TRANSLATE?

As you are reviewing all of these strategies for making the target language comprehensible, you may be asking yourself: Why can't I just translate? A translated word here or there can't do much harm, can it? While it is certainly tempting (and oftentimes quicker) just to give the student the English translation of a word they don't understand, there are a few important reasons why doing so will undermine your classes and your students' language development.

Students form habits: The more comfortable students are asking for and getting translations of words they don't know, the more they will do it. Although it may save time in the short term, reliance on translation in the long term will lead to more and more demands for translations by students, which slows down language acquisition.

Slippery slope: Teachers, like their students, also form habits! The more comfortable you get just translating a few words into English, the more likely *you* are to do it. Avoid the slippery slope to predominant English use!

Comfort with ambiguity: Evidence points to correlations between tolerance of ambiguity and success in language learning (Saville-Troike & Barto, 2017). In language learning, being tolerant of ambiguity means that you are okay with having a *pretty good idea of* what something means; you don't need to always have a precise and definitive understanding of every single thing. Providing students with translations of words they don't know, instead of using the comprehensible input strategies presented in this chapter, will undermine their ability to develop tolerance of ambiguity.

Translation ≠ Lexical Knowledge: Knowing the *translation* of a word is only one part of actually knowing a word—what's known as *lexical knowledge*. Nation (2013) identifies three categories that make up lexical knowledge: **form, meaning,** and **use.** Because of these factors, a one-to-one translation is not always so simple. Knowing the **form** of a lexical item means that you know how it sounds and how it is written. Knowing the **meaning** of the word is more complex than just knowing a direct translation. The word may have different meanings, and thus different translations, depending on the context in which it is used. The innocent word *bread*, for example, can be a verb meaning "to coat something with bread crumbs"; or it can be a noun referring to the food item that is used to make a sandwich; or it can be a synonym for money. The **use** of the lexical item involves understanding patterns of how it is used in context, collocations (other words that are often or always used with the word), and constraints on register (when the word is or is not appropriate to use). In American English, for example, we make a distinction between *bread* (in our mind, this is sandwich bread) and *fresh bread*. In France, on the other hand, *bread* will only ever be thought of as *fresh*, so saying "fresh bread" in French *(du pain frais)* doesn't make any sense. Rather, the French will distinguish between *bread* (always fresh bread) and *sandwich bread (du pain à sandwich)*. In short, developing real lexical knowledge requires encountering the word many times through authentic language input. A simple translation ignores the complexity of lexical knowledge and takes time away from input and interaction.

Teaching in the target language 90% or more of instructional time can easily be achieved using the strategies provided here. There is no one-size-fits-all strategy, however, and you will likely use these strategies in combination. Carefully planning your lesson and selecting your comprehensible input strategies will make a world of difference in your classroom. At first, you may spend more time planning as you adjust to a 90%+ classroom, but in little time, you and your students will adjust to the new reality, and you won't want to go back.

Tech Zoom

Providing teacher language input using technology to support in-person, flipped learning or a hybrid or distance learning environment can easily be accomplished with some careful planning. Here are some strategies and tools that support teacher target-language use for synchronous or asynchronous virtual learning.

- Virtual classroom survival language: When you meet with students in person, you teach them basic classroom survival language, such as "take out your book" or "work with a partner." To navigate a virtual class, students need to learn different terminology, such as words for "mute" or "breakout rooms." If you are meeting with students online, try using a virtual etiquette template like the one featured in Figure 2.8. These basic classroom directions and expectations can be presented to students every day to begin the virtual class and remind them of class norms.

FIGURE 2.8.
Virtual Etiquette in the Target Language

Translation from left to right, top to bottom:
- *Turn off microphone*
- *Be respectful in the chat*
- *Have a charger for your equipment*
- *Have the necessary materials*
- *Arrive on time*
- *Raise your hand to speak*

- Teacher-made videos: If you are working with students remotely or want to "flip" your classroom (provide teacher presentations for students to watch before they come to class), you can provide teacher target-language input by creating your own videos. These do not need to be fancy, but they do need to draw on basic strategies for providing comprehensible input, such as using gestures and visuals. Easy-to-use tech tools, such as Screencastify and Zoom, allow you to record while sharing your screen. Be sure that you are also visible when you record so that students can see any gestures or body language you use as you speak. Preparing slides to use with visuals and written text to reinforce your oral language helps ensure comprehensibility for students. Your videos can include basic directions for independent student work or vocabulary presentations in which you use the vocabulary in context to present cultural information or any other topic connected to your thematic unit. Try to keep these videos fairly short (under 5 minutes) to best hold students' attention.

- Virtual checks for understanding: In an in-person learning environment, you can read students' body language to figure out if they understand what is being said in the target language. It is much harder to judge this online, so you will need to be more deliberate in gauging the students' level of understanding during online synchronous classes. If the students' cameras are on, you can ask them to give a thumbs-up or thumbs-down to show they have understood. If students are not using their cameras, then you can ask them to write quick responses in the chat box or have them click on the appropriate reaction button. Here are some other easy tech tools that can help you check for understanding:

  - *Nearpod or Pear Deck:* Both of these platforms integrate with presentation slides and include numerous templates you can use to check for understanding. Some of the templates included ask students to identify how they feel, to summarize what they just learned, or to agree or disagree with a statement. By integrating these templates directly into your class slides, you can check for understanding during a lesson and get immediate feedback.

  - *Flipgrid:* Flipgrid allows you to set up a prompt for students (using text, images, videos, or audio recordings), which students need to respond to with a video recording. In addition to being a great tool for interpersonal speaking, this platform is also useful for formative checks for understanding. You can ask students to record takeaways from the lesson, a 3-2-1 (three things they learned, two questions they have, and one part of class they enjoyed), or a response to a prompt that asks them to use the target language focusing on the day's learning. You can then respond to students individually or address questions with the entire class the following day.

  - *Polls:* Platforms such as Mentimeter, Slido, or the poll function in Zoom will allow you to easily create polls or surveys, which you can use to assess student understanding in real time. You get immediate feedback on what was understood by the students and can also share the results with the class.

  - *Virtual whiteboards:* There are many tools that replicate a class whiteboard but have more interactive and dynamic features, such as Google Jamboard or Padlet. You can ask your students to respond to a question, post a picture or video, or self-reflect against the learning outcomes. Both platforms will be viewable by all students, however, so you will want to use this only when you want all students to see each other's responses.

  - *Seesaw:* Particularly for younger learners, Seesaw is an excellent tool for many different uses. You can create any number of activities that can serve as formative checks for learning. The platform is incredibly user friendly, and many younger learners are able to navigate it independently.

Now that we've looked at different ways to ensure that your target-language use is comprehensible to students, we're going to walk through two *Classroom Close-Ups* that show us how teachers of two different languages and working with students of two different proficiency levels apply this to their own teaching. In *Classroom Close-Up* 2.2, we'll also show how the teacher adapts the model for a hybrid or distance learning environment. You'll find a lesson plan template in Appendix B.

Classroom Close-Ups
Classroom Close-Up 2.1: Day One, Level One
Lesson developed by Catherine Ritz

COURSE OVERVIEW	
Course Name	Any Language, Level 1
Course Proficiency Target	Novice High

LESSON OVERVIEW	
Unit Theme	Getting to Know You
Lesson Learning Outcome	I can greet someone and exchange basic information.
Core Vocabulary and Forms	• Hello • How are you? • What's your name? • Other basic questions and responses
Material and Resources	No materials are needed. The teacher may choose to supplement gestures with prepared slides that include images, but this is optional.
Lesson Length	45-55 minutes

LEARNING SEQUENCE		
Focus of Learning	• Teacher greets students at the door in the target language.	*Time:* 1 min
Preview of Learning	• Teacher invites a student to read the lesson learning outcome (in English) by gesturing to them and pointing to the learning outcome on the overhead slide.	*Time:* 1 min

Primetime 1	1. Teacher begins modeling basic conversation using gestures and asking for whole class repetition:
	    a. Hello!
	    b. How are you? I'm good/bad/okay.
	    c. What is your name? My name is...
	    d. Where do you live? I live in...
	    e. *May add more depending on how quickly students pick up meaning and are able to repeat.*
	2. Teacher shifts from whole class repetition to asking individual students to answer questions, being sure to ask each and every student. (This should move quickly, keeping a good pace.)
	3. Teacher then adds having students also ask the question to another student in the class, still as a whole class.
		Time:
		15-20 min

Downtime	4.	Maintaining the target language and using gestures, the teacher indicates to students that they will now work in pairs to ask and answer the questions they have been practicing.	*Time:* 5 min
	5.	Two students are invited to model this for the class.	
	6.	Students are then put in pairs and begin the conversation.	
Primetime 2	7.	Using gestures, the teacher invites each pair of students to stand and share their conversation with the class.	*Time:* 10-15 min
	8.	The teacher then uses body language and gestures to teach basic classroom directions, including:	
		a. Work in pairs.	
		b. Get out your book.	
		c. Raise your hand.	
		d. Write this down.	
		e. *And so on, as appropriate.*	
Celebration of Learning		The teacher returns students' attention to the learning outcome. One student is asked to read it aloud (in English) and the teacher gestures for a thumbs-up/thumbs-down/thumbs-in-the-middle to get feedback	*Time:* 2 min

In this sample lesson, students are beginning their language studies on the very first day of class. The teacher intends to use the target language for 100% of class time to establish a clear expectation for the year. Additionally, the teacher wants students to engage in a simple conversation and begin to understand some classroom instructions. Since students are only beginning their language studies, no prior knowledge of the language is expected. There is an intentional use of oral language *only* in this first class; the target-language expressions used in this lesson are never written, so that students will focus their attention only on hearing and speaking.

Building a Basic Conversation: Whole Class
The teacher greets students at the door as they enter the classroom with a greeting in the target language and a handshake or other culturally-appropriate greeting. Once students are seated, the teacher opens the class by again greeting students in the target language while also waving. The teacher encourages students to repeat the greeting.

The teacher then shows the objective and agenda slide on the overhead and asks a student to read the objective by gesturing to the student and pointing to the slide. Figure 2.9 shows the objective and agenda slide.

The teacher now begins leading students in building their basic conversation by saying hello in the target language again while waving and encouraging students to repeat. The teacher may choose to use a slide with an image, such as the one in Figure 2.10.

The teacher then introduces the first simple question: *What's your name?* The teacher uses hand gestures to encourage students to repeat the question, then gestures to themselves and says, *My name is....* The teacher may choose to use name tags or have name cards available on each student's desk. Through this process students begin to understand that they are talking about their names. The teacher then gestures to one student after another, asking them what their name is and always using the target language. The teacher prompts students to say, *My name is...* before their name. The teacher moves quickly around the class to ask each student their name.

Objective:
I can greet someone and exchange basic information.

Agenda:
1. Greetings & Introductions: Building a Basic Conversation
2. Following Classroom Directions

FIGURE 2.9.
Objective & Agenda Slide

FIGURE 2.10.
Image Slide to Support Making Greetings

FIGURE 2.11.
Image Slide to Support Asking How You Are

FIGURE 2.12.
Image Slide to Support Instructing Students to Take Out a Book

The teacher now adds another simple question: *How are you?* Again, the teacher asks for the whole class to repeat a few times, then answers by saying and gesturing: *I'm fine* (points to themselves while smiling and giving thumbs-up); *I'm bad* (points to themselves while frowning and giving thumbs-down); *I'm okay* (points to themselves while shrugging and waving hand back and forth). Generally, a few students pick up on what is being said fairly quickly, while others need to see their classmates respond before understanding the meaning. The teacher leads the class once more in a whole class repetition of the question and the possible answers with gestures and may choose to also include a slide with images such as the one in Figure 2.11. The teacher then begins asking students one at a time, prompting them if necessary on how to respond. The teacher may also ask the class to repeat responses from their classmates, saying, *Emma is feeling good, bad, or so-so?* for example.

This sequence is repeated to include additional questions, such as *Where do you live? Where are you from? How old are you?* as well as one or two ways to say good-bye, always using questions and answers that are culturally appropriate in the target-language context. The teacher can adjust the number of questions depending on how quickly the students are catching on. For example, many students may already be familiar with *hola* [hello] and *¿cómo estás?* [how are you?] in Spanish class. The teacher will need to move quickly with these first expressions, and be ready to add more if students appear to already know these first ones. In classes with younger learners, on the other hand, the teacher may choose to focus on fewer expressions to give students more time to learn them. The number of question/answer sequences introduced to the class depends on the language being taught and the age group of the learners.

Building a Basic Conversation: In Partners
Once the class has reviewed the questions and responses, the teacher asks a few students to model the full conversation with them. The teacher can first lead with the questions, then ask the student to lead with the questions. The teacher then indicates to the class that they will work in pairs (gesturing to two students to indicate meaning) and do the whole conversation with each other. The teacher circulates as students talk, providing prompts as needed. This lasts approximately 3-4 minutes. Students are then asked to stand and share out their conversation in pairs. If the size of the class permits, having every pair present their short conversation is preferable. The teacher encourages students to applaud after each presentation.

Following Classroom Directions
For the final segment of the class, the teacher uses body language and gestures to build student comprehension of simple oral classroom directions, such as *work in pairs, open your book, raise your hand,* and so on. Students are asked to show their understanding by following the directions (raising their hand, for example, when the teacher instructs them to). The teacher may choose to additionally use slides with images (but not printed text!) to support comprehension, such as in Figure 2.12. This can last 8-10 minutes.

The teacher then concludes the class by showing the learning outcome on the overhead (Figure 2.13), and asking a student to read it: *I can greet someone and exchange basic information.* They ask students to give a thumbs-up, thumbs-down, or thumbs-in-the-middle to indicate whether they feel they have met this objective. The teacher then says good-bye to students as class ends, and encourages them to say good-bye in the target language as well.

Classroom Close-Up 2.2: Hosting & Hospitality

This classroom example was shared by Katie Quackenbush, Arabic teacher at Boston Latin Academy, Boston, MA.

This lesson was developed for a first-year 8th and 9th grade Arabic class at a public middle and high school. The lesson is part of a unit around the theme of hosting and hospitality, which is an important aspect of Arab culture and a cultural theme that is introduced to the students early in their Arabic studies. At this point in the curriculum, students have recently finished learning the Arabic alphabet and how to read and write all of the Arabic letters.

Objective:

I can greet someone and exchange basic information.

FIGURE 2.13.
Learning Outcome Reflection Slide

COURSE OVERVIEW	
Course Name	Arabic 1
Course Proficiency Target	Novice High

LESSON OVERVIEW	
Unit Theme	Hosting and Hospitality
Lesson Learning Outcome	I can say what drink(s) I like/would like and do not/would not like when asked by a host.
Core Vocabulary and Forms	• Do you/would you like...? • I like/would like • I do/would not like • Coffee • Tea • Water • Orange juice • Mango juice
Materials and Resources	• Screenshots of videos from https://www.qfi.org/for-teachers/teacher-resources/jusuur-series-videos/ • Slides prepared and uploaded to Peardeck.com
Lesson Length	45 minutes

LEARNING SEQUENCE		
Focus of Learning	Students engage in a do-now, reading aloud some key vocabulary with a partner.	Time: 3 min
Preview of Learning	The teacher presents the learning outcome and agenda.	Time: 1 min

Primetime 1	1. The teacher presents vocabulary in context using screenshots from the authentic video. The teacher builds in Turn and Talks during this presentation so that students practice with the vocabulary and structures.
	
	 2. The teacher does a check for understanding
	
	      a. In person: The teacher asks different students in the class to answer questions on what they like/ don't like.
	
	      b. Remote: Students use Peardeck.com to drag a dot to different images on an interactive slide indicating what they like/don't like.
		Time: 15 min

Downtime	3. Students are now directed to work with a partner (either in person or through a breakout room if remote). Students will use a prepared Google Jamboard slide to record the likes and dislikes of their partner.	Time: 10 min
Primetime 2	4. Students now are asked to share out what their partner likes or dislikes.	Time: 15 min
Celebration of Learning	The teacher shows the student learning outcome and asks for a thumbs-up/thumbs-down self-reflection.	Time: 1 min

The teacher begins the class by showing the objective and agenda slide, shown in Figure 2.14, and students complete a do-now. Since students have recently finished learning all of the letters of the Arabic alphabet and are still building reading skills, the do-now asks students to work with a partner to read aloud several vocabulary words that will be introduced to them in the upcoming lesson. If this class were meeting virtually, students would be asked to join the slideshow on Pear Deck (this requires giving students a link to Pear Deck and a code to join), and would then be asked to read the do-now to themselves.

The teacher then begins the lesson by presenting a scenario to students in which a woman visits the home of a friend and is offered a beverage, as is customary in Arab culture. Using screenshots from an authentic video (found on https://www.qfi.org/for-teachers/teacher-resources/jusuur-series-videos/), the teacher models how students can ask and answer questions such as *Do you like coffee?* with a positive and negative response. Students may be asked to turn to a partner to ask the question and respond before moving on to other words such as tea, water, or juice. The teacher has chosen culturally-relevant images and ensures that vocabulary is used in context. In a virtual class, instead of having students Turn and Talk after each question, they could instead have students write whether they like or do not like the drink in the chat box. Figures 2.15 and 2.16 show slides that include the images, questions, and model responses.

After modeling the vocabulary words in context, the teacher does a check for understanding. For in-person instruction, the teacher asks students individually to respond to questions about whether they like certain kinds of drinks. For remote learning, the teacher would use an interactive slide on Pear Deck that allows students to individually drag an image on the slide to indicate their response. Figure 2.17 shows the interactive slide in Pear Deck. Students see a dot that they are able to drag to "I like" or "I do not like" in response to the question about liking mango juice.

The teacher then uses more screen shots from the authentic video to continue modeling a conversation that would take place when hosting guests and offering them something to drink. The teacher ensures that students are comfortable and comprehending the language before moving on to allow them to practice in pairs. When the teacher feels students are ready, students are told they will work with a partner to have a short conversation (or put in a breakout room with a partner if the class is meeting online). The teacher models the directions with the class before students begin working in pairs. Students will use Google Jamboard to record what drinks their partner does and does not like. The teacher will need to have prepared a separate slide in Google Jamboard for each pair of students. Students will ask each other questions such as *Do you like coffee?* then write an X for drinks their partner does not like and draw a heart for drinks their partner does like. Figure 2.18 shows a sample slide from Google Jamboard.

After students have had time to complete the conversation with their partner, they would then be asked to share out a few responses of drinks they like or do not like. In a virtual learning environment, this could be done using a student poll. The teacher would then return students' attention to the learning outcome and ask students to give a thumbs-up/thumbs-down as a self-assessment of learning.

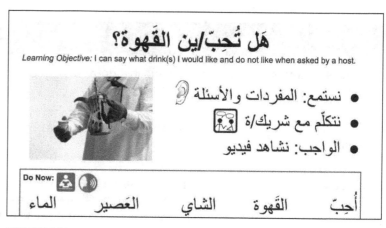

FIGURE 2.14.
Objective and Agenda Slide

Translation of Agenda:
- *We listen: vocabulary and questions*
- *We speak with a partner*
- *Homework: we watch a video*

Translation of Do Now (from right to left): I love...coffee...tea...juice...water

FIGURE 2.15.
Slide Modeling Question with a Positive Response

Translation:
Do you like coffee?
I like coffee.

FIGURE 2.16.
Slide Modeling Question with a Negative Response

Translation:
Do you like coffee?
I do not like coffee.

FIGURE 2.17.
Interactive Slide for Formative Check for Learning

Translation:
Top: And you?
Left: I like mango juice.
Right: I do not like mango juice.

FIGURE 2.18.
Sample GoogleJamboard Slide

Reflection and Next Steps

In this chapter, we have defined when English can be used to support language development and when teachers must remain in the target language. English (L1) use should be reserved for supporting *processing* of learning, such as in goal setting, self-reflection, assessment prompts, and so on. The target language, on the other hand, should be used for any and all *content*—what you are teaching. With a clear distinction for English vs. target-language use in hand, you can use both languages purposefully to best support and develop your students' language proficiency. This chapter also looked closely at specific strategies for ensuring your target-language use is comprehensible to your learners. Teachers are the most important source of language input for students, so you need to be sure that when you speak the target language, it is comprehensible to them. Strategies such as using body language or gestures, incorporating images, modifying your language, modeling expectations for language use, building in classroom routines, and more are all important ways that you can remain in the target language while ensuring that your learners understand you. Maintaining 90%+ target-language use that is comprehensible to your learners is an essential piece in developing their language proficiency.

Before moving on, take some time to reflect and assess your own practice. Consider how you are applying or would like to apply the practices and strategies discussed in this chapter. Where are your strengths? Where would you like to grow your practice? What actions will you take to move forward? This one-point rubric is designed to help you reflect and assess your own target-language use.

One-Point Rubric: Teacher Target-Language Use

GLOW	CRITERIA	GROW	TAKE ACTION
Where are my strengths related to this practice?	What should I be looking for in my own teaching?	Where do I need to grow or expand my practice?	What steps will I take to move my practice forward?
	I use the target-language 90% or more of instructional time.		
	I use numerous strategies to ensure my target language use is comprehensible to my students (such as body language, images, modeling, and so on).		
	I use English 10% or less of instructional time and only to support student processing of learning (not for content).		
	I avoid translation of the target language into English.		

Level Up Your Learning

- **Annenberg Learner. (2016). Teaching foreign languages K-12: A library of classroom practices. https://www.learner.org/series/teaching-foreign-languages-k-12-a-library-of-classroom-practices/**
  The Annenberg Learner series contains videos of world language classrooms in a range of languages and levels. In every video, you will find teachers using the target language with their students (and asking their students to use the language as well!). This resource includes overviews of each lesson to give you some background into the class, and each video is aligned to the World-Readiness Standards, so you can see which standards are covered in each lesson.

- **Crouse, D. (2012, October). Going for 90% plus: How to stay in the target language.** *The Language Educator, 7*(5), 22-27.
  This excellent article provides clear and applicable strategies and suggestions for achieving 90%+ target-language use in your classes. It also discusses the question of when to use English and provides some guiding questions for you to work through if you think you want to reduce your use of English and are not sure how to avoid speaking English.

- **Teacher Effectiveness for Language Learning (TELL). (2014).** *Teacher target language use focused feedback tool.* **http://www.tellproject.org/wp-content/uploads/2014/07/TELL_FeedbackTool_TeacherLanguageUse.pdf**
  The TELL Project provides a comprehensive framework for effective world language teacher practice, and includes numerous tools and resources. One excellent tool is a suite of Focused Feedback Tools, including one specifically designed for teacher target-language use. You can use this to either self-assess your own practice or invite a colleague to observe you and provide some feedback.

Chapter 2 References

ACTFL. (2010). Position statement on the use of the target language in the classroom. https://www.actfl.org/advocacy/actfl-position-statements/use-the-target-language-the-classroom

Annenberg Learner. (2016). *Teaching foreign languages K-12: A library of classroom practices.* https://www.learner.org/series/teaching-foreign-languages-k-12-a-library-of-classroom-practices/

Bex, M. (n.d.). *How to circle.* Comprehensible Classroom. https://comprehensibleclassroom.com/how-to/essential-strategies-for-tprsci-teachers/how-to-circle/

Crouse, D. (2012, October). Going for 90% plus: How to stay in the target language. *The Language Educator, 7*(5), 22-27.

De La Campa, J. C., & Nassaji, H. (2009). The amount, purpose, and reasons for using L1 in L2 classrooms. *Foreign Language Annals, 42*(4), 742–759. https://doi.org/10.1111/j.1944-9720.2009.01052.x

Ellis, R. (2012). *Language teaching research and language pedagogy.* Wiley-Blackwell.

Ellis, R., & Shintani, N. (2014). *Exploring language pedagogy through second language acquisition research.* Routledge.

Gass, S. M., & Mackey, A. (2015). Input, interaction, and output in second language acquisition. In B. VanPatten & J. Williams (Eds.), *Theories in second language acquisition,* (pp. 181–206). Routledge.

Krashen, S. (1985). *The input hypothesis.* Longman.

Nation, I. S. P. (2013). *Learning vocabulary in another language* (2nd ed.). Cambridge University Press.

Pufahl, I., & Rhodes, N. C. (2011). Foreign language instruction in U.S. schools: Results of a national survey of elementary and secondary schools. *Foreign Language Annals, 44*(2), 258–288. https://doi.org/10.1111/j.1944-9720.2011.01130.x

Ray, B., & Seely, C. (1999). *Fluency through TPR storytelling: Achieving real language acquisition in school.* Command Performance Language Institute.

Saville-Troike, M., & Barto, K. (2017). *Introducing second language acquisition* (3rd ed.). Cambridge University Press.

Teacher Effectiveness for Language Learning (TELL). (2014). *Teacher target language use focused feedback tool.* http://www.tellproject.org/wp-content/uploads/2014/07/TELL_FeedbackTool_TeacherLanguageUse.pdf

VanPatten, B. (2017). *While we're on the topic: BVP on language, acquisition, and classroom practice.* ACTFL.

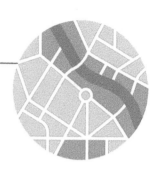

CHAPTER 3

Providing Input
Through Authentic Resources

B eing able to successfully read or listen to something in another language is an exciting and motivating experience for learners. When what they are reading or listening to is an *authentic resource*—something made by native speakers for other native speakers—students get the feeling of lifting the veil and peeking into another world. They are able to connect directly with the culture. Authentic resources are exciting because they are *authentic*. They provide learners with a chance to engage with the language unfiltered and see the culture on its own terms. For younger learners, authentic resources can be incorporated along with glossed resources, in the same way that learners would experience both leveled readers and more whole language books as they learn to read in their L1 using a balanced literacy approach.

Using authentic resources and guiding learners to interpret them is one of ACT-FL's (n.d) Core Practices. These practices are considered foundational for world language teaching and learning. But why do authentic resources and the student task of interpretation have such a powerful effect on learners' language development?

First, an important consideration is student comprehension and proficiency development in the language. You may be surprised to learn that student comprehension is actually higher when reading or listening to an authentic resource compared to non-authentic, simplified, or teacher-made resources (Crossley, Louwerse, McCarthy, & McNamara, 2007; Maxim, 2002; Young, 1999). Of course, authentic resources need to be carefully selected for the proficiency level of the learners, but by giving learners access to authentic language in context, often accompanied with contextual images and structural support, authentic materials become more comprehensible than their simplified counterparts. Authentic resources also are excellent sources of needed language input for learners, showing them how language is used in real-world contexts.

But authentic resources support more than just language acquisition. Since these materials come from a culture where the target language is spoken, they are naturally imbued with elements of that culture. They may also provide interdisciplinary information, connecting language learning to other content areas, including social studies, the arts, science, math, and so much more (Glisan, 2012; Hlas & Hlas, 2012). Culture and Connections (meaning connections to other content areas) are two of the 5 Cs of the World-Readiness Standards for Learning Languages (National Standards Collaborative Board, 2015). When you use authentic resources as part of your curriculum, culture and content are naturally integrated.

In addition to their impact on language development, their natural integration of culture, and their interdisciplinary connections, authentic resources have another advantage over simplified texts: they are more motivating and engaging for students. Researchers have identified using authentic materials as a key factor for student engagement (Cox & Montgomery, 2019). Zoltán Dörnyei (1994) has consistently pointed to authentic materials as a way to "increase the attractiveness of the course content" and generate motivation in language learners (p. 281; see also Guilloteaux & Dörnyei, 2008). Authentic resources are motivating because they are real.

But how can you select authentic resources that support learners at different proficiency levels, even if they are Novice Low or Novice Mid? How do learners process what they are reading or listening to when they encounter authentic resources?

And how can you design lessons to support your learners in the interpretation of such resources? In this chapter, we tackle these important questions so that you will be able to effectively integrate authentic resources into your teaching and guide your learners to interpret them with ease.

Understanding How Learners Process What They Listen to, Read, or View

Take a look at the images and text in Figure 3.1. Whether you speak Portuguese or not, we are going to go out on a limb and say that you probably have a pretty good idea what this is about.

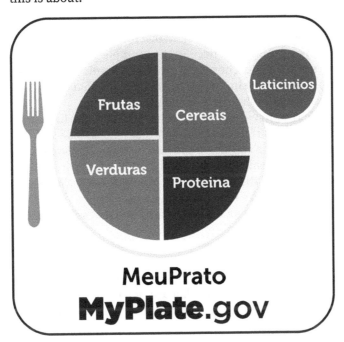

FIGURE 3.1.
Sample Portuguese Authentic Resource

Source: U.S. Department of Agriculture, n.d.

But—assuming you are Novice Low or below in Portuguese, as we are—how did you understand this without speaking the language? How do you interpret things that you read, listen to, or view, even when they're in another language? Everyone draws on two different processing approaches when trying to make meaning: top-down processing and bottom-up processing (Shrum & Glisan, 2016). Top-down processing draws on contextual clues and background knowledge to help make meaning of what is read, heard, or viewed. In our Portuguese example, a reader will look at the text and immediately notice the images, color coding, and organizational structure. The plate shape and colors immediately trigger background knowledge for readers, who may already be familiar with the English version of MyPlate.gov from their schoolwork. The image immediately elicits the thought of a plate of food, and the color scheme connects to colors associated with certain food groups (green vegetables, red fruit, or brown grains, for example). Before even looking at any of the individual words in this text, the learner is able to understand quite a bit through top-down processing. Attention then shifts to taking a close look at the individual words, phrases, or other items in the text. This text includes some cognates that will likely be recognizable to speakers of English, such as *cereais* and *frutas*. Students are now drawing on bottom-up processing to decode the individual linguistic items in the text closely. Readers rely on both bottom-up and top-down processing to make meaning of text, and in fact, language learners often find that top-down processing is more useful when they encounter a misunderstanding (Shrum & Glisan, 2016, p. 178).

Selecting Authentic Resources

An authentic resource is typically defined as something developed by a native speaker for a native speaker. However, since defining who a "native speaker" is isn't as simple as it may seem, it might be easier to define an authentic resource as something that was *not* created for a second language learner. Authentic resources—whether they are reading materials, audio, video, a combination of all three, or only images—provide rich content for learners, naturally integrate culture, and are often more engaging for students than simplified materials. In addition, being able to understand authentic resources can be a very rewarding accomplishment for learners, and thus a powerful motivator for them to continue on their proficiency journey.

While many teachers feel that they cannot use authentic resources with Novice-level learners, in fact authentic resources are easily accessible for beginning students when carefully chosen—as you probably noticed in the example above. Novice-level learners have many more skills than teachers may give them credit for! By tapping into their top-down and bottom-up processing skills, you can ensure that carefully selected authentic resources are easily comprehensible for your learners.

To select appropriate authentic resources, you need to consider both the linguistic elements of the resource—which draw on learners' bottom-up processing skills—and non-linguistic factors which draw on learners' top-down processing skills. For Novice-level learners, the non-linguistic factors will be more significant in supporting comprehension. As learners move up toward the Advanced level, it becomes easier for them to make meaning from materials that have fewer non-linguistic elements. Here are some important considerations for selecting an authentic resource that will be appropriate for the proficiency level of your students.

Visual Support
In the same way that integrating visuals into your lessons makes your target-language use more comprehensible, selecting authentic materials that are rich in images will make them more accessible to your learners, especially those at the Novice level.

Organization/Structure
Authentic resources that include some kind of organizational structure—whether numbers to indicate steps, a side-by-side comparison of two images, or another format that is familiar to learners—will support the use of top-down processing skills.

Background Knowledge
Selecting authentic resources for which students have some background knowledge allows them to draw on what they already know to make meaning. However, teachers can also build learners' background knowledge by asking them to interpret resources on less familiar topics.

Relevance/Interest for Learners
Selecting authentic material that will excite and engage your learners has the added bonus of supporting comprehension. If you select a text that naturally interests learners, they are more likely to have background knowledge on the topic, they are more likely to pay attention to it when they read or listen to it, and they are more likely to want to talk about it afterward.

Length and Complexity
Learners at different proficiency levels will be able to handle authentic materials of different lengths. An Advanced-level learner will likely be able to pay attention to and make meaning of material that is longer and more complex than the texts a Novice-level learner can manage. Without editing an authentic text, you can still use a longer one with Novice or Intermediate Low students by using only one paragraph or only the title and subheadings, for example.

Vocabulary

While students do not need to understand every single word in the authentic resource you choose, they should certainly know many or most of them. If you scan the resource and find that students will likely only know half of the words, this should tell you that it is too challenging for them. Likewise, if students know every single word in the text, it may not push them beyond their proficiency level. Look for authentic resources that include roughly 80–90% of words and phrases that your learners already know.

Target Structures

In any given lesson or unit, you are likely working with learners on how to use certain grammatical forms or structures in the target language. An authentic resource is an excellent way to provide learners with more input on how those forms or structures are used in context, and the fact that you have been focusing on these structures in your unit already will support their comprehension of the material.

Writing System or Script

For languages that use a writing system that is new to learners (for example, a non-Roman script for native speakers of English), the script used in printed and online authentic resources may have a bigger impact on comprehensibility than you initially realize. Reading authentic material that is printed in a less-familiar script reduces reading speed and fluency, and thus may impede access to the content. In addition, depending on the technology available to learners, some characters may not render correctly on screen or when printed out.

Table 3.1 provides a summary of considerations for selecting authentic materials for use with your learners.

TABLE 3.1. CONSIDERATIONS FOR SELECTING AN AUTHENTIC RESOURCE	
Non-Linguistic Factors *(drawing on top-down processing)*	**Linguistic Factors** *(drawing on bottom-up processing)*
Visual support	Vocabulary
Organization/structure of text	Grammatical forms and structures
Background knowledge	
Relevance/interest for learners	
Length and complexity	
Writing system/script	

So what do all of these important features look like in practice? Check out Box 3.1 for an annotated authentic resource that shows them in a real-world example. And if you are not sure where to start looking for authentic resources, head to Box 3.2 for some tips as you start your search.

BOX 3.1. SO WHAT DO ALL OF THESE IMPORTANT FEATURES LOOK LIKE IN PRACTICE?

Visual support: The image of the woman wearing a mask helps give readers an initial idea of what this infographic is all about. The icons next to each section of text provide further clues as to the context.

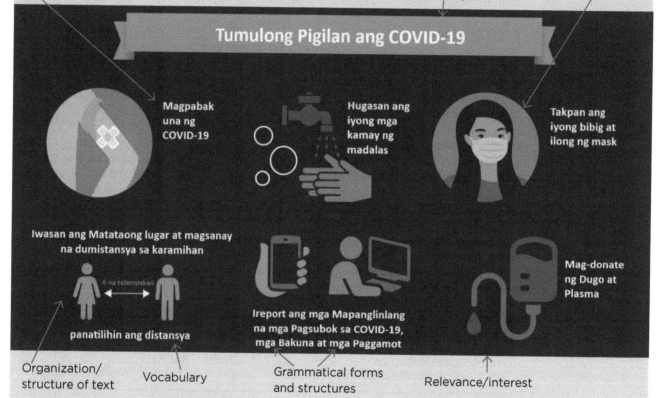

Source: U.S. Food and Drug Administration, n.d.

Organization/structure of text: Each of the sections of text is chunked, making it less overwhelming for readers, and easier for them to associate the text with the icon next to it.

Background knowledge: In today's world, any reader will bring some background knowledge to this infographic. The images of hand-washing, wearing masks, and social distancing will make any reader think of COVID-19, and their background knowledge will help tell them that this infographic likely has something to do with how to stay safe from COVID.

Relevance/interest: Whether an authentic resource is relevant or of interest to your learners will depend on who they are, where they live, how old they are, and their personal interests.

Length and complexity: This infographic uses sentence-level discourse, but the text is chunked so that readers focus on one part at a time, making it more easily accessible.

Vocabulary: In addition to seeing COVID-19 in the title, readers will encounter a few cognates in the text.

Grammatical forms and structures: This infographic uses a few structures repeatedly, including *ang* [the], *ng* [a/an], and *mga* [the marker for plural]. This resource would provide meaningful input for learners to see how articles are used in context.

BOX 3.2. TIPS FOR FINDING AUTHENTIC RESOURCES

Finding just the perfect authentic resource can be time-consuming, but you are not alone in your search. Here are some tips and resources to help you:

- Google: Try an image search in Google by entering a key word in the target language. Better yet, use the version of Google from your target culture, such as Google.de (Germany), Google.es (Spain), Google.com.br (Brazil), and so on.

- Pinterest: Pinterest can be used to both search for and save authentic resources. Many teachers have created Pinterest boards on different themes, and you can easily copy their boards to your own page and add to it. Note in particular Leslie Grahn's treasure trove of resources at www.pinterest.com/grahnforlang. You will find curated resources in a range of languages and topics.

- Social Media: Social media platforms such as Twitter, Instagram, and TikTok are great places to search for resources. Try searching for a key structure in quotes (such as *il faut que* in French) to see what comes up. You will find many authentic examples of how the target structure is used in real life. You can also use these platforms to search for cultural topics, current events, people, and organizations that are relevant to your theme.

- YouTube: You can find almost anything on YouTube! If you are looking for music videos, commercials, clips of TV shows, movie trailers, news broadcasts, and more, YouTube is a great place to search. Search using a key word or expression in the target language.

- Netflix and Kanopy: Both of these streaming sites have tons of films and TV shows from around the world in many different languages. While Netflix requires a subscription, Kanopy may be available through your school or local library.

- Looking for travel reviews? Try TripAdvisor for reviews in the target language.

The Interactive Model for Interpretive Communication

With a carefully selected authentic resource in hand, you now face the question of how to use it in the classroom. Certainly you want to do more than just ask students to read or listen to it, right? Enter the Interactive Model for Interpretive Communication, which provides a clear and well-structured framework for using authentic resources with your students (Glisan & Donato, 2017; Shrum & Glisan, 2016). This model moves away from traditional reading and listening exercises and draws on learners' top-down and bottom-up processing skills to support meaning making. It also connects interpretive reading and listening to the interpersonal and presentational modes, encouraging students to actively discuss what they have read or listened to (interpersonal) as well as use the information gained to write or prepare an oral presentation (presentational). The Interactive Model can be used with all levels, age groups, and languages. It provides a framework for engaging students with authentic material and leading them toward meaningful interaction as they discuss what they have learned from the resource.

The Interactive Model includes five phases:

1. The Preparation Phase
2. The Comprehension Phase (parts 1 and 2)
3. The Interpretation/Discussion Phase
4. The Creativity Phase
5. The Extension Phase (optional)

Here we provide an overview of the phases and some specific activities you can use as part of each one. In the *Classroom Close-Up* section, you will find two detailed examples that put the Interactive Model to work.

Phase 1. The Preparation Phase

Before reading, listening to, or viewing an authentic resource, students need some time to prepare. Spending time activating or building background knowledge, previewing new key vocabulary, establishing purpose, or predicting meaning will help make the text more accessible to your learners. This phase can last 10 minutes or an entire class period, depending on the complexity of the topic and the resource. An important consideration as you begin is the *purpose of the text* and the *purpose for reading, listening, or viewing*. Questions to ask yourself as the teacher are *Why this text?* and *What is the goal of having my students read this particular text?* If the answer is just to practice reading, that should be a red flag. Define the purpose for reading or listening before you begin. What do you want students to learn about or discover? What will students do with the knowledge they gain from reading or listening to this text? Students should not just be reading or listening for the sake of reading or listening. Rather, they should be reading with a purpose. Part of the Preparation Phase is to establish this goal through an essential question, a stated learning outcome, or articulation of what students will be doing after they read or listen to the text. Box 3.3 outlines some strategies you might try during this phase.

BOX 3.3. STRATEGIES TO USE AS PART OF THE PREPARATION PHASE

Here are some activities that work well to support the Preparation Phase:

- Categorization: To help students review key vocabulary, the teacher provides students with a small set of vocabulary words on index cards, a slideshow or another format. Students are asked to place the words into categories to show where they belong. For example, are the words drinks or food items? Positive or negative? Opposites?

- Hold Ups: To help students review key vocabulary, the teacher gives the students manipulatives that were prepared ahead of time, such as image cards, toys, or maps. The teacher calls out a statement, and the student responds by holding up the appropriate manipulative to show their understanding.

- Guiding Questions: To help tap into background knowledge, the teacher prepares a number of guiding questions connected to the theme. If students are going to be reading an authentic infographic on food, for example, the teacher provides questions such as "What do you usually eat for breakfast?" or "What kind of food do you really hate to eat?" Students are asked to do Turn and Talks with their partners, then share out a few responses to the whole class.

- Predictions: To help students predict the meaning of the text, the teacher can show a few images (screenshots from the authentic resource or related images) or words that represent concepts in the text or video. The students are asked to come up with some ideas to predict what the text might be about. After reading the text, students can look back to see if their original predictions were correct or not.

Phase 2. The Comprehension Phase, Parts 1 and 2

After preparing students to read, listen to, or view the text, you are now ready to dive in. Students should be engaged in an activity while reading or listening, rather than just quietly listening or following along as someone else reads. Recall that you have established a purpose for reading or listening to this text—students are reading with a goal in mind. That goal can and should be incorporated in what you ask students to do during the Comprehension Phase. Will you give students a graphic organizer to jot down notes as they read? Will you provide guiding questions for learners to focus their attention? While reading or listening, how will learners be active in a way that connects to the purpose you have established for the text?

The Comprehension Phase should be composed of two parts, so that students read or listen to the text twice, each time being active in different but connected ways. The first time students read or listen to the text, you should ask them to focus on the main idea and a few details about the text. In the second reading or listening you can ask students to delve deeper into the text so that they focus more deeply on additional details and guess the meaning of some unknown words by using context.

For example, if you have given students a graphic organizer for note-taking as they listen, perhaps during the first listening they can take notes in the part of the graphic organizer that focuses on the main idea. Then, in the second listening session, they can take notes in a different section of the graphic organizer that helps them pay attention to more details. Box 3.4 provides some ideas for activities and strategies to use as part of the Comprehension Phase.

BOX 3.4. ACTIVITIES TO USE AS PART OF THE COMPREHENSION PHASE

- Listen and Draw: To help students focus on specific details of the text, the teacher asks them to draw a few key images (this works best with an audio resource). Students are asked not to start drawing until they have finished listening to the entire passage, and the teacher can specify what should be drawn. For example, if the resource is about types of sports that adolescents in the target culture participate in, students could be asked to draw a picture of one sport they like and one sport they do not like.

- Picture Sequencing: To help students focus on specific details of the text, the teacher gives them a series of images and asks them to place the images in order based on what they understood from the text. The images could be screenshots, if a video resource is being used, or general images that represent key points from the text.

- Story Maps: To help students focus on the main idea and supporting details, the teacher can use a story map (a type of graphic organizer) to guide identification of the main idea, setting, characters, problem and solution, and so on. Students are asked to complete one part of the story map after the first reading of the text, focusing more on the main idea, and another part of the story map after the second reading to help them focus on supporting details.

- Guiding Questions: To help students focus on the main idea and supporting details and even guess meaning from context, the teacher prepares a number of guiding questions connected to the theme. These questions should first guide students in thinking about the main idea for Part 1 of the Comprehension Phase. Questions such as *Who is the audience for this article?* can help students think about the big picture of the text. Part 2 questions should lead students to focus on more details from the text, but can also ask them to make guesses about words that they do not know but should be able to figure out from the context. For example, ask them, *Which of these words would be a good synonym for...?* Students can ask each other the questions in short Turn and Talks before sharing out with the whole class.

Phase 3. The Interpretation/Discussion Phase

After reading or listening to the text twice and completing two active tasks connected to the purpose, teacher and learners shift to the next phase for interpretation and discussion of what they have read, listened to, or viewed. This can be done through providing discussion questions and asking students to work in small groups, using a structured activity that further focuses learners' attention on the text, or using the notes from the Comprehension Phase to make comparisons. The main focus of this phase is on interpersonal communication, where learners are actively engaging in text-based discussions. Box. 3.5 provides activity ideas to support the Interpretation/Discussion Phase.

Phase 4. The Creativity Phase

Following engagement in discussions around the text, students move to the Creativity Phase, which allows them to apply what they have learned in creative ways in either the interpersonal or the presentational mode of communication. They may be asked to make their own version of what they read or listened to, write a different ending, create a video, or any other creative idea that connects to the original purpose of reading or listening to the text. Box 3.6 provides additional ideas for the Creativity Phase.

BOX 3.5. ACTIVITIES TO USE AS PART OF THE INTERPRETATION/DISCUSSION PHASE

- Question/Image Cards: To support student discussion and interpretation, the teacher prepares a series of cards with either questions or images on each one. Students are given the cards to discuss in small groups. For Novice-level classes or younger language learners, the teacher can include simple questions for students to practice with or images connected to the authentic resources that learners can describe. For Intermediate- or Advanced-level classes, students could be asked to generate their own questions.

- Explain a Quote: To support student discussion and interpretation, and ensure that students are focusing closely on the text, the teacher identifies a series of quotes from the text or video. These are provided as paper handouts or shared on the whiteboard (in face-to-face instruction) or shared screen (in online instruction). Students work in small groups or pairs to identify the context of each quote and paraphrase it in their own words.

- Hashtags: To support student discussion and interpretation in an Intermediate- or Advanced-level class, students work in small groups or pairs to come up with keywords or phrases from the text that identify some of the themes, concepts, or opinions. Students turn these phrases into hashtags like those used on social media. Students should be ready to share their hashtags and explain their relevance to the text. As a follow-up activity, students might be asked to write a short statement from the perspective of one of the characters in the text using one of the hashtags. These could be posted on an online class discussion board.

- Venn Diagram: To support student discussion and interpretation when students are comparing two perspectives from the text, students are first assigned one of the two perspectives and asked to jot down key points on the Venn diagram. Each student is then paired with a classmate who was assigned the opposite perspective, and they must work together to find common ground and figure out where they overlap. The teacher can provide guiding questions for discussion, if needed.

BOX 3.6. ACTIVITIES TO USE AS PART OF THE CREATIVITY PHASE

- Role Play: For interpersonal speaking, the teacher can design an authentic speaking task in which the students role-play different characters based on the authentic resource. For example, one student could be a traveler looking to book an AirBnB while the other student is the host who wants to rent their property. To maintain interpersonal communication, the teacher can allow students time to practice speaking with a partner in class, but then call names randomly when it is time to perform the role play. This gives students some practice speaking, but also prevents them from writing a script that they memorize, since students do not know ahead of time who they will be performing the role play with.

- Text Messages: For presentational communication, the teacher can give students a template for writing a text message exchange between two characters from the authentic resource. This activity can be scaffolded by providing students with the dialogue for one character and asking them to write what they think the other character would say in response.

- Create a Product: For presentational communication, students can create their own version of the authentic resource, such as making an invitation, creating a menu, designing a proposal for a socially responsible company, or making a public service announcement video.

- Interview: For interpersonal communication, students can be asked to interview a native speaker from their community or students from a partner school in another country to find out more about the topic. Students can also be connected virtually to native speakers using sites such as epals.com. If students are unable to connect with native speakers, they can also try interviewing students from a higher-level language class within their own school. Students can record the interview on their mobile phones or using a tech tool such as Screencastify or Zoom. Depending on their proficiency level, students may need support in preparing interview questions and practicing with classmates before conducting the actual interview.

Phase 5. The Extension Phase (optional)

One of the many benefits of using authentic resources is the ability to provide different perspectives from the target culture or cultures, while also affirming the identities of the students in your own classroom (Glynn, Wesley, & Wassell, 2014). For this reason, you may use a number of authentic resources on a common theme. The Extension Phase encourages teachers to extend the theme by introducing another authentic resource that provides a different perspective or engages learners with a different skill (reading instead of listening, for example). Perhaps you first use a video clip and go through the phases of the Interactive Model. Then, wanting to extend the learning, you introduce an article on the same topic for students to read the following day—essentially re-starting the Interactive Model and working through each phase with this new resource. Although it is listed as the final step, you may decide to use the Extension Phase before the Creativity Phase. You may, in fact, decide to use three or even four authentic resources on the same theme, going through the Preparation Phase, Comprehension Phase, and Interpretation/Discussion Phase with a different resource each day. Finally, after working through a few authentic resources, you are ready to move students to the Creativity Phase where they are asked to work on a creative project that pulls all their learning together. Table 3.2 shows a possible week-long lesson overview using the Interactive Model with multiple authentic resources.

TABLE 3.2. WEEK-LONG LEARNING SEQUENCE USING THE INTERACTIVE MODEL AND MULTIPLE AUTHENTIC RESOURCES ON THE SAME THEME

Monday	Tuesday	Wednesday	Thursday	Friday
Authentic Resource 1	*Extension:* Authentic Resource 2	*Extension:* Authentic Resource 3	*Extension:* Authentic Resource 4	Creativity Phase
• Preparation Phase	• Preparation Phase	• Preparation Phase	• Preparation Phase	
• Comprehension Phase, Part 1	• Comprehension Phase, Part 1	• Comprehension Phase, Part 1	• Comprehension Phase, Part 1	
• Comprehension Phase, Part 2	• Comprehension Phase, Part 2	• Comprehension Phase, Part 2	• Comprehension Phase, Part 2	
• Interpretation/ Discussion Phase	• Interpretation/ Discussion Phase	• Interpretation/ Discussion Phase	• Interpretation/ Discussion Phase	

Tech Zoom

When using authentic resources and the Interactive Model, you can easily integrate technology into in-person classes, use a flipped classroom model, or adapt activities to a hybrid or distance learning environment. When possible, the Interpretation/Discussion Phase should be prioritized for synchronous time with students so that they can interact with you and each other using the target language. *Classroom Close-Up 3.1* gives a detailed example of how this model can work in a hybrid or distance learning class. While tech tools often change and new resources are constantly being developed, these tips and suggestions can help you think about ways to integrate technology, whether you're working with students in the face-to-face classroom, in a hybrid model, or in a distance learning model.

• Comprehension or interpretation tools: Students can be asked to read, listen to, or view the authentic resource independently. These interactive tools can help scaffold student comprehension while also checking for understanding.

  • Edpuzzle: This tool lets you add videos (either those you create yourself and upload or ones available online) and insert questions. The video pauses when there is a question, and students need to answer it to move on.

- Pear Deck and Nearpod: Both of these sites let you create interactive slides where you can poll students, have them post comments, ask open-ended questions, and more. You can use the slides when meeting synchronously with students, or students can work through the slides independently.

- Seesaw: Seesaw can be used to create activities for students that are essentially interactive slides in which you can embed authentic resources. Students can record audio or video, manipulate images, and more. Older learners may prefer Classkick, which has many of the same features.

- Interactive games: There are many online game platforms that will allow you to develop customized games for your learners, such as Wordwall, Kahoot, and Gimkit. Each of these sites will let you build your own games, and they can be fun ways for students to show understanding of interpretive content.

- Discussion tools: Although it is preferable to engage students in target-language discussions during synchronous class time, many tools allow for student interaction on asynchronous platforms.

  - Zoom and Google Meet: If you are meeting synchronously with students, these two sites allow you to put students in breakout groups for discussions. You can also assign students to meet on their own using one of these platforms and record their conversation to submit, depending on the age of the students.

  - Flipgrid: Flipgrid allows you to post questions, audio or video prompts, or images and then ask students to respond by recording their own video asynchronously. Other students are able to watch the video and reply. Students can choose to insert an emoji over their face if they prefer not to be seen in the video.

  - Virtual bulletin boards: Padlet and similar platforms can be used for asynchronous discussions, as well as for comprehension or interpretation activities. As with a virtual bulletin board, you can post a question, image, or video and then ask students to respond by typing or posting a video. Students are able to see each other's responses and reply to each other.

Now that you have looked at how to select an authentic resource, how to integrate it into the Interactive Model for Interpretive Communication, and how to identify some specific strategies to use with each phase of the model, you are ready to walk through two *Classroom Close-Ups* that show how teachers of two different languages, working with students at two different proficiency levels, apply the model in their own teaching. In *Classroom Close-Up 3.1*, you will also see how the teacher adapts the model for a hybrid or distance learning environment.

Classroom Close-Ups
Classroom Close-Up 3.1: My School Life at Home
Lesson developed by Catherine Ritz

COURSE OVERVIEW	
Course Name	French 1B, 7th Grade
Course Proficiency Target	Novice Mid-High

LESSON OVERVIEW	
Unit Theme	A Day in the Life
Lesson Learning Outcome	I can compare an ideal and real daily routine for children at home during quarantine.
Core Vocabulary and Forms	• Telling time • Daily activities/routines • Using infinitives and present-tense verbs
Materials and Resources	Two authentic resources from https://vifamagazine.ca/comprendre/role-du-parent/horaires-et-routines-pendant-la-crise-du-coronavirus-organiser-le-quotidien-a-la-maison-avec-les-enfants/: • *"Horaire Maison"* [*"Home Schedule"*] • *"Horaire Maison revue et corrigée"* [*"Home Schedule: Revised and Corrected"*] Students each need their own tablet or laptop. Account on Peardeck.com or Nearpod.com with prepared interactive slides and account on Seesaw.com with prepared interactive activity.
Lesson Length	60 minutes

LEARNING SEQUENCE		
Focus of Learning	Question posted on slides: *Quelle est ta routine matinale?* [What is your morning routine?] Students either Turn and Talk (in-person) or post responses in the chat (virtual). Students are also instructed to join the Nearpod slides.	*Time:* 2 min
Preview of Learning	The teacher presents the learning outcome and reviews the agenda.	*Time:* 1 min
Learning Episode		
Primetime 1	1. The teacher uses a poll to survey students about their daily routine. (Slides are prepared using Nearpod.) 2. The teacher pauses after each question to share the survey results and ask follow-up questions regarding each question. 3. The teacher presents the ideal class schedule and models the structure: *Pendant le confinement, l'idéal est de...à...* [During quarantine, the ideal is to...at...] 4. As a whole class, students use the sentence frame to read the ideal schedule. 5. The teacher then presents the real schedule and models the structure: *Mais en réalité, à...* [But in reality, at...] 6. As a whole class, students use the sentence frame to read the real schedule.	*Time:* 15 min

Downtime	7. Students work independently to draw a comparison between the real and ideal schedules using the interactive drawing slide feature on Nearpod.	*Time:* 5 min
Primetime 2	8. The teacher invites a few students to share their drawings and explain what happens during the real and ideal schedules.	*Time:* 10 min
Brain Break	Students are given a 60-second stretch break. The teacher plays Francophone music while students are allowed to get up and move around.	*Time:* 1 min
Learning Episode 2		
Primetime 1	9. The teacher instructs students to read the two schedules again and work independently to complete a drag-and-drop activity in Seesaw.	*Time:* 5 min
Downtime	10. Students are instructed to work in small groups (2 or 3 students) and discuss the two schedules. They are given the discussion guide, including sentence frames. (Students work in small groups for in-person or are put in breakout groups for virtual.)	*Time:* 10 min
Primetime 2	11. A few groups are asked to share out from their group discussions.	*Time:* 10 min
	12. The teacher presents that students will now begin developing their own ideal schedule. Students are given a template and the teacher asks students to share some ideas for their ideal schedule. Students will create their own schedule as homework and will be ready to share during the following class.	
Check for Learning	Students are asked to write down one real and one ideal activity for their quarantine schedule. (For in-person, students can write this on an index card to hand in; for virtual, students can write in the chat box.)	*Time:* 10 min
Celebration of Learning	The teacher returns students' attention to the learning goal and asks for a thumbs-up/thumbs-down self-reflection.	*Time:* 10 min

In this lesson focused on the theme of daily life, the teacher is using blended instruction to integrate technology and shift between whole class and individual or pair work. The lesson is designed for either in-person instruction with students using tablets or laptops or over a synchronous live streaming platform. To increase the interactive content of the lesson, the teacher uses a site such as Pear Deck or Nearpod. The example that follows shows sample slides from Nearpod.

Preparation Phase
As students join the class, a question is presented on the slides for them to discuss (classes meeting in person can have students Turn and Talk; classes meeting virtually can have students post a response in the chat): *Quelle est ta routine matinale?* [What is your morning routine?] Students are given a minute or two to discuss the question or

post a response. The teacher then greets the students and goes over the objective and agenda for the lesson. The teacher begins with whole class instruction using the poll function on Nearpod to ask students a few simple questions on the topic of daily routines. Figures 3.3 and 3.4 show the objective/agenda slide, followed by one of the polling questions. Students are able to respond on their devices and the results can be shared in real time. The survey is designed to activate background knowledge and review key expressions and vocabulary that students will encounter when reading the authentic resources. The teacher pauses after each survey question to ask individual students to elaborate and ask follow-up questions.

Comprehension Phase, Part 1
The teacher now shares the first of two authentic resources with students. Because the goal is to support comparisons between the ideal and the real schedule for children during the quarantine, the teacher has placed the two authentic resources next to each other, but begins by showing the ideal schedule. Students are asked to read aloud using the sentence frame: *Pendant le confinement, l'idéal est de... à...* [During confinement, the ideal is to... at...] Students then supply the activity in the first blank and the time in the second. Figure 3.5 shows the authentic resource with the ideal schedule.

The teacher then shows the second authentic resource, the "real" schedule. Again, students are asked to read using a sentence frame: *Mais en réalité, à...* (time + activity). [But, in reality, at ... time + activity.] Figure 3.6 shows the authentic resource with the real schedule.

The teacher then uses the interactive drawing slide feature on Nearpod to ask students to work independently to draw two pictures to demonstrate comprehension, the first focusing on one activity from the ideal schedule and the second focusing on one activity from the real schedule. The teacher is able to see and show the images drawn by students and can ask a few students to explain what they drew. Figure 3.7 shows the interactive drawing slide from Nearpod.

Comprehension Phase, Part 2
Students are now asked to read the schedules again and complete some independent work using Seesaw. The teacher has created an interactive assignment on Seesaw where students drag an image to a time slot for either the ideal or real schedule (Figure 3.8). This activity helps students focus on more details from the text and begin to compare the two schedules.

Interpretation/Discussion Phase
Moving now to interpretation and discussion, the teacher either pairs students in class or uses the breakout feature on the platform to put students in small groups. The teacher has prepared some sentence frames and guiding questions to support students, who likely need a good amount of scaffolding at this proficiency level to facilitate their conversation. Figure 3.9 includes the discussion guide given to students to use during the discussion. The teacher tells students to be ready to report back to the whole class when the discussion ends; this helps keep them accountable and on-task during discussion time.

Creativity Phase
While the teacher may choose to integrate additional authentic resources connected to this theme (Extension Phase) before moving to Creativity, in this example, the teacher moves students to a short Creativity Phase in which they create their own ideal schedule for conducting school from home during quarantine. A template is given to students for this work, seen in Figure 3.10. The teacher asks students to share what their ideal activities are. Students will complete their ideal schedule as homework and will share it during the following class. As a quick check for learning, the teacher asks students to write one real activity and one ideal activity, either on an index card for in-person instruction or in the chat box for virtual.

Français 1B - *La Routine Confinement!*

Objectif: I can compare an ideal and real daily routine for children doing school at home during quarantine.

Emploi du temps:

1. Sondage
2. La routine confinement: l'idéal vs. la réalité
   a. Lisons!
   b. Dessinons!
   c. Discutons!
3. Ta routine confinement

FIGURE 3.3.
Objective and Agenda Slide

Translation
French 1B - The quarantine routine!
Objective: I can compare an ideal and real daily routine for children doing school at home during quarantine.
Agenda:
1. Survey
2. The quarantine routine: the ideal vs. the real
   a. Let's read!
   b. Let's draw!
   c. Let's discuss!
3. Your quarantine routine

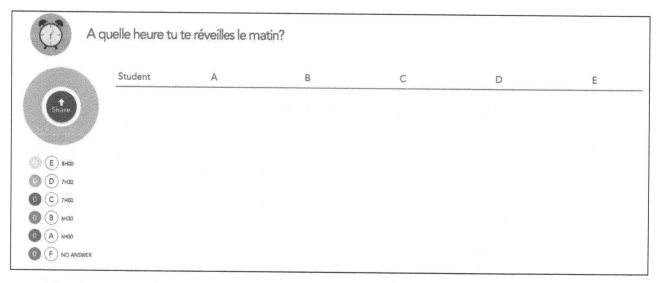

FIGURE 3.4.
Sample Polling Question Using Nearpod

Translation
What time do you wake up in the morning?

HORAIRE MAISON

8H00-9H00	ON DÉJEUNE ET ON S'HABILLE
9H00-10H00	JEUX À L'EXTÉRIEUR OU JEUX LIBRES
10H00-11H00	ON TRAVAILLE SUR NOTRE PROJET!*
11H00-12H00	PÉRIODE DE DEVOIRS
12H00-12H30	DÎNER
12H30-13H30	ON PARTICIPE AU MÉNAGE. À LA CUISINE...
13H30-14H30	JEUX À L'EXTÉRIEUR OU JEUX LIBRES
14H30-15H30	PÉRIODE DE DEVOIRS
15H30-16H30	ON AVANCE NOTRE PROJET!*
16H30-18H00	PÉRIODE LIBRE
18H00-19H30	SOUFER ET BAINS
19H30-21H00	TEMPS D'ÉCRAN ET DODO

*UN PROJET SPÉCIAL SUR LE LONG TERME. CRÉATION. CONSTRUCTION DE LEGO. PROJET DE JARDINAGE. ÉCRIRE ET ILLUSTRER UNE HISTOIRE. ETC.

ta tribu

FIGURE 3.5.
Ideal Schedule Authentic Resource

Translation
Home Schedule
8:00 - 9:00: We have breakfast and we get dressed.
9:00 - 10:00: Outdoor games or free game time
10:00 - 11:00: We work on our project.
11:00 - 12:00: Homework time
12:00 - 12:30: Lunch
12:30 - 1:30: We do chores. In the kitchen...
1:30 - 2:30: Outdoor games or free game time
2:30 - 3:30: Homework time
3:30 - 4:30: We make progress on our project!
4:30 - 6:00: Free time
6:00 - 7:30: Dinner and bath
7:30 - 9:00: Screen time and bedtime
*A special long-term project: Creation and construction of Legos, garden project, write and illustrate a story, etc.

Source: Poulin-Chartrand, 2020a

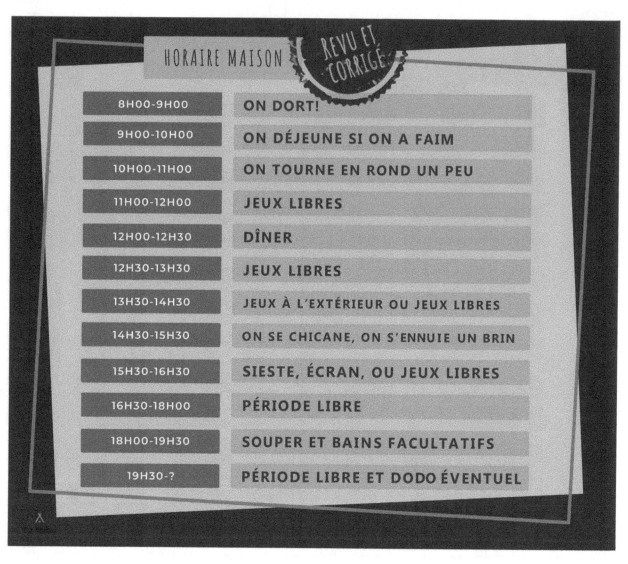

FIGURE 3.6.
Real Schedule Authentic Resource

Translation
Home Schedule - Revised and corrected
8:00 - 9:00: We sleep!
9:00 - 10:00: We have breakfast if we're hungry
10:00 - 11:00: We run around in circles a bit
11:00 - 12:00: Free time
12:00 - 12:30: Lunch
12:30 - 1:30: Free time
1:30 - 2:30: Outdoor games or free games
2:30 - 3:30: We fight with each other, we're a bit bored
3:30 - 4:30: Nap, screen, or free game time
4:30 - 6:00: Free time
6:00 - 7:30: Dinner and optional bath
7:30 - 9:00: Free time and possible bedtime

Source: Poulin-Chartrand, 2020b

FIGURE 3.7.
Interactive Drawing Slide from Nearpod

Translation
Draw two activities from your quarantine routine - one activity from the ideal routine and one activity from the real routine.

	Move the images to the time that best matches the schedule.	
L'idéal	**Heure**	**La réalité**
	8h00 - 9h00	
	9h00 - 10h00	
	10h00 - 11h00	
	11h00 - 12h00	
	12h00 - 12h30	
	12h30 - 13h30	
	13h30 - 14h30	
	14h30 - 15h30	
	15h30 - 16h30	
	16h30 - 18h00	
	18h00 - 19h30	
	19h30 - 21h00	

FIGURE 3.8.
Drag-and-Drop Activity on Seesaw

Translation
Drag the image to the corresponding space.
The Ideal - Time - the Reality

Discutons!

Compare the ideal and real schedule. Use the sentence frames on the right to help your discussion.

- What should the children do each day (ideal)?
- But, what do they actually do each day (real)?
- What would you do if you were these children?

Be ready to share out:

- Two differences in the schedules
- One thing that you would prefer to do during confinement

Sentence Frames:

- Pendant le confinement, les enfants doivent _____ , mais en réalité _____ .
- Il est bien de _____ , mais les enfants préfèrent _____ .
- Moi, je préfère _____ pendant le confinement.

FIGURE 3.9.
Discussion Guide

Translation
Sentence frames:
• *During quarantine, children should _____, but in reality _____.*
• *It's good to _____, but children prefer _____.*
• *Me, I prefer _____ during quarantine.*

Create your own ideal schedule for confinement! Please follow this template.

Mon emploi du temps **idéal** pendant le confinement!

Heure	Activité	Dessin/Image
Ex. 7h30	Je me réveille.	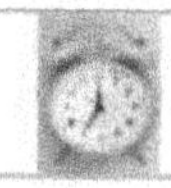

FIGURE 3.10.
Student Template for Creating Their Own Schedule

Translation
My ideal schedule during quarantine!
Time - Activity - Drawing/Image
Ex. 7:30 - I wake up.

Classroom Close-Up 3.2: Exploring Habana
Lesson developed by Christina Toro

COURSE OVERVIEW	
Course Name	Spanish 2, High School
Course Proficiency Target	Intermediate Low

LESSON OVERVIEW	
Unit Theme	Travel/City Life
Lesson Learning Outcome	I can describe characteristics of major Spanish-speaking cities.
Core Vocabulary and Forms	• Places in a city • Modes of transportation • Tiene/Es/Está/Hay (It has/It is/It is/There is)
Materials and Resources	An authentic video from: https://www.youtube.com/watch?v=qWs8eMUqII4&t=54s
Lesson Length	55 minutes

LEARNING SEQUENCE		
Focus of Learning	The teacher asks the students to come up with five things that they know about Cuba, then share out with the whole class.	*Time:* 5 min
Preview of Learning	The teacher goes over the objective and the agenda for that day.	*Time:* 1 min
Learning Episode 1		
Primetime 1	1. The teacher asks the students to copy down a graphic organizer into their notebooks. The two categories are transportation and places in a city. Then the teacher posts the words for the students to see.	*Time:* 3 min
Downtime	2. The students work in pairs to categorize the words. The teacher checks for understanding and clarifies any misunderstandings.	*Time:* 5 min
Primetime 2	3. The teacher then shows the students a 2-minute video about Havana and asks them to jot down places or types of transportation that they heard in the video. 4. The students compare their answers with a classmate before sharing out what they learned. 5. The teacher plays the video a second time. This time, students dig deeper to identify places or types of transportation that are unique to Cuba by matching an image to a word.	*Time:* 15 min

Brain Break	Students listen to salsa from Celia Cruz, one of Cuba's best-known singers.	*Time:* 2 min
Learning Episode 2		
Primetime 1	6. The teacher gives the students another graphic organizer: a Venn diagram. If the students need more support, the teacher can provide pictures of students' own community and Havana. The teacher explains that they will be comparing the two communities. For students that need more support, the teacher can provide guiding questions to give them food for thought.	*Time:* 2 min
Downtime	7. Students work in pairs to come up with statements that show what the two communities have in common and what differences they have. The teacher calls on different groups to share what they wrote.	*Time:* 10 min
Primetime 2	8. The teacher now asks the students to choose between two different cities they have explored—Mexico City and Havana—and write an email describing which city the school should visit on a school trip and why. They will need to describe the features of the city and give their opinion about the city.	*Time:* 10 min
Check for Learning	The teacher asks the students to write down five things they learned about Havana.	*Time:* 1 min
Celebration of Learning	The teacher brings back the first slide to reflect on the student learning outcome.	*Time:* 1 min

The unit is designed to introduce students to different cities in the Spanish-speaking world. Students have previously explored other cities, such as Madrid and Mexico City, and this lesson focuses them on the city of Havana, Cuba.

Preparation Phase
To start the lesson, the teacher reviews the agenda and learning outcome, seen in Figure 3.11, and then asks students to share with their partner what they already know about Cuba. After coming up with a short list, the students are asked to share out a few things with the whole class. The teacher expects that students may mention something about Fidel Castro, American cars, or Cuba's location in the Caribbean Sea. Figure 3.12 shows the opening discussion slide that helps students tap into their background knowledge.

¡LA HABANA, CUBA!

Objetivo: I can compare what places there are in different Spanish-speaking cities.

Actividades:

1. Hablar de Cuba
2. Describir partes de una ciudad
3. Describir la ciudad de la Habana
4. Comparar la Habana con Boston
5. Escribir sobre la Habana

FIGURE 3.11.
Objective and Agenda Slide

Translation
Havana, Cuba!
Objective: I can compare what places there are in different Spanish-speaking cities.
Activities:
1. Talk about Cuba
2. Describe parts of a city
3. Describe the city of Havana
4. Compare Havana and Boston
5. Write about Havana

FIGURE 3.12.
Background Knowledge Slide

Translation
What do you know about Cuba?
Write 5 things.
Compare your list with a partner.

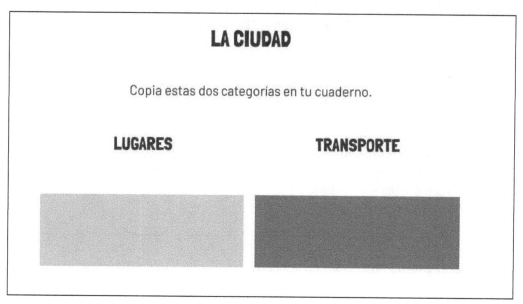

FIGURE 3.13.
Slide of Categorization Graphic Organizer

Translation
The City
Copy these two categories in your notebook.
Places - Transport

Next, the teacher asks students to copy a quick graphic organizer into their notebooks, which they will use to categorize key vocabulary words. Figure 3.13 shows the graphic organizer that the teacher has projected on the slide for students to see.

Once the students are ready, the teacher projects a list of vocabulary words on the board. Students are asked to place the vocabulary into one of the corresponding categories: places in a city *(lugares)* or modes of transportation *(transporte)*. This activity is designed to review key vocabulary that students will encounter in the authentic video and engage higher-order thinking skills by analyzing the words and placing them in categories. Figure 3.14 shows the slides with the vocabulary words for students to categorize. After students have finished, the teacher does a quick check for understanding and clarifies any misunderstood words.

Comprehension Phase
With the vocabulary fresh in students' minds, the teacher now plays the video and asks students to jot down a few places or modes of transportation that they hear. This first viewing of the video helps students to consider a few details. Students are asked to compare their list with a partner, and then share out some of the main places or modes of transportation that are highlighted in the video.

The teacher now plays the video a second time, asking students to focus on some concepts that they might not have picked up during the first viewing. The teacher shows a slide where some of the words that students may not have understood are projected, along with images. As they listen, students are asked to match the words to the pictures. This second viewing helps students focus on more details, as well as guess the meaning of certain words from context. For example, students will notice the cognate *taxi*, and using bottom-up processing they will figure out that a *cocotaxi* is a rickshaw-type taxi in the shape of a coconut (hence the word *coco*). Figure 3.15 shows the teacher's slide with the vocabulary and images for students to match. After reviewing the matched words and images, students will be asked to do a quick Turn and Talk in which they reflect on which modes of transportation are popular in Havana compared to where they live.

LA CIUDAD
Pon las palabras en la categoría apropiada.

EL MUSEO	LA PLAZA	EL TAXI	EL PALACIO
EL AUTOBUS	EL TEATRO	EL ESTADIO	EL CENTRO
EL PARQUE	EL MONUMENTO	LA CATEDRAL	EL CENTRO COMERCIAL
EL METRO	EL RESTAURANTE	LA CALLE	EL MERCADO

FIGURE 3.14.
Vocabulary Words Slide

Translation
The City
Put the words in the appropriate category.
(Words, from left to right and top to bottom):
The museum, The square, The taxi, The palace
The bus, The theater, The stadium, The center
The park, The monument, The cathedral, The mall
The metro, The restaurant, The street, The market

Interpretation/Discussion Phase

Before being put into small groups for discussion, students are asked to jot down some key characteristics of Havana and where they live using a Venn diagram graphic organizer (shown in Figure 3.16). After a few minutes, students are moved into groups and given some discussion questions that encourage them to reflect on what they learned about Havana and make comparisons to their own hometown. By noticing similarities and differences between the two communities, students begin to reflect on the relationship between Cuba and the United States. They are asked to report out on their discussion, with each group sharing key takeaways for a different question. Figure 3.17 shows the discussion question used during the group discussion.

Creativity Phase

The teacher has explored other Spanish-speaking cities with students using authentic resources in a previous lesson, so they are now ready to move on to the Creativity Phase. The teacher has developed a writing task for students that they will begin to draft during class time, seen in Figure 3.18. Students will choose one of the different Spanish-speaking cities they have explored—Mexico City or Havana—and write an email in which they describe some of the great features of that city to help decide which location the school should visit on a school trip. Students begin drafting their email during the remainder of class time and will continue and finalize their writing the following day.

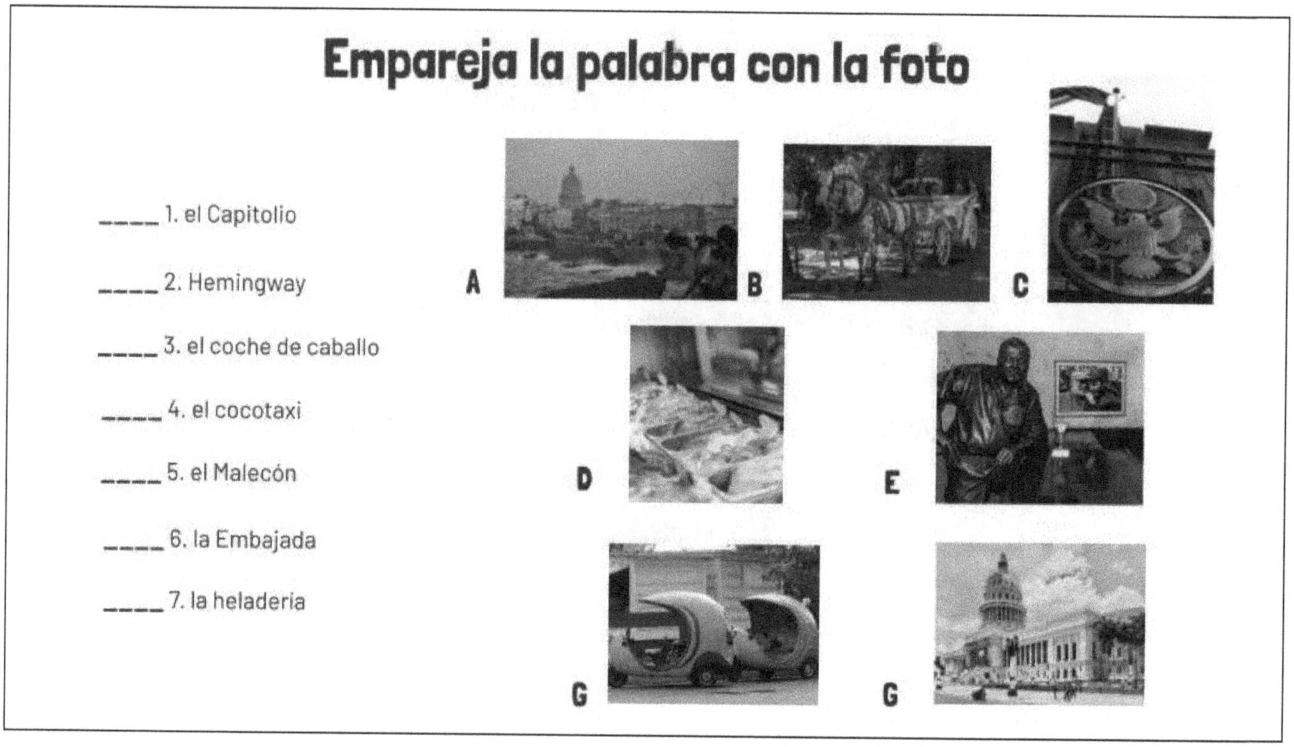

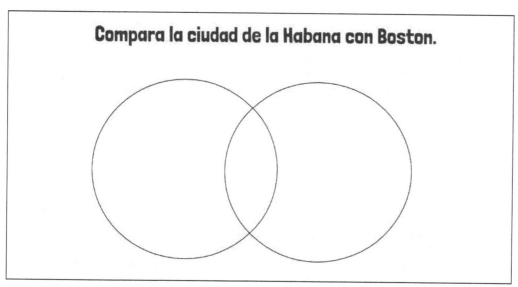

FIGURE 3.15.
Vocabulary and Image Matching Slide

Translation
Match the word with the photo
1. *The Capitol building*
2. *Hemingway*
3. *Horse-drawn carriage*
4. *The cocotaxi*
5. *The esplanade*
6. *The embassy*
7. *The ice-cream shop*

FIGURE 3.16.
Venn Diagram Slide

Translation
Compare the city of Habana with Boston.

Contesta estas preguntas con tu pareja.

1. ¿Quiénes son Fidel Castro, Che Guevara, Hemingway y José Martí?

2. ¿Cómo son similares y diferentes Boston y la Habana?

3. ¿Por qué son similares y diferentes?

4. ¿Qué tipo de persona le gustaría visitar la Habana? ¿Cómo es?

5. ¿Cuáles son sus intereses? ¿Qué le gusta hacer?

FIGURE 3.17.
Discussion Question Slide

Translation
Answer these questions with your partner.
1. Who are Fidel Castro, Che Guevara, Hemingway, and José Martí?
2. How are Boston and Havana similar and different?
3. Why are they similar and different?
4. What type of person would like to visit Havana? What are they like?
5. What are their interests? What do they like to do?

¡A ESCRIBIR!

Purpose: Your school wants to take students abroad for the 2021-2022 school year. The options are Mexico City, Mexico or Havana, Cuba. Your teacher wants to know which city the students might be more interested in going to, which has the best attractions, and the easiest to move around. After studying the issue, you will present your recommendations.

FIGURE 3.18.
Writing Prompt for Creativity Phase

Translation
Let's write!

Reflection and Next Steps

In this chapter, you have looked at how learners process meaning when reading, listening to, or viewing texts, called top-down and bottom-up processing. This understanding allows you to determine important criteria for selecting authentic resources to use with learners at different proficiency levels. You need to consider both linguistic and non-linguistic factors when selecting resources, such as the organizational structure of the resource, the vocabulary and target structures learners will encounter, whether the resource includes images that will support comprehension, whether your learners have background knowledge about the topic, and whether it is relevant and interesting to them. Using well-selected authentic resources with your learners has the potential to engage and motivate them by bringing real-world concepts and context to your classes. Authentic resources also enable you to show different perspectives from the target cultures and reflect the variety of identities of your learners. The Interactive Model for Interpretive Communication provides a framework for using authentic resources with your students, moving from the Preparation Phase to the Comprehension Phase (parts 1 and 2), the Interpretation/Discussion Phase, the Creativity Phase, and the optional Extension Phase. You can use any number of strategies and activities in each phase that are appropriate for your students and support the goal you are working toward, as you saw in the two *Classroom Close-Up* examples.

Before moving on, take some time to reflect and assess your own practice. Consider how you are applying or would like to apply the practices and strategies discussed in this chapter. Where are your strengths? Where would you like to grow your practice? What actions will you take to move forward? This one-point rubric is designed to help you reflect and assess your own teaching on using authentic resources and the Interactive Model for Interpretive Communication.

One-Point Rubric: Using Authentic Resources and the Interactive Model

GLOW	CRITERIA	GROW	TAKE ACTION
Where are my strengths related to this practice?	*What should I be looking for in my own teaching?*	*Where do I need to grow or expand my practice?*	*What steps will I take to move my practice forward?*
	I regularly incorporate authentic resources connected to the theme of my unit.		
	I select authentic resources that will be comprehensible to my students by considering the linguistic and non-linguistic features that will support their top-down and bottom-up processing skills.		
	Before asking my students to read, listen to, or view an authentic resource, I prepare them by articulating a purpose, anticipating key vocabulary, activating background knowledge, and making predictions about the text. (Preparation Phase)		

	When my students read, listen to, or view an authentic resource, they are engaged in tasks that help their comprehension. These tasks include two readings of the text and two different activities. (Comprehension Phase)		
	I engage my students in discussion of the authentic resource using appropriate scaffolds. (Interpretation/Discussion Phase)		
	When my students are ready, I engage them in a task in which they apply what they have learned from the authentic resource in a creative product. I provide appropriate scaffolds as needed. (Creativity Phase)		
	I use multiple authentic resources on the same theme to provide different perspectives and new information. (Extension Phase)		
	My students and I use the target language 90% or more of lesson time. I do not translate text or ask students to translate as one of their activities.		
	I use a communicative learning outcome, which is shared with students. All activities used reflect steps toward attainment of the student learning outcome.		

Level Up Your Learning

- **Glisan, E. W., & Donato, R. (2017).** *Enacting the work of language instruction: High-leverage teaching practices.* **ACTFL.**
  If you want to delve more deeply into the Interactive Model, this book is a must. You will find a clear research base for and explanation of the Interactive Model and will also be able to explore the other High-Leverage Teaching Practices (HLTPs). This book has lots of great information and is essential for all world language teachers.

- **Grahn, L. (2017). Tips for finding authentic resources.** *The Language Educator,* **12(4), p. 41.**
  Looking for more suggestions on how to find authentic resources? This short article is full of quick tips and ideas for efficiently searching online for authentic resources and using Pinterest effectively.

- **Spangler, D., & Mazzante, J. A. (2015).** *Using reading to teach a world language: Strategies and activities.* **Routledge.**
  Looking for more strategies to use as part of the Interactive Model? This book includes 37 strategies and 30 activities to support reading in your classroom. You will find simple explanations and clear steps to help you put these strategies and activities into practice.

Chapter 3 References

ACTFL. (n.d.). *Guiding principles for language learning.* https://www.actfl.org/resources/guiding-principles-language-learning

Cox, C. B., & Montgomery, C. (2019). A study of 21st century skills and engagement in a university Spanish foreign language classroom. *Foreign Language Annals, 52*(4), 822–849. https://doi.org/10.1111/flan.12426

Crossley, S. A., Louwerse, M. M., McCarthy, P. M., & McNamara, D. (2007). A linguistic analysis of simplified and authentic texts. *Modern Language Journal, 91*(1), 15–30. https://doi.org/10.1111/j.1540-4781.2007.00507.x

Dörnyei, Z. (1994). Motivation and motivating in the foreign language classroom. *Modern Language Journal, 78*(3), 273–284. https://doi.org/10.1111/j.1540-4781.1994.tb02042.x

Glisan, E. W. (2012). National Standards: Research into practice. *Language Teaching, 45*(4), 515–526. http://www.journals.cambridge.org/abstract_S0261444812000249

Glisan, E. W., & Donato, R. (2017). *Enacting the work of language instruction: High-leverage teaching practices.* ACTFL.

Glynn, C., Wesley, P., & Wassell, B. (2014). *Words and actions: Teaching languages through the lens of social justice* (2nd ed.). ACTFL.

Grahn, L. (2017). Tips for finding authentic resources. *The Language Educator, 12*(4), p. 41.

Guilloteaux, M. J., & Dörnyei, Z. (2008). Motivating language learners: A classroom-oriented investigation of the effects of motivational strategies on student motivation. *TESOL Quarterly, 42*(1), 55–77. https://doi.org/10.1002/j.1545-7249.2008.tb00207.x

Hlas, A. C., & Hlas, C. S. (2012). A review of high-leverage teaching practices: Making connections between mathematics and foreign languages. *Foreign Language Annals, 45*(s1), s76–s97. https://doi.wiley.com/10.1111/j.1944-9720.2012.01180.x

Maxim II, H. H. (2002). A study into the feasibility and effects of reading extended authentic discourse in the beginning German language classroom. *Modern Language Journal, 86*(1), 20–35. https://doi.org/10.1111/1540-4781.00134

National Standards Collaborative Board. (2015). *World-readiness standards for learning languages.* ACTFL.

Poulin-Chartrand, S. (2020a, March 14). *Inspirée par mon amie Martine qui a préparé un super horaire pour ses enfants, j'ai pensé faire ceci…* [Facebook post]. Ta Tribu. https://www.facebook.com/tatribufamilles/photos/2739700699440795

Poulin-Chartrand, S. (2020b, March 15). *Loin de moi l'idée d'ajouter au bruit ambiant de performance de parentalité et d'enfants pris dans un…* [Facebook post]. Ta Tribu. https://www.facebook.com/tatribufamilles/photos/2741746885902843

Shrum, J. L., & Glisan, E. W. (2016). *Teacher's handbook: Contextualized language instruction* (5th ed.). Heinle Cengage Learning.

Spangler, D., & Mazzante, J. A. (2015). *Using reading to teach a world language: Strategies and activities.* Routledge.

U.S. Department of Agriculture. (n.d.). MyPlate graphics. https://www.myplate.gov/resources/graphics/myplate-graphics

U.S. Food and Drug Administration. (n.d.). Zumulong Pigilan ang Pagkalat ng coronavirus at Protektahan ang Iyong Pamilya. https://www.fda.gov/consumers/consumer-updates/tumulong-upang-mapahinto-ang-pagkalat-ng-coronavirus-protektahan-ang-iyong-pamilya

Young, D. J. (1999). Linguistic simplification of SL reading material: Effective instructional practice? *Modern Language Journal, 83*(3), 350–366. https://doi.org/10.1111/0026-7902.00027

CHAPTER 4

Input Processing Instruction

H ave you ever explained a grammar rule to your students that you thought was really easy, only to be surprised when—the very next day or even moments later—they were unable to use the rule when they spoke or even wrote? A simple rule such as using certain verb endings in the present tense may be easy to *teach*, but can be difficult for our learners to *acquire*. For many years, language teachers have used a "presentation plus practice" approach to teaching grammatical rules. This means that the teacher presents (teaches) the grammar rule, and then the students practice it through the use of worksheets or grammar exercises. It should follow that students would then be able to use the rule when they communicate, but more often than not they struggle to do so.

Teachers want their students to learn more than the mechanics of the language. In proficiency-based instruction, the goal is not that learners master present-tense verb conjugation, for example, but that they are able to *use* the present tense in order to convey real meaning, that is, to communicate. Grammar does not drive the curriculum in such a classroom, therefore, but instead is incorporated in the service of communication.

An input-first approach to teaching grammar helps students build a conceptual understanding of how grammar is used in context before they are asked to produce it when they speak or write. Rather than starting by presenting the grammar rule to students in a decontextualized way, the input-first approach starts by providing meaningful language input that uses the target grammatical form in context. Students are exposed to the grammatical form and can begin to make meaning and connections to it, all the while keeping a primary focus on meaning; they are reading or listening to content in order to learn about the topic, not just to learn a grammar rule. By starting with input, learners develop an idea of the general *concept* of what the target grammatical structure means.

Teaching grammar as a concept and using it in context has been identified as a core practice by ACTFL (n.d.). Having a conceptual understanding of a grammatical structure means that learners have an idea of the general meaning, but do not necessarily know the abstract rule. For example, in first-year French classes, learners are often taught how to say "I would like" *(je voudrais)*— the conditional tense. They are not taught the abstract rule for the conditional, but instead develop a general conceptual understanding that this form has to do with politeness.

Abstract rule: How to conjugate the conditional tense.

Conceptual understanding: This form is used to be polite.

Starting with input allows learners to develop conceptual understandings and provides them with many examples of how the structure is used in context. To help learners focus on specific features of language input, strategies from input processing instruction—such as using *enriched input* (selecting a resource that includes the target grammar form with high frequency) or *enhanced input* (where teachers highlight key grammar forms)—can help ensure that students notice what the teacher wants them to notice.

Input processing instruction builds from an important area of research in second language acquisition: input processing, which studies how learners make connections between language forms and their meanings (VanPatten, 2015). Input processing instruction applies this research to the classroom. Using an understanding of how learners process input, teachers can develop activities that help learners notice and make meaning of grammatical forms. By first providing input and language in context, then supplementing the input with input processing activities, teachers equip learners to notice grammatical structures and develop conceptual understandings of them as a precursor to understanding and being able to use the structures in their own output.

But what does input processing say about how learners make meaning of what they hear and read? And how can teachers apply those understandings in ways that keep learners engaged and focused on meaning, while also paying attention to grammatical forms? In this chapter, we will start by looking at the research base for input processing and the input processing principles that can guide the design of classroom material. We will then explore input processing instruction, looking at specific strategies you can use to effectively apply this practice in your classes. We will also connect input processing to the Interactive Model (discussed in Chapter 3) so that you can keep a focus on meaning while also tackling the ever-challenging grammar question.

Research Base: Input Processing

To understand input processing, it is important to start with a clear definition of what is meant by *processing*. Processing happens when learners make connections between a *form* and its *meaning* (VanPatten, 2015). This is different from *comprehensible input* (discussed in Chapter 2) and from *noticing* features of the input without actually understanding them. Here is a simple example. Say a learner hears, "Go get two books from the table." If the learner gets up and gets two books from the table and brings them back, the teacher can reasonably assume that the input has been understood, that is, it was comprehensible input. However, there is no indication of what the learner actually *noticed* or *processed* in the input. Perhaps the learner only noticed and processed "two book" and "table" and was able to use that information to follow the direction. Perhaps the learner understood and processed "two book" and "table" and also noticed that the teacher actually said "books" but has no idea what that -s is doing there or what it means. In order to say that the learner *processed* the -s—that is, made a connection between the form and its meaning—we would need some evidence that they know that -s means "more than one." If, for example, the learner hears, "Please go get the books from the table" (rather than *two* books, which would be a clue), and the learner gets both books, this could be evidence that they have made a connection between the -s and the meaning "more than one." This is *processing*.

Input processing research investigates "what happens during comprehension" by looking at how learners make form-meaning connections, why learners make some form-meaning connections but not others, and what strategies learners use to make sense of input (VanPatten, 2015, pp. 113–114). The research in input processing leads to a number of principles about how learners process input, summarized in Table 4.1 with example sentences and explanations. Read through this carefully before moving on.

TABLE 4.1. PRINCIPLES OF INPUT PROCESSING WITH EXAMPLES AND EXPLANATIONS

Principle	Sentence Example	Explanation
Primacy of Content Words Learners will process content words before anything else.	"The **sky** is **blue**."	Learners will focus first on *sky* and *blue* to derive meaning.
Lexical Preference Learners will process lexical items before grammatical ones, particularly when they encode the same meaning.	"I walk**ed** to the store **yesterday**."	Learners will first use *yesterday* to understand the past time frame of this sentence, rather than the -ed in *walked*.

Preference for Non-Redundancy Learners will process non-redundant grammatical markers before redundant ones.	"The two gir**ls** are watch**ing** T.V."	The -s in *girls* is redundant, since *two* also encodes the meaning of "more than one." The -ing in *watching*, however, is the only place that learners will get the meaning "in the process of"; -ing is non-redundant, and therefore learners are more likely to process it.
Meaning Before Non-Meaning Learners will process meaningful grammatical markers before non-meaningful ones.	"**Do** you have the book**s**?"	*Do* is used here to indicate a question, but it is meaningless in and of itself. Learners are more likely to process the -s in *books* since it encodes the meaning of "more than one" and is non-redundant.
First Noun Learners are likely to assume that the first noun they encounter in a sentence is the subject.	"The **letter** was mailed."	The first noun here is *letter*, although this sentence uses a passive construction and does not explicitly name the active agent (the person who sent the letter). In English, the first noun is always the subject, but in other languages the first noun can instead be a direct or indirect object.
L1 Transfer Learners will use their L1 structures to help with processing.	"A Sofia le llamó Juan." (Literally, "To Sofia her called Juan," meaning "Juan called Sofia.")	Spanish has a more flexible word order than English, and Spanish Speakers can put the indirect object where English speakers would instead put the subject. L1 English speakers may process this sentence assuming that Sofia is the subject and not Juan (this also reflects the *First Noun* principle).
Sentence Location Learners are more likely to process grammatical markers and lexical items when they come at the beginning of a sentence.	"The **two shiny round red** balloons were popped by the girl." vs. "The girl popped the **two shiny round red** balloons."	Learners are more likely to process the English adjective order number [*two*] before quality [*shiny*], shape [*round*], and color [*red*] if it is in the beginning of the sentence, as opposed to the end or middle.
Event Probability, Lexical Semantics, and Contextual Constraints Although these are three different principles, each considers the likelihood of whether a statement is logical, which may force learners to re-process or draw on other processing principles to make sense of it.	"The complex houses married and single soldiers and their families."	This is a confusing sentence! Learners will likely initially process *houses* as the first noun and assume it is the subject, when in fact *complex* is the first noun and *houses* is the verb. Learners will likely pause initially when they put *complex* and *houses* together—how can houses be complex? If initially processed with *complex houses* as the subject, the learner will invariably stumble with the rest of the sentence, since it makes no sense. The illogic of what follows will force learners to revisit the sentence and draw deeply on their processing skills.

Source: Adapted from VanPatten, 2015.

While input processing principles do not explain everything that is happening in learners' minds when they encounter input, it does provide important information about how and why learners make meaning. These principles can also help teachers understand why certain forms that they think are really easy for learners to understand are in fact incredibly difficult. Take, for example, adjective endings in Spanish, which are commonly taught in first-year Spanish classes. In Spanish, adjectives must agree in number and gender with the noun they qualify. So, if you want to say "the comfortable chair," you must make the adjective feminine to agree with chair, which is a feminine noun: *la silla cómoda*. Although this may appear to be a simple rule to explain (use -a for feminine nouns and -o for masculine ones), looking at it through the lens of input processing shows that making a form–meaning connection is in fact incredibly challenging for learners. The -a ending is a form that is both *meaningless* (that is, it encodes no meaning in and of itself) and *redundant* (that is, the lexical item *silla* tells learners the word is feminine, which in and of itself is also meaningless). Given this, it is no surprise that learners struggle with adjective endings! While the grammar rule may be simple, *processing* it (making connections between the form and its meaning when encountering it in the input) is something that comes much later in learners' language development.

Another classic example of learners struggling to acquire seemingly simple rules comes from English: the ever-challenging third-person -s. This is another very simple grammatical rule to explain to learners: for he/she/it, add -s to the verb in the present tense. Sounds easy? Listen to some advanced English language learners, and you are likely to hear them say "he walk" or "she eat," repeatedly omitting the third person -s in conversation. Why? Well, principles of input processing show that this form is both meaningless (can you give a definition of the third person -s?) as well as redundant (learners know you are talking about a he/she/it from the subject). Since this form is not likely to be *processed* when learners encounter it in the input, it is less likely to become part of their internal language system, which they draw from when they speak spontaneously.

Input Processing Instruction

The basic premise of input processing instruction is to apply what is known from the principles of input processing in teaching. Using the principles of input processing outlined above, teachers can use input to help learners *notice* and *process* certain forms, be they lexical or grammatical. In the example used above, where the teacher told a student, "Go get two books from the table," an understanding of the principles of input processing shows clearly that learners will process *two* before they process the plural -s due to Lexical Preference (learners will process the lexical item *two* before the grammatical item -s) and Preference for Non-Redundancy (learners are more likely to process grammatical items when they are not redundant, but in this case they can get the meaning of -s from the word *two*). If your goal is to help learners *notice* and *process* the plural -s, they will be less likely to do so when you use the qualifier *two*. If, instead, you tell them, "Please get the books," they will only complete the instructions correctly if they *notice* and *process* the plural -s since it is now non-redundant and is not competing with a lexical item that encodes the same meaning. If the learner responds to your direction by giving you *one* book, you might repeat, "No, please get the books," which would force the learner to process that -s means more than one.

Teachers can use authentic resources or teacher-made material to draw learners' attention to particular lexical items or grammatical forms that they want to highlight as part of their instruction. There are a few key ways in which this can be accomplished, including using *enriched input, enhanced input,* and *structured input* activities.

Enriched Input

Also referred to as "input flooding" (Ellis, 2012), enriched input is language input that includes the target lexical item or grammatical form with high frequency. Selecting an authentic resource or creating a teacher-made resource that includes the target feature repeatedly (while still naturally) provides the learner with many exposures to the feature, with the goal of helping them notice and process it. While you may want to strive for authentic resources (as discussed in Chapter 3), teacher-made resources can provide useful supplements. You should be careful, however, to incorporate the target form naturally so that it isn't overly obvious to students. Figure 4.1 provides an example of an authentic song that includes many instances of the preterite and imperfect tenses being used in Spanish. This is an example of enriched input or input flooding and could be used if the teacher were trying to focus learners' attention on how these forms are used; learners will be repeatedly exposed to both tenses as they listen to or read this song.

Figure 4.2 provides an example of a teacher-made resource in French. The teacher wants to draw learners' attention to negative constructions, so she has written a short story about all the things she will not eat (she's a picky eater!). This story is intended to naturally feature the negative form repeatedly (the *ne...pas* as well as *ne...ni* constructions, meaning *not* and *neither*, respectively), so it provides a good example of enriched input or input flooding. The teacher can either present the story to be read by students or can tell this story orally in class.

Authentic Resources for Storytelling
In addition to using either authentic resources or teacher-made resources, teachers may choose to bridge both options by using authentic resources as platforms for creating their own stories or telling simplified versions of authentic stories (Jacobs, 2016). In one technique, teachers select a music video from the target language and use screenshots from it to put together a teacher-made story. For example, the music video for the song "Mon précieux" by the singer Soprano (2017) is rich with engaging images on a relevant topic for adolescent learners: how cell phones (which Soprano refers to as "precious ones") have influenced people's daily lives. Using screenshots from the video, a teacher can engage students in a dialogue that features reflexive verbs. Showing a screenshot of Soprano going to bed while looking lovingly at his cell

Lyrics from "Llegaste tú," by Jesse & Joy (2006)

Hundida yo estaba, ahogada en soledad
Mi corazón lloraba, de un vacío total
Todo lo intenté, por dondequiera te busqué
Eras tú mi necesidad

Triste y desolada, ya no pude soportar
Más desesperada era imposible de estar
Todo lo intenté, por dondequiera te busqué
Eras tú mi necesidad

FIGURE 4.1.
Authentic Resource Used for Enriched Input

Madame est difficile!

Je suis difficile! J'aime manger, bien sûr, mais je n'aime pas manger beaucoup de nourriture. J'aime les fruits, mais je n'aime pas manger ni les framboises, ni les mûres, ni le pamplemousse. Je mange beaucoup de légumes, mais je ne mange ni des asperges, ni des artichauts, ni des aubergines. Et la viande? Eh ben, je suis végétarienne! Je ne mange pas de viande du tout!

FIGURE 4.2.
Teacher-Made Resource Used for Enriched Input

Translation
Title: "Your Teacher is picky!"
Text: I am picky! I like to eat, of course, but I do not like to eat a lot of food. I like fruit, but I do not like to eat raspberries or blackberries or grapefruit. I eat a lot of vegetables, but I do not eat asparagus or artichokes or eggplant. And meat? Well, I am vegetarian! I do not eat meat at all!

phone, the teacher says, *"Soprano se couche tous les soirs en regardant son portable. Et vous? Regardez-vous vos portables avant de vous coucher?* [Soprano goes to bed every night by looking at his cell phone. And you? Do you look at your cell phone before going to bed?]" In another part of the video, Soprano and his family eat breakfast while all looking at their cell phones. The teacher narrates this by saying, *"La famille de Soprano ne se parle pas pendant le petit déjeuner parce qu'ils regardent tous le portable. Et dans votre famille? Est-ce que vous vous parlez? Ou vous regardez les portables pendant le repas?* [Soprano's family doesn't talk to each other during breakfast because they all look at their cell phones. And in your family? Do you talk to each other? Or do you look at your cell phones during meals?]" By selecting images from music videos, films, or other authentic materials, teachers can develop their own narratives that feature a high frequency of a target structure to provide enriched input.

Enhanced Input

Enhanced input is essentially the same as enriched input but takes the additional step of highlighting the target feature to further draw learners' attention to it. Electronic highlighting tools such as Scanmarker or LINER allow you to highlight PDFs or websites if you are using authentic resources and want to enhance certain features in the input. Features in teacher-made resources can be highlighted using boldface, underlining, or colored highlights. If input is being provided orally, teachers can enhance the target form by putting emphasis on certain words when they are speaking (VanPatten, 2017).

In Figure 4.3, the teacher has searched Twitter for a particular French structure to highlight: *"la raison pour laquelle,"* meaning "the reason for which." The teacher has found a few Tweets that naturally include the target structure and has copied them onto a document. Then, the teacher has highlighted the target structure.

Structured Input

Structured input can build from enriched or enhanced input to force learners to process particular features in order to demonstrate understanding. Essentially, the "input is manipulated to push learners to process something they might miss otherwise" (Van-Patten, 2017, p. 106), and learners show comprehension and evidence of processing by responding in non-verbal or minimally verbal ways. These responses could be ones in which learners supply simple information, reply to a survey, match items, answer questions with binary responses (true/false, yes/no, etc.), order or rank information, or select alternatives (Guilloteau, 2010). Structured input is more complicated to apply than enhanced or enriched input, since the activity is designed by drawing on one or more of the principles of input processing outlined in Table 4.1.

Revisiting adjective agreement in Spanish shows how a structured input activity can be designed. This example, created by Spanish teachers Mike Travers and Maria DiPietro (Travers, 2019), forces learners to process adjective endings (that is, connect the *meaning* and the *form*) by deciding which adjectives describe the celebrities Bradley Cooper and Lady Gaga. Students are presented with a simple table, with the adjectives in the leftmost column (see figure 4.4). This draws on the Sentence Location Principle: learners are more likely to process something when it comes first (in this case, in the first column they read). This activity also draws on the Preference for Non-Redundancy Principle: there are no competing words that also encode the designation of masculine or feminine. For example, learners are forced to read *rubia* [blonde] alone and can only use this word to figure out whether it is masculine or feminine, that is, whether it applies to Lady Gaga or Bradley Cooper. It is important to note that this activity maintains a primary focus on meaning. Learners are *not* completing a mechanical drill. This activity is being used to provide input to learners on the topic while also forcing them to process a target grammatical structure to make meaning. The focus of the lesson is *describing people*, not adjective agreement. Our two *Classroom Close-Ups* at the end of this chapter will include more examples of how to design and integrate structured input in your lessons.

- "la raison pour laquelle je pleure c'est tout simplement parce que tu me manques" (Belin, 2020)

- "tu es la raison pour laquelle je suis heureux" (Gars Wifi, 2020)

- "Personne ne peut changer une personne mais quelqu'un peut être la raison pour laquelle une personne change" (IRRÉVERSIBLE, 2020)

- "Soyez la raison pour laquelle quelqu'un continue de croire que les bonnes personnes existent" (Ideal isco, 2020)

FIGURE 4.3.
Authentic Resource Used for Enhanced Input

Translation
- *the reason for which I cry is quite simply because I miss you*
- *you are the reason for which I am happy*
- *No one can change another person but someone can be the reason for which a person changes*
- *Be the reason for which someone continues to believe that good people exist*

¿A quién describe? Es...	Lady Gaga	Bradley Cooper	¿Estás de acuerdo?
1. rubia.			□ sí □ no
2. guapo.			□ sí □ no
3. extraña.			□ sí □ no
4. alto.			□ sí □ no
5. baja.			□ sí □ no
6. extrovertida.			□ sí □ no
7. simpático			□ sí □ no

Ahora, ¿cuáles son tres palabras más para describir a Lady Gaga y Bradley Cooper?

Lady Gaga	Bradley Cooper
1. 2. 3.	1. 2. 3.

FIGURE 4.4.
Sample Structured Input Activity (Spanish Adjective Agreement)

Note: The left-hand column includes a list of adjectives that are either feminine or masculine. Students are asked to indicate who is being described by each adjective: Lady Gaga or Bradley Cooper. Then, students are asked to provide three additional adjectives to describe each person.

Source: Travers, 2019

Embedding Input Processing Tasks Within the Interactive Model

In Chapter 3, we looked closely at the Interactive Model for Interpretive Communication, which uses an authentic resource as a platform for interpersonal and presentational communication. The model has five phases: Preparation, Comprehension (parts 1 and 2), Interpretation/Discussion, Creativity, and Extension. Input processing instruction can easily be embedded within this framework to keep a primary focus on meaning, while also helping learners notice and process key lexical items and grammatical forms that are important for communication on the topic. Table 4.2 summarizes the phases of the Interactive Model and outlines where you can insert aspects of input processing instruction.

As you have seen, both the Interactive Model and input processing instruction keep a clear and strong focus on *meaning*, not grammatical forms in isolation. The goal is not to use input processing instruction to transition into a drill-based grammar exercise or lesson. Instead, the goal is to remain focused on the topic that students are learning about (food, politics, current events, fashion, school life, and so on) while also helping them notice and process particular features in the input that they may otherwise miss. Research shows that when grammatical forms are "divorced from the communicative needs and activities of the students, only short-term effects are obtained" (Lightbown, 1992, cited in Ellis, 2012, p. 299). A direct grammar lesson on the abstract rule may result in short-term understanding, but without any real long-term gains in language proficiency. While there is mixed research on the overall benefits of input processing instruction resulting in acquisition of particular features of language (Ellis, 2012; VanPatten, 2017), couching all learning in communicative activities and continuously providing meaningful input that includes the target feature is your best bet for achieving long-term acquisition (Ellis, 2012).

Tech Zoom

Input processing instruction is easily used with various digital platforms for in-person instruction, flipped classrooms, distance or hybrid learning, or providing independent work that students complete during class time or at home. Here are some tech tools and tips to get you started:

- Enriched Input/Input Flooding
  - Twitter: In addition to being a great site for collaborating with other world language teachers across the country and around the world, Twitter provides a wealth of target-language material that you can find in a few ways. First, if you're looking for a particular resource, try sending out a Tweet using the hashtag #authres. Another world language teacher may have ideas for resources or have already searched for (and found!) the same resources you are looking for. Second, if you want authentic texts in which speakers use a particular language structure, you can often find them on Twitter. Searching for target structures such as *"il faut que," "deberías," "das gefällt mir"*—or any other language structure—will lead you to examples from any Twitter user who has used that expression in a Tweet. You can then copy and paste whichever ones you like to use with your students.
  - VEED.IO (https://www.veed.io/tools/auto-subtitle-generator-online/video-caption-generator): If you're creating your own material to use for enriched input, you may want to record yourself, allowing students to watch the video at home or during independent work. VEED.IO lets you up your game by automatically adding captions when you speak. Speech recognition is supported in over 100 languages, so adding captions while speaking in the target language may be an easy way to further enhance your input.

- Enhancing Input
  - LINER (https://getliner.com/en): This GoogleChrome extension allows you to highlight PDFs or websites in a range of colors. It is a simple and easy tool for drawing students' attention to target grammar structures and vocabulary.

TABLE 4.2. THE INTERACTIVE MODEL WITH INPUT PROCESSING INSTRUCTION

The Phases of the Interactive Model	Overview	Input Processing Instruction
Pre-Interactive Model	The teacher chooses an appropriate authentic resource (or teacher-made resource, if appropriate) for the theme/topic.	*Enriched Input:* The teacher selects a resource that naturally includes the target lexical item or grammatical form with high frequency.
Preparation	The teacher prepares learners to read/listen to/view the authentic resource by • establishing a purpose, • activating/developing background knowledge, • anticipating and pre-teaching key vocabulary, and • predicting meaning.	
Comprehension, Part 1	Learners engage in a *first* read/listen to/view of the authentic resource that actively engages them in understanding the main idea and some key details.	*Enriched Input:* During the first read/listen to/view, learners focus entirely on the content. No special attention is paid to the target feature in the input.
Comprehension, Part 2	Learners engage in a *second* read/listen to/view of the authentic resource that actively engages them in understanding more key details and guessing meaning of key words from context.	*Enhanced Input (optional):* The teacher may present learners with an enhanced version of the authentic resource (with the target feature highlighted) for the second read. *Structured Input Activity:* Learners complete a structured input activity to support comprehension of the text and support processing of the target feature.
Interpretation/ Discussion	Learners engage in guided discussion of the text.	
Creativity	Learners develop a product or performance connected to the learning from the authentic resource.	
Extension	Learners read/view/listen to another authentic resource on the same theme/topic.	

- GoogleDocs (https://docs.google.com): As a collaborative writing tool, GoogleDocs is hard to beat. If you are creating your own enhanced input or if you are copying over authentic resources into GoogleDocs, you can easily highlight target structures and even color code different features.

- Structured Input Activities
  - Games: Digital game platforms such as Kahoot, Quizlet Live, or Blooket can turn a structured input activity into a fun class competition. You can create your own quiz games using images or text, and then students compete against one another as they play. While many teachers already use these platforms for vocabulary review, a structured input activity can easily be created as well.

  - Nearpod or Classkick: Using the Quiz function in Nearpod or Classkick, you can create a slideshow of structured input questions, with embedded audio, video, images, web content, or text for each question. After saving the slides to Nearpod, select Student Paced. You then get a link and code to share with students who can work on the assignment on their own. (Be sure to select "Require student submissions" so that you can collect student responses.)

  - Edpuzzle: This platform allows you to add existing videos or upload your own, and then embed questions. The video stops playing when a question comes up, and students need to respond before moving on. If you are using an interpretive listening resource connected to your structured input activity, you can insert questions for students that help them process the target structure while also demonstrating comprehension of the content.

Now that we have looked at principles of input processing instruction, how to select or create enriched input, how to enhance input, and how to create structured input activities, we will move to two *Classroom Close-Ups* that show how teachers of two different languages working with students at two different proficiency levels apply these concepts in their own teaching. In *Classroom Close-Up 4.2*, you will also see how the teacher adapts the model for a hybrid or distance learning environment.

Classroom Close-Ups

Classroom Close-Up 4.1: Fantasy Novels

This classroom example was shared by Victoria Pascual, English as a foreign language teacher at the Monte Tabor Schoenstatt School, Madrid, Spain.

COURSE OVERVIEW	
Course Name	English 2, Middle/High School
Course Proficiency Target	Intermediate Low

LESSON OVERVIEW	
Unit Theme	Fantasy Novels
Lesson Learning Outcome	I can tell someone what happens in a fantasy novel using simple and connected sentences.
Core Vocabulary and Forms	• Fantasy novel key vocabulary, such *as elf, wizard, danger* • Third person -s, present tense • Sequencing transition words, such as *first, next, then*
Materials and Resources	Copies of book review of "Harry Potter and the Chamber of Secrets" from https://www.pluggedin.com/book-reviews/harry-potter-and-the-chamber-of-secrets/

Lesson Length	60 minutes	

LEARNING SEQUENCE		
Focus of Learning	Students are given one question to discuss in pairs: What do you know about the Harry Potter novels?	*Time:* 1 min
Preview of Learning	The teacher goes over the agenda and student learning outcome.	*Time:* 1 min
Learning Episode 1		
Primetime 1	The teacher shows images from the Harry Potter books on slides, asking students to share what they know about each character. Students do short Turn & Talks for each image before sharing with the whole class.	*Time:* 5 min
Downtime	The teacher hands out copies of the Harry Potter book review. Students work in partners to read the book review aloud to each other. Students additionally complete comprehension questions. Students share answers with the whole class. The teacher provides a sentence-completion activity. Students read the book review a second time (individually) and complete the sentence-completion activity. Students share answers with the whole class.	*Time:* 15 min
Primetime 2	The teacher provides the structured input activity. Students can complete this in pairs or individually. The teacher then reviews responses with the full class.	*Time:* 10 min
Brain Break	The teacher may use a short brain break, such as playing the trailer from the Harry Potter movie or giving students a chance to stand and stretch before moving on.	*Time:* 1 min
Learning Episode 2		
Primetime 1	The teacher now explains that students will retell the Harry Potter story using the information they just read about in the book review. The teacher presents sequencing expressions on the overhead for students to use as scaffolds and asks one student to model this in front of the whole class.	*Time:* 5 min
Downtime	Students engage in an inside-outside circle activity in which they rotate partners every 2-3 minutes. The sequencing expressions remain projected on the overhead for students to refer to.	*Time:* 10 min
Primetime 2	The teacher asks for a few students to share how they re-told the story during the inside-outside circle activity.	*Time:* 10 min
Check for Learning	Students are given an index card on which they are asked to write down two things that happen in the Harry Potter story, and they must hand this to the teacher as they leave class.	*Time:* 1 min
Celebration of Learning	The teacher projects the student learning outcome on the overhead and asks for a thumbs-up/thumbs-down from the students as self-reflection and feedback.	*Time:* 1 min

The teacher begins the class by presenting the lesson objective and class agenda, shown in Figure 4.5. The teacher engages students in a short do-now by providing one question for students to discuss in pairs: What do you know about the Harry Potter novels? Students discuss for 1-2 minutes, then share briefly as a whole class.

Goal: I can tell someone what happens in a fantasy novel.

Agenda:

1. What do you know about Harry Potter?
2. Vocabulary
3. Book Review:
   Harry Potter and the Chamber of Secrets
4. Retell the story!

FIGURE 4.5.
Lesson Objective and Agenda Slide

Preparation Phase

The teacher has selected a book review of *Harry Potter and the Chamber of Secrets* as the authentic resource for this lesson. The book review includes a high frequency of the target grammatical structure (enriched input/input flooding): the third person singular. The teacher begins the Preparation Phase by showing students a few images of characters from the Harry Potter novels. Students do a Turn and Talk to tell their partner if they know the Harry Potter characters in the images and to describe them. The teacher then previews key vocabulary by having students do an image matching activity: students are asked to match words such as "elf," "wizard," and "danger."

Comprehension Phase, Part 1

The teacher now gives students copies of the book review, along with comprehension questions focusing on the main idea (Figure 4.6), and asks them to read the passage aloud with a partner. The teacher has used boldface to highlight the third person singular verbs (input enhancement), as shown in the first paragraph of the book review here:

> After a particularly horrible summer at home with the Dursleys, Harry can't wait to return to Hogwarts for his second year. Banished to his bedroom, Harry **receives** a visit from an elf named Dobby, who **warns** him that he must not return to the school, for great danger **awaits** him there. Finally, he is rescued from his bedroom prison by Ron and his brothers in their flying car. Despite Dobby's warnings, Harry **returns** to Hogwarts and **stumbles** right into the mystery of the Chamber of Secrets.
> Source: Plugged In, 2020.

Comprehension Phase, Part 2

Students are then asked to read the book review for a second time (reading individually), now focusing more closely on specific details. They are given sentences to complete as they read, shown in Figure 4.7. The teacher has once again highlighted the third person -s to help draw students' attention to the target grammatical structure while still keeping the primary focus of the lesson on meaning.

Comprehension Questions:

1. What is the story about?

2. Does the description happen in the present, the past or the future?

3. Who are the main characters?

4. What novel of the saga does this review refer to?

5. What's the danger at Hogwarts?

FIGURE 4.6.
Comprehension Questions

DETAILS:
What happens in *Harry Potter & the Secret Chamber?*

1. Harry receive**s** a visit from _____.
2. Harry return**s** to _____.
3. Who warn**s** Harry about a great danger? _____
4. The Chamber of Secrets contain**s** a _____.
5. Harry meet**s** and defeat**s** _____.
6. "The heir" in the message refer**s** to a descendant of one of the school's four founders, Salazar Slytherin _____.

FIGURE 4.7.
Sentence Completion Activity

Before moving to the Interpretation/Discussion Phase, the teacher engages students in a structured input activity. Drawing on the Sentence Location Principle, the teacher has designed an activity where students must determine which of the characters does each of the described actions. This activity (shown in Figure 4.8) forces students to process the third person -s in order to find the answer, but the primary focus is again on meaning. When students share their answers with the full class, the teacher may briefly point out the third person -s, particularly if a student gives an incorrect answer. The teacher may choose to give a brief but explicit explanation, saying, for example, "Notice when it's the third person—he, she, or it—you add an -s to the end of the verb." However, the teacher would quickly move back to the primary focus on the meaning of the book review.

Interpretation/Discussion Phase

Students now engage in an Interpretation/Discussion activity in which they retell the story based on the book review using an interpersonal inside-outside circle technique (see Chapter 5 for details on this technique). The teacher projects some previously learned sequencing expressions, shown in Figure 4.9, for students to use as scaffolds for this activity. Students have 2-3 minutes to retell the story with the person they are facing in the circle, and then rotate to a new partner. Students would be expected to use the present tense during this activity, and therefore they have the opportunity to use the third-person singular in context.

The teacher asks a few students to retell the story to the whole class after the inside-outside circle activity has ended. The teacher then returns students' attention to the learning outcome—*I can tell someone what happens in a fantasy novel*—and asks for a thumbs-up/thumbs-down for students to self-reflect on their attainment of the learning outcome. Students are additionally given index cards on which to write down two things that happen in the Harry Potter story. They hand these in to the teacher as they leave (exit tickets), which allows the teacher to check for learning.

Who does what?

1. ... **receives** a visit from an elf named Dobby.
2. ... **warns** him that he must not return to the school.
3. ... **find** a message painted on a wall.
4. ... **returns** to Hogwarts.
5. ... **contains** a deadly monster.
6. ... **refers** to a descendant of one of the school's four founders.
7. ... **meets** and defeats Voldemort.
8. ... **solve** the mystery.
9. ... **goes** beyond petrifaction and kills again.
10. ... **opens** the Chamber of Secrets.

a.   Harry
b.   Harry and his friends
c.   Ron and Hermione
d.   The monster
e.   The Chamber of Secrets
f.   Voldemort
g.   The Heir
h.   Dobby

FIGURE 4.8.
Structured Input Activity

Retell the story!
Use some sequencing expressions...

Beginning:
- First...
- First of all...
- Initially...
- To begin with...

Continuing:
- Then...
- After that...
- Next...
- As soon as...
- ...but then...

Interruptions:
- Suddenly...
- Unexpectedly...
- All of a sudden...

Ending:
- Finally...
- In the end...
- Eventually...

FIGURE 4.9.
Scaffold for Inside-Outside Circle

Classroom Close-Up 4.2: Career Day
Lesson developed by Christina Toro

COURSE OVERVIEW	
Course Name	Spanish 5
Course Proficiency Target	Intermediate High

LESSON OVERVIEW	
Unit Theme	Career Day
Lesson Learning Outcome	I can describe my future career interests.
Core Vocabulary and Forms	• Professions • I want to be • When I am older
Materials and Resources	• Article from http://www.bbc.co.uk/spanish/specials/1631_museo/page3.shtml • Video from https://www.instagram.com/p/B_iC_v0Hwsf/ • Song lyrics from "Cuando Sea Grande"
Lesson Length	Two classes, 55 minutes each OR one 90-minute block

LEARNING SEQUENCE		
Focus of Learning	Teacher asks students to come up with a list of 10 popular careers and to categorize them by their field (arts, science, etc). Each pair shares out items from their list.	*Time:* 7 min
Preview of Learning	Teacher presents the objective and reviews the agenda for the day.	*Time:* 1 min

Learning Episode 1		
Primetime 1	The teacher asks students to match vocabulary to an image. The teacher then does a quick check for understanding.	*Time:* 7 min
Downtime	The students are placed into pairs to answer questions about different jobs. The students share what they discussed with the class.	*Time:* 7 min

Primetime 2	The teacher asks the students to read an article from BBC Mundo about people's careers. In pairs, the students identify what the people wanted to be as children and what they are now. After students finish discussing, the teacher checks for understanding before asking them to identify why these people have the jobs they do.	*Time:* 20 min
Brain Break	Students get up and stretch or do a 2-minute Zumba video.	*Time:* 2 min
Learning Episode 2		
Primetime 1	The teacher introduces the structured input activity. The students identify who said the statement by looking at the first word for each statement.	*Time:* 5 min
Downtime	The students ask each other questions about what careers they wanted to have as children and what they now want to be when they grow up.	*Time:* 10 min
Primetime 2	Students listen to a song and then receive the lyrics so they can follow along. In pairs, they identify what each worker does. Then, the students answer true or false questions about the song. Students have to look at a series of statements and decide who said them based on the verb in the sentence.	*Time:* 25 min
Check for Learning	The students write down what they want to be and why as an exit ticket.	*Time:* 5 min
Celebration of Learning	The teacher returns to the student learning outcome and asks for students to self-reflect on their learning.	*Time:* 1 min

This lesson focuses on how to describe what career students are interested in by using the complex sentence *"Cuando sea grande, quiero ser + career"* [When I am older, I want to be + career]. This sentence construction uses the subjunctive in the dependent clause, a difficult topic for learners to grasp due to its abstract nature and the fact that English rarely uses the subjunctive form. The teacher has selected an article from the online news source BBC Mundo as well as a song in which the target structure is used naturally and in the context of the thematic topic of professions. This lesson is designed as a distance learning lesson but can easily be adapted for in-person or hybrid learning. It takes two 55-minute class periods or one 90-minute block to complete.

Day 1
As class begins, students see the agenda and learning objective shared by the teacher as they enter the virtual learning platform (Figure 4.10). The teacher greets students and briefly reviews the learning objective and lesson agenda.

Agenda - Español V AP

Objetivo: Puedo describir cual podrá ser mi futura carrera.

Actividades del día:

1. Identificar 10 carreras populares
2. Contestar algunas preguntas sobre una futura carrera
3. Leer unos comentarios sobre las carreras y contestar preguntas
4. Decidir quién dijo cada frase
5. Escuchar una canción y contestar preguntas
6. Entrevistar a amigos y miembros de mi familia sobre las carreras

FIGURE 4.10.
Objective and Agenda Slide

Translation
Objective: I can describe which could be my future career.
Daily activities:
1. Identify 10 popular activities
2. Answer questions about a future career
3. Read some commentaries about careers and answer the questions
4. Decide who said each phrase
5. Listen to a song and answer the questions
6. Interview friends and members of my family about careers

Preparation Phase
Given the high proficiency level of this class, students have learned some careers in previous Spanish courses, so the teacher activates their background knowledge by asking them to generate their own list of careers. Students then work in breakout groups to come up with at least ten possible careers and categorize the careers by field (careers in the arts, careers in science, etc.). Students are given 5 minutes to work and are then asked to share out in the main session. While the students are presenting their lists, the teacher shares the slide and adds the responses from each group for all the class to see, as shown in Figure 4.11.

The Preparation Phase continues with the goal of filling any gaps in students' vocabulary knowledge. Students work in pairs for 2-3 minutes to match the careers shown in Figure 4.12 with the corresponding images. The teacher asks them to write down the answers in their notebooks or use a tech tool like Pear Deck to draw on the slide. After doing a quick check for understanding, the teacher assigns students in new pairs and sends them into breakout groups so that they can engage in an interpersonal discussion. Students have access to the discussion questions, shown in Figure 4.13, and are given 10 minutes to discuss them with their partners.

Identifica 10 carreras y el campo al que pertenecen

1. Ejemplo - Un terapeuta - (j)
2.
3.
4.
5.
6.
7.
8.
9.
10.

a. Agricultura
b. Arquitectura
c. Arte
d. Comunicación
e. Educación
f. Gobierno
g. Ley y Justicia
h. Manufactura
i. Negocios y Finanza
j. Salud
k. Servicios
l. Turismo

FIGURE 4.11.
Background Knowledge Slide

Translation
Identify 10 careers and the category to which they belong.
a. Agriculture, b. Architecture, c. Art, d. Communication, e. Education,
f. Government, g. Law and Justice, h. Manufacturing, i. Business and Finance,
j. Health, k. Service, l. Tourism

Identifica la foto con la profesión

 1.
 2.
 3.
 4.

 5.
 6.
 7.
 8.

 9.
 10.
 11.
 12.

Un(a) arqueólogo(a)

Un(a) contador(a)

Un(a) cirujano

Un(a) diseñador(a)

Un(a) guía

Un(a) ingeniero(a)

Un(a) juez(a)

Un(a) mecánico(a)

Un(a) panadero(a)

Un(a) programador(a)

Un(a) sastre

Un(a) terapeuta

FIGURE 4.12.
Vocabulary and Matching Slide

Translation
Match the photo with the profession
An archaeologist, A storyteller, A surgeon, A designer, A guide, An engineer, A judge, A mechanic,
A baker, A programmer, A tailor, A therapist

Contesta las preguntas en pareja

1. ¿Cuáles son los trabajos mejores pagados? ¿Por qué?

2. ¿En cuáles trabajos se necesita mucha educación?

3. En tu familia, ¿hay un trabajo que es muy común?

4. ¿Hay alguien en tu familia que te haya inspirado a estudiar una carrera en particular?

5. ¿Qué tipo de influencia ha tenido tu familia en tu decisión?

FIGURE 4.13.
Discussion Questions Slide

Translation
Answer the questions in pairs
1. Which jobs are the best paid? Why?
2. Which jobs require a lot of education?
3. In your family, which type of job is the most common?
4. Is there someone in your family that has inspired you to study for a particular career?
5. What type of influence has your family had on your decision?

Comprehension Phase
The teacher has two sources of input for the students, one focusing on the past and present tenses (from BBC Mundo) and the second on the present and future tenses. They both use a similar sentence structure (I want[ed] to be + career), which forces the students to focus on the verb forms (want vs. wanted) instead of the content words in the sentence. The teacher begins with the source that includes the timeframes the students already are familiar with: the past and present. After assessing students' understanding of this material, the teacher adds a second source of input that includes new information.

Figure 4.14 depicts a slide used to show students quotes from the BBC Mundo source, which includes personal stories about people's careers, describing what they wanted to be as children, what they currently are, and why.

Comprehension Phase, Part 1
In this phase, the students work in pairs using the chart to identify what the people wanted to be and what they are now. Students record their answers in their notebooks or in a teacher-made Google Form, shown in Figure 4.15.

Comprehension Phase, Part 2
After reviewing the chart, the teacher asks the students to find the reason why the person does or does not have the profession that they dreamed of having as a child. Depending on the time, the teacher could ask for them to jot the answers down in their notebooks or submit their answers electronically, as shown in Figure 4.16.

Having generated background knowledge on the topic, the teacher introduces the structured input activity. Based on the sentence given, the students have to decide whether a presenter or a student at a career day said the statement, shown in Figure 4.17. The only way they can determine this is by looking at the conjugation of the first word because it will tell the student if the verb is in the past tense or the present tense.

Fuente #1

Cuando era chico vivía en la ciudad de México cerca del aeropuerto y **yo quería ser** piloto aviador, por azares del destino terminé viviendo en la provincia y soy operador de maquinaria, mecánico y hago lo que más me gusta conducir, algún día seré piloto.
Mauricio Guevara Aguilar,
Zinapécuaro, Michoacán, México

Cuando era niña, yo quería ser como Valentina Tereshkova y viajar por el espacio. Cuidé mucho mis dientes para que nada me impidiera pasar los exámenes médicos para el entrenamiento como astronauta y estudié mucho pensando graduarme algún día en Física Teórica. Terminé estudiando Derecho y trabajando en comunicaciones, pero aún sigo soñando.
Diana Casas,
Huancayo, Perú

Bueno, **yo de grande quería ser** abogada, o entonces médica o arquitecta. En realidad quería cualquier profesión que no fuera profesora, pues los profesores no tienen un buen sueldo en mi país. Pero, adivine qué hago... soy profesora y muy feliz en mi profesión.
Michelle Lopes,
Cascavel, Brasil

Yo **cuando estaba pequeño deseaba** ser militar y recuerdo que me encantaba ver los desfiles militares y me imaginaba vestido con mi uniforme de oficial, pero bueno la vida da muchas vueltas y hoy en día soy historiador.
José Betancourt,
Caracas, Venezuela

De pequeña **quería ser** veterinaria para sanar a todos los animales sufrientes...pero cuando vi que para aliviar el dolor a veces tendría que eutanasiar, no me atreví. Luego **quería ser** antropóloga...y hoy me dedico, desde la filosofía al tema de los derechos animales y el medioambiente.
Fabiola Leyton Donoso, Roma, Italia

http://www.bbc.co.uk/spanish/specials/1631_museo/page3.shtml

FIGURE 4.14.
Input Source #1 Slide

Translation
Source #1
When I was younger, I lived in Mexico City near the airport and I wanted to be an aviation pilot. By chance I ended up living in the province and I am the machine operator, mechanic, and I do what I like the most driving, one day I'll be a pilot.

When I was a child, I wanted to be like Valentina Tereshkova and travel through space. I took care of my teeth so that nothing could prevent me from passing my medical exams for training as an astronaut and I studied a lot thinking of graduating some day in Theoretical Physics. I finished studying law and am working in communications but I still continue to dream.

Well, as a youth, I wanted to be a lawyer, or doctor or architect. In reality, I wanted to be whichever profession was not a teacher. Well, teachers don't have a good salary in my country. But guess what I do...I am a teacher and I am happy in my profession.

When I was small, I wanted to be a soldier and I remember that I loved watching military parades and I imagined myself dressed with an official uniform, but well life takes many turns and today I am a historian.

As a child, I wanted to be a veterinarian to cure all the suffering animals...but when I saw that to alleviate pain sometimes you have to euthanize, I did not dare. Later, I wanted to be an anthropologist...and today I dedicate myself to the philosophy of animal rights and the environment.

Escribe lo que quería ser de niño y la carrera que tiene ahora.

Nombre	Que quería ser de niño/a	La carrera que tiene ahora
Mauricio Guevara Aguilar		
Diana Casas		
Michelle Lopes		
Jose Betancourt		
Fabiola Leyton Donoso		

FIGURE 4.15.
Comprehension Phase, Part 1 Slide

Translation
Write what the person wanted to be when they were young and what they are now.
Name... What they wanted to be when they were young... The career they have now

Escribe la razón porque no tiene la carrera que quería tener cuando era niño.

Nombre	La razón porque no tiene la carrera que quería cuando era niño
Mauricio Guevara Aguilar	
Diana Casas	
Michelle Lopes	
Jose Betancourt	
Fabiola Leyton Donoso	

FIGURE 4.16.
Comprehension Phase, Part 2 Slide

Translation
Write the reason why the person does not have the career they wanted when they were young.
Name... The reasons why they do not have the career they wanted when they were young.

This draws from the sentence location principle of input processing. If the verb is in the past, then it would describe what the presenter wanted to be in their youth. The present-tense sentence would describe the career that the students want to have when they grow up. Students work in pairs to complete the structured input activity.

Decide quién dijo cada frase

Un presentador	Un estudiante	Yo....
_____	_____	Quiero ser piloto aviador.
_____	_____	Quería ser piloto aviador.
_____	_____	Quería ser abogada.
_____	_____	Quiero ser abogada.
_____	_____	Quería ser historiador.
_____	_____	Quiero ser historiador

FIGURE 4.17.
Structured Input Activity Slide

Translation
Decide who said each phrase.

A presenter   A student   I...
want to be an aviation pilot.
wanted to be an aviation pilot.
wanted to be a lawyer.
want to be a lawyer.
wanted to be a historian.
want to be a historian.

The teacher asks students to share responses, and then moves them into breakout groups for pair discussion of what they wanted to be when they were children and what they want to be now. Students use the discussion prompts shown in Figure 4.18. After a few minutes of discussion, the teacher asks students to share what they learned about their partner with the class. The teacher ends this lesson by returning students' attention to the learning outcome and asking for feedback on whether students feel they have achieved the day's objective.

Day 2
Preparation Phase
To start the next day, the teacher greets students and shares the student learning outcome and agenda. The teacher begins the lesson by playing a video published by the Ricky Martin Foundation which shows young children dressed up as some of the careers that have been important during the pandemic: teachers, doctors, farmers, and scientists, to name a few. The teacher plays the short video, and then asks students to do a quick Turn and Talk to discuss the importance of the video and what it means to them.

Contesta con tu pareja

De niño(a)

1. ¿Querías ser maestro/a/x?
2. ¿Querías ser actor/actriz?
3. ¿Querías ser astronauta?
4. ¿Querías ser presidente?
5. ¿Querías ser deportista profesional?

Y ahora....

1. ¿Quieres ser maestro/a/x?
2. ¿Quieres ser actor/actriz?
3. ¿Quieres ser astronauta?
4. ¿Quieres ser presidente?
5. ¿Quieres ser deportista profesional?

FIGURE 4.18.
Discussion Questions Slide

Translation
Answer with your partner.
As a child
1. *Did you want to be a teacher?*
2. *Did you want to be an actor/actress?*
3. *Did you want to be an astronaut?*
4. *Did you want to be president?*
5. *Did you want to be a professional athlete?*

And now...
1. *Do you want to be a teacher?*
2. *Do you want to be an actor/actress?*
3. *Do you want to be an astronaut?*
4. *Do you want to be president?*
5. *Do you want to be a professional athlete?*

Comprehension Phase, Part 1
The teacher then introduces a song, "Cuando sea grande" by Flavia Palmiero, that will serve as the second main source of input for this lesson sequence. The song naturally includes many instances of the target structure: *"Cuando sea grande, quiero ser..."* As they listen to the song and read along with a printed version of the lyrics, students describe what the singer says that each worker does. They complete the chart in Figure 4.19, either with their partner or individually.

Comprehension Phase, Part 2
Next, the students listen to the song a second time to dig deeper. They are now asked to decide if the statement in Figure 4.20 is true or false and provide evidence to support their choice. The teacher plays the song a second time, then puts students in pairs in breakout rooms to allow them time to work with the material and consider the evidence to support each statement.

After students share out their responses from this activity, the teacher prepares them to engage in the second structured input activity, shown in Figure 4.21. As with the first structured input activity, students will be asked to decide who would say the statements presented: an adult or a student. The teacher has used the clauses *"cuando sea grande"* [when I will be an adult] and *"cuando era niño"* [when I was a child] in the activity. Students must look closely at the verbs to determine which person said the statement. Students work with their partners and then share out responses and discuss with the full class.

Identifica lo que hace estas personas según la cancion.

La carrera	Lo que hace
El bombero	
El piloto aviador	
El astronauta	
El presidente	
El marinero	

FIGURE 4.19.
Comprehension Phase, Part 1 Slide

Translation
Identify what these people do according to the song.

Career   *What they do*
The firefighter
The aviation pilot
The astronaut
The president
The sailor

Decide si la frase es cierto o falso. Después, da evidencia del texto para apoyar tu respuesta.

Cierto o Falso	Frase	Evidencia
	El texto describe las ventajas y desventajas de diferentes carreras.	
	La persona es muy optimista sobre el futuro.	
	Esta persona es un adulto.	

FIGURE 4.20.
Comprehension Phase, Part 2 Slide

Translation
Decide if the statements are true or false. After, give evidence from the text to support your answer.
True or False   Statement   Evidence
The text describes the advantages and disadvantages
of different careers.
The person is very optimistic about the future.
The person is an adult.

Creativity Phase

The teacher is now ready to move students forward to the Creativity Phase. Students are told that they will interview four adults and four adolescents about their career choices as a homework assignment (shown in Figure 4.22). The next day in class the students will have to report what they learned using the sentence structure appropriate to the people they interviewed: *"cuando sea grande"* or *"cuando era niño."* The teacher closes class by returning attention to the student learning outcome and asking students to reflect and provide feedback on their learning.

Decide quién dijo cada frase -
un adulto o un adolescente

Cuando sea grande...   Cuando era niño...   Yo....

_____   _____   Quería ser bombero.

_____   _____   Quiero ser bombero.

_____   _____   Quiero ser presidente

_____   _____   Quería ser presidente.

_____   _____   Quería ser arquitecto.

_____   _____   Quiero ser arquitecto.

FIGURE 4.21.
Structured Input Activity Slide

Translation
Decide who said each phrase - an adult or an adolescent.

When I am older   When I was young   I...
wanted to be a firefighter.
want to be a firefighter.
want to be president.
wanted to be president.
wanted to be an architect.
want to be an architect.

Ahora, entrevista 4 adultos y 4 adolescentes sobre las carreras.

1. **Para los adultos, identifica lo que querían ser de niño y lo que son ahora y por qué**

2. **Para los adolescentes, describe lo que quieren ser cuando sean grandes y por qué**

FIGURE 4.22.
Directions for Interview Slide

Translation
Now, interview 4 adults and 4 adolescents about professions.
1.   For the adults, identify what they wanted to be as a child and what they are now and why
2.   For the adolescents, describe what they want to be when they grow up and why

Reflection and Next Steps

This chapter has looked at research into input processing and how teachers can use input to help learners focus on form—in other words, how they can use input to teach grammar in context. Input processing helps teachers understand how learners make form-meaning connections when they encounter input and why they make some connections but not others. The principles of input processing can be applied to teaching through input processing instruction. First, teachers can select authentic resources or use their own teacher-made or adapted resources to provide learners with *enriched input:* input that naturally features a target structure with high frequency. Then, they can *enhance* the input by highlighting the target structure and drawing learners' attention to it. They can design *structured input* activities that force learners to process the target structure while demonstrating comprehension, drawing from the principles of input processing outlined in Table 4.1. Input processing instruction can be embedded in the Interactive Model to keep a primary focus on content (that is, meaning) rather than practice and memorization of grammar. An input and meaning-based approach to teaching grammar in context can help learners engage with relevant content. It can provide rich input so learners see and hear how the target structure is used in context, and it has the potential to more effectively advance student language proficiency when compared to a traditional grammar-driven approach.

Before moving on, take some time to reflect and assess your own practice. Consider how you are applying or would like to apply the practices and strategies discussed in this chapter. Where are your strengths? Where would you like to grow your practice? What actions will you take to move forward? This "one-point" rubric is designed to help you reflect and assess your own teaching practice in selecting resources, enhancing input, developing structured input activities, and embedding input processing instruction in the Interactive Model.

GLOW Where are my strengths related to this practice?	CRITERIA What should I be looking for in my own teaching?	GROW Where do I need to grow or expand my practice?	TAKE ACTION What steps will I take to move my practice forward?
	I select authentic resources that include target structures with high frequency, or I create my own resources, ensuring that the target structure is used naturally. (Enriched Input/Input Flooding)		
	I keep a primary focus on meaning when using interpretive resources with my students.		
	I use the structure of the Interactive Model for Interpretive Communication to engage students in the selected resources.		
	I use enhanced input (where the target structure is highlighted) to draw students' attention to the target feature.		

	I engage students in structured input activities, drawing on the principles of input processing.		
	I do not engage students in drill-based exercises in which they practice grammar in isolation (with no communicative context).		
	My students and I use the target language 90% or more of lesson time. I do not translate text or ask students to translate as one of their activities.		
	I use a communicative learning outcome, which is shared with students. All activities used reflect steps toward attainment of the student learning outcome.		

Level Up Your Learning

- **VanPatten, B. (2015). Input processing in adult SLA. In B. VanPatten & J. Williams (Eds.),** *Theories in second language acquisition* **(pp. 113-134). Routledge.**
  Bill VanPatten is unquestionably the best-known researcher in the area of input processing and input processing instruction. If you are looking for more information on the research into input processing principles, this chapter provides a clear and concise overview with straightforward examples.

- **VanPatten, B. (1996).** *Input processing and grammar instruction: Theory and research.* **Ablex.**
  Although it may be hard to get your hands on a copy, this book presents VanPatten's pioneering work in input processing instruction. In addition to a thorough research base, you will also find examples and a sample lesson.

- **Travers, M. (2019, February 8). Structured input.** *Diaries of a mad foreign language teacher.* **https://madlanguageteacher.weebly.com/teaching-grammar/structured-input**
  If you are looking for more teacher-made examples of structured input activities, Mike Travers' blog is a great place to start. In addition to structured input, Mike Travers also discusses how he is applying other input-based approaches to teaching grammar in context.

- **VanPatten, B. (2017).** *While we're on the topic: BVP on language, acquisition, and classroom practice.* **ACTFL.**
  A fun, engaging read that outlines six principles of communicative language teaching, including: "Any focus on form should be input-oriented and meaning-based." VanPatten succeeds in pulling together his deep understanding of second language acquisition research into concise principles, while also giving the reader just enough background in the research to walk away with a solid understanding.

Chapter 4 References

ACTFL. (n.d.). *Teach grammar as concepts in meaningful contexts in language learning.* https://www.actfl.org/resources/guiding-principles-language-learning/teach-grammar-concepts-meaningful-contexts-language-learning

Belin, L. [@lou_belin]. (2020, October 31). la raison pour laquelle je pleure c'est tout simplement parce que tu me manques [Tweet]. Twitter. https://twitter.com/lou_belin/status/1322663887091761154

Ellis, R. (2012). *Language teaching research and language pedagogy.* Wiley-Blackwell.

Gars Wifi. [@WifiGars]. (2020, October 30). tu es la raison pour laquelle je suis heureux [Tweet]. Twitter. https://twitter.com/WifiGars/status/1322329198749487104

Guilloteau, N. (2010). Vocabulary: Lesson 4: Input to output. In C. Blyth (Ed.), *Foreign language teaching methods.* COERLL, The University of Texas at Austin. https://coerll.utexas.edu/methods/modules/vocabulary/04/input.php

Ideal isco. [@IscoIdeal]. (2020, October 26). Soyez la raison pour laquelle quelqu'un continue de croire que les bonnes personnes existe [Tweet]. Twitter. https://twitter.com/IscoIdeal/status/1320846475048476673

IRRÉVERSIBLE. [@MulumbaMr]. (2020, October 28). Personne ne peut changer une personne mais quelqu'un peut être la raison pour laquelle une personne change [Tweet]. Twitter. https://twitter.com/MulumbaMr/status/1321345579197321217

Jacobs, K. (2016). *Canela.* Comprehensifying and extending authentic resources. http://www.ceauthres.com/p/click-here-for-link-to-slideshow-for.html

Jesse & Joy. (2006). Llegaste tú [Song]. On *Esta es mi vida.* Warner Music Latina.

Plugged In. (2020). Harry Potter and the Chamber of Secrets [Review of the book *Harry Potter and the chamber of secrets*, by J. K. Rowling]. *Focus on the Family's Plugged In.* https://www.pluggedin.com/book-reviews/harry-potter-and-the-chamber-of-secrets/

Soprano. (2017, September 1). *Soprano - Mon précieux (Clip officiel)* [Video]. YouTube. https://www.youtube.com/watch?v=OVmfGb8XKSg

Travers, M. (2019, February 8). Structured input. *Diaries of a mad foreign language teacher.* https://madlanguageteacher.weebly.com/teaching-grammar/structured-input

VanPatten, B. (1996). *Input processing and grammar instruction: Theory and research.* Ablex.

VanPatten, B. (2015). Input processing in adult SLA. In B. VanPatten & J. Williams (Eds.), *Theories in second language acquisition,* (pp. 113–134). Routledge.

VanPatten, B. (2017). *While we're on the topic: BVP on language, acquisition, and classroom practice.* ACTFL.

CHAPTER 5

Interaction in a Learner-Centered Classroom

F or most language learners, using the target language in class—in front of all of their peers!—can be an incredibly intimidating experience. It is natural for students to feel nervous or self-conscious when they try to speak in another language. They are, after all, taking a risk by speaking. As language learners, they are perfectly aware how *imperfect* their language skills are. They will make mistakes, they will lack vocabulary, they will get flustered and say the wrong thing. Your job as a world language teacher is to let students know that this is okay and in fact is an important part of the process. But for students to take risks in your classroom, you need to first ensure that they feel comfortable and supported and that they understand that what you are asking them to do is *communicate*, as messy as that may be.

Making students feel comfortable and supported starts with building a positive and inclusive classroom culture by getting to know your students, honoring their backgrounds, treating every student with dignity and respect, and regularly giving them a chance to have their voice heard in class. World language teachers often worry about the "affective filter" of their students (Krashen, 1985), interpreting that to mean that students should have a low stress level in class. Krashen's original definition of the affective filter, however, was that it is a "mental block" that is triggered when students are "unmotivated, lacking in self-confidence, or anxious" (p. 3). While some teachers may interpret this to mean that students should not be encouraged or required to speak the language before they are "ready" (meaning they choose to speak on their own), we disagree. We want all students to feel prepared and supported *before* they are asked to speak, and teachers need to carefully plan and prepare students for language output, but research indicates that some level of "tension" in language learning is actually beneficial for learners (Spielmann & Radnofsky, 2001, qtd. in Lightbown & Spada, 2013, p. 85). Tension means that students are actively engaged and challenged, while not being overwhelmed. Positive relationships with their teacher and working in small groups when using the language can help reduce anxiety while also maintaining a level of tension that engages students (Gass, 2013). Furthermore, when students speak—or, in technical terms, produce *output*—they must actively draw on their knowledge of the language to create comprehensible utterances. This is known as *comprehensible output* or *pushed output*, and it is a powerful learning experience for students. Learners get feedback on their language use, are able to test what they know (or think they know) about the language, develop more automatic language use, and focus on actively using the language (Gass, 2013). While you want to maintain a positive and supportive classroom atmosphere, you also should not shy away from pushing your students to use the language even at early Novice levels.

Another important consideration as you seek to encourage student target-language use in your classes is how much you are focusing on language practice and accuracy versus true communication. The way you interact with your students in the target language lets them know what is important in your class, and the way that you ask questions and listen to the answers plays a large role in the communicative dynamic of your classroom. Additionally, the types of classroom activities you engage students in may or may not be truly communicative in nature. Do your class activities have a communicative purpose, or are they designed for students just to practice language?

Also, when you ask students to use the target-language, how much of it is presentational communication (rehearsed and practiced) versus interpersonal communication (spontaneous and two-way)? Supporting interaction in a learner-centered classroom means emphasizing meaningful communication over language practice, both in how you speak to your students and how you ask them to speak to each other.

So what does teacher talk that values communication and interaction sound like? And how can you design classroom activities that truly engage students in interpersonal (interactive) communication? In this chapter, we will examine how teachers interact with their students by looking at teacher talk and question types, as well as different types of learning experiences and the difference between exercises, activities, and tasks. We will look at the SCRAP Framework that supports teachers in crafting real-world, authentic tasks to imbue communicative purpose in class learning experiences. We will also walk through numerous interpersonal strategies and show how they can be adapted in different learning environments.

Re-Thinking Teacher Talk

So you want your students to talk more in class? (In the target language, of course!) One of the best ways to encourage student talk is to re-examine teacher talk and make some small but significant shifts in the way you interact with your students. When you talk to students in the target language, are you actually interested in what they have to say or are you just listening for correctness? When you ask students questions, do you give them space to elaborate, or do you get one-word answers and find yourself constantly telling them to use complete sentences? The way you talk to your students lets them know what you value: communication (mistakes and all) or accuracy above all else. Here are some ways you can shift teacher talk to cultivate a learner-centered classroom that values meaningful interaction.

IRE vs. IRF

When you ask your students a question, how do you respond to what they say? If you find yourself saying "good job" or "no, that's not right," you are likely using what Glisan and Donato refer to as IRE: Initiate, Respond, Evaluate (2017, p. 42). In the following student-teacher interactions, the teacher is more interested in *how* the student says something than *what* the student actually says.

> Initiate (Teacher): "How are you?"
> Respond (Student): "Good."
> Evaluate (Teacher): "No, say, 'I'm fine, thank you.'"
>
> Initiate (Teacher): "What did you do this weekend?"
> Respond (Student): "I went to the café." or "Went to the café."
> Evaluate (Teacher): "Good."

As you can see, in the first example the teacher cares very little for whether the student is doing well or not; they just want to be sure the student uses a complete sentence. And in the second example, the teacher is not really interested in what the student did over the weekend. Instead of responding to the content of the student's response, the teacher *evaluates* the response by telling the student, "Good."

The problem with IRE is that it lets students know that meaningful communication is not really important in your classes. Keeping a focus on communication in your classes means that you interact to exchange information, not just to use language for the sake of practice (VanPatten, 2017). Rather than evaluating students each time they speak, you need to think about engaging students in meaningful conversation. IRE can therefore be re-configured as IRF: Initiate, Response, *Feedback* (Glisan & Donato, 2017). Here is an example of how this sounds in practice:

> Initiate (Teacher): "How are you?"
> Respond (Student): "Good."
> Feedback (Teacher): "Glad to hear it! What did you do this weekend?"
> Respond (Student): "I went to the café."
> Feedback (Teacher): "That sounds like fun! Did you go with some friends?'"

As you can see, the teacher is listening to the student not just for complete sentences or accuracy, but for information—what the student is saying. The teacher then responds in a way that continues the conversation naturally. While this shift in teacher language may seem small, it can have a significant impact on how your students view language use in your classes.

Teacher Questions

Another way to shift teacher talk is to consider the types of questions that you ask students and whether they actually give students space to push beyond Novice-level (single word) responses and use higher-order thinking skills. Closed-response questions—such as yes/no, either/or, or simple *what, where, when, who* questions—can usually be answered with a single word. Often, teachers find themselves telling students to respond with a complete sentence. The teacher asks, for example, "What's your name?" and the student responds, "Paul." If the teacher then says, "Complete sentence, please!" the student gets the message that what is important is not *what* they say (communication), but *how* they say it (accuracy). This type of exchange follows the IRE model and is called a "display question," where teachers already know the answer and are just checking for accuracy in student language (Lightbown & Spada, 2013). With the IRF model, if a student has successfully responded to a question with only one word, rather than force the student to repeat themselves while using a complete sentence, you can instead ask follow-up questions that require elaboration.

What types of questions are you typically asking your students? If the majority of your questions are closed-response and can be answered successfully with only one word, your students won't be challenged to push beyond the Novice level. Recall that Novices exhibit *word-level* discourse; they are comfortable producing single-word utterances. If you want your students to advance to the Intermediate level, you need to give them opportunities to produce *sentence-level* discourse. And if you are working with Intermediate-level students, to move to Advanced they need to be given opportunities to produce *paragraph-level* discourse. Rather than telling your students, "Complete sentence, please!" ask them questions that they need and want to answer with more than one word in order to keep the emphasis on meaningful communication while also encouraging them to produce more complex output.

Clementi and Terrill (2017) provide a hierarchy of questions that can serve as a guide in structuring your questions. Table 5.1 summarizes the hierarchy and includes sample questions. As you move down the list of question types, you will see that each question demands a more robust student response.

TABLE 5.1. HIERARCHY OF QUESTIONS WITH SAMPLES

Question Type	Sample Question
Yes/No	Did you have a good weekend?
Which?	Which activities did you do this weekend?

Either/Or	Did you play soccer or football?
What? When? Where? Who?	What did you do this weekend? Where did you go?
How? Why?	How did you spend your weekend? Why did you play soccer this weekend?
Can you describe...?	Can you describe what that was like?
Can you tell me about...?	Can you tell me about the soccer game?
What if...?	What would you have done instead if it had rained this weekend?

Source: Adapted from Clementi & Terrill, 2017.

Talking Less So Students Talk More

As you know, teacher talk is the most important source of target-language input for your students. Students need to hear you speak the target language! However, this should not be interpreted to mean that you are running a teacher-centered classroom where your voice is the only one heard. If you want to support student language use and interactions, you need to give students space to speak.

What does this mean in practice? It means that students should get more airtime than you do each and every day. It means that every single student should have a chance to speak in the target language every day, multiple times a day. It means that you plan for interactive student activities throughout each class session and limit your teacher presentations to keep them short and sweet. Here are some quick tips to speak less so that your students speak more:

- Build in regular Turn and Talks during teacher presentations.

- Keep teacher presentations brief (5-10 minutes maximum).

- Incorporate regular and frequent student-centered communicative tasks.

- Be wary of "teachable moments" that tempt you to talk more, especially if you tend to go off on a tangent that goes on and on.

- Spend more time planning and less time teaching; become the guide on the side during class time.

- Make sure that every student talks every day, multiple times a day.

Student Target-Language Use Expectations

One of the great frustrations for world language teachers happens when they put students in small groups to start an interpersonal task, and—as soon as the teacher is out of earshot—the students start using English instead of the target language. This experience can be really discouraging, especially when the teacher tries telling students, *"en français!"* ["in French!"] to move them back into the target language, but ends up sounding like a broken record when students need reminding again and again.

At the secondary (middle and high school) and post-secondary levels, student reluctance to use the target language in class can be viewed as a classroom management issue. Imagine that instead of using English each time you put them in groups, students start texting on their cell phones. Student use of cellphones in class for non-educational purposes is clearly a classroom management issue, and teachers dedicate lots of time to addressing it. The same can be said for students' English use in world language classes.

Think about how much class time you waste by asking students to use the target language again and again. Rather than *asking* them to use the target-language, you need to establish target-language use as a basic *expectation* in any and all world language classes.

But getting students to use the target-language need not be or feel punitive. Rather, it should be something that is fun and engaging, while also building classroom community. Using a technique called Responsibility Training (Jones, 2014), you can harness the power of collaboration and community to build student responsibility for and ownership of class target-language use. Responsibility Training is essentially using a game or fun strategy that incentivizes collective use of the target-language. What exactly this game or strategy is depends entirely on what will work with your students. The strategy itself doesn't matter! What does matter is that you set a basic expectation in your class that *all students will use the target-language exclusively during class time and will only use English after asking for permission.*

Here are some Responsibility Training strategies for establishing an expectation of target-language use. As you read them, consider ways you might implement or adapt them for your own classes. If your students are already using the target-language throughout your classes, you may not need these strategies.

Target-Language Stuffy

Choose a stuffed animal (any one will do, but culturally relevant ones are great to use for this strategy). Introduce the stuffed animal to the class and explain (in English if necessary) that the stuffed animal is joining the class to help everyone use the target language. Starting at the next class session (to give students time to mentally prepare), any time you hear someone using English without having first asked permission, they will be given the stuffed animal. If you hear any other students speak English, you will then move the stuffed animal to their desk. Whichever student has the stuffed animal at the end of class will be asked to speak to you for 30-60 seconds at the end of class using the target-language (or any other "consequence" that you feel is appropriate). Students can talk about whatever they like in the target-language. Figure 5.1 shows a possible target-language stuffy, ready to do his job!

FIGURE 5.1.
Target-Language Stuffy

Chat Box

Grab a large jar, cookie tin, or other container of your choice. Type up 20 or so questions in the target-language. Open-ended questions are preferable; they should be level appropriate so that most students in your class will be able to understand and answer them. Explain to the class that, starting at the next class session, whenever you hear anyone use English without first asking permission, you will jot down their name. At the end of class, the students who spoke English will be asked to pull a question out of the chat box, read it, and then answer in the target-language.

Class Competitions

If you teach more than one class group, assign each one a team name in the target-language and post them all in the room. Explain to each class group that you will now be holding weekly competitions to see which group can stay in the target-language the most. Each Monday, give each class group 10 points, writing this next to each class's name. Any time a student uses English without first asking permission, that student's class group will lose a point. On Friday, the group with the most remaining points wins and can choose a small reward for the following Monday (such as playing a game in class or watching a target-language music video). Caution! If you have a class that knows it will never win, the students will no longer be motivated to play. Use a different target-language strategy for that class.

Secret Student

Every few days in class, tell your students that you have chosen one of them to be the "secret student." If the secret student does not speak English at all during that day's class, the whole class will be rewarded (with, for example, an in-class game or watching a target-language music video). At the end of class, you will announce who the secret student was *only if they did not use English*. If the secret student was successful, you can celebrate them in front of the whole class and the class gets the reward. If the secret student did speak English, however, do not reveal their name. Tell the class that they did not make it today, but you will try again tomorrow. Caution! On the first day you try this strategy, be sure that the secret student is successful. If they are not, just switch to another student who was—you want success on the first day, otherwise students will quickly lose motivation to participate. (A special thanks to Spanish teacher Zach Bagan of Hingham, MA, who developed and shared this strategy.)

TALK Rubric

A TALK score or TALK rubric (Shrum & Glisan, 2016; Grahn & McAlpine, 2017) can be an effective tool to promote student target-language use during interpersonal speaking tasks or group work. The TALK rubric (shown in Table 5.2) is handed out to students during small group activities. Students can self-assess or peer-assess, and the teacher can additionally keep notes for each student and provide individual feedback after the activity.

TABLE 5.2. SAMPLE TALK RUBRIC		
TALK	**✓- ✓ ✓+**	**Feedback**
T: Target Language *I only use the target language in class.*		
A: Accuracy *Most of what I say is understood by others.*		
L: Listens *I actively listen to classmates when they speak.*		
K: Kind *I am kind and understanding when others speak and offer help when needed.*		

The strategy you use will depend on your students (their age and interest) and your own personal preferences. There is no one "right" strategy—whatever achieves the goal is great. You need to put the use of English to an end quickly and efficiently, while also maintaining a positive atmosphere in the class. Some teachers will try assigning "participation points" when students use the target language. If this works for you, then by all means, this could be an effective strategy. For many teachers, however, running the class while also tracking participation points can be a lot to manage all at once. Additionally, through experience, we have found that positive rewards and encouragement of target-language use do not seem to be as effective as *mandating* target-language use in a way that is fun and engaging. And finally, if your class is already using the target-language without one of these strategies, fantastic! You don't need to use one of these strategies.

Moving from Exercises to Tasks

Making shifts in teacher talk and setting a target-language use expectation can help establish a classroom culture that supports communication and interaction. However, you also need to take a close look at the types of learning experiences that you engage students in during class time. Do these learning experiences support or undermine an interactive classroom culture?

VanPatten (2017) distinguishes three types of learning experiences: exercises, activities, and tasks. While teachers often refer to learning experiences generally as "activities," VanPatten defines this term in a specific way that we will clarify here. Using the lens of supporting a communicative, interactive class culture, our identification of the type of learning experience comes down to whether students are expressing or interpreting *meaning* in order to engage in the learning experience and whether there is a *communicative purpose* for the learning experience. A communicative purpose means that students are using language to convey information, not just for the sake of using language or practicing.

Exercises

Learning experiences that would be considered *exercises* require no student expression or interpretation of meaning and have no communicative purpose. These traditional practices (sometimes referred to as *drill and kill*) should look very familiar. Take a look at Figure 5.2. Students are given a verb that they need to conjugate. Without knowing the meaning of the sentence, students are able to complete the exercise correctly if they know the pattern for conjugation. There is no expression or interpretation of meaning, and there is no communicative purpose. Exercises tell students that the primary goal of class is accuracy. Think about how the exercise below would be graded. There are clear right and wrong answers, and the only feedback to students is on correctness. When considering which learning experiences to use with our students, exercises like this should no longer be used (Wong & VanPatten, 2003).

Fill in the sentence with the correct form of the -ER verb in the present tense.

1. Je _____ au téléphone. (parler)
2. Paul _____ son petit-déjeuner. (manger)
3. Nous _____ un film. (regarder)
4. Tu _____ au foot? (jouer)
5. Sophie et Jeanne _____ bien en classe? (écouter)

FIGURE 5.2.
Sample Exercise

Translation
1. I _____ on the phone. (to talk)
2. Paul _____ his breakfast. (to eat)
3. We _____ a film. (to watch)
4. You _____ soccer? (to play)
5. Do Sophie and Jeanne _____ well in class? (to listen)

Activities

Activities differ from exercises in that they require an expression or interpretation of meaning. Like exercises, however, they do not have a communicative purpose. Look at the sample activity in Figure 5.3. As a do-now activity, students are told to ask five of their classmates what their favorite free-time activity is. Students will need to interpret meaning (the favorite activity) in order to write it down. However, many will be left asking the question: *Why are we doing this?* If the answer to that question is that the teacher wants to practice verbs the students recently learned (to play sports, to read a book, and so on), the activity clearly has no communicative purpose. Use of activities that are no more than "communicative drills" (Wong & VanPatten, 2003, p. 406) should be limited, but with some modifications they can be incorporated into meaningful tasks.

Do Now:

Find out the favorite free-time activity of five of your classmates.

FIGURE 5.3.
Sample Activity

Tasks

Tasks take activities and give them a communicative purpose. Consider the activity above. By giving this activity a purpose, you can use it meaningfully in your classes. The task description shown in Figure 5.4 does just that. Students are still asked to collect information on their classmates' favorite free-time activities, but now they are going to use this information to create a graph and compare what they learn from their e-pals in the target culture. Incorporating tasks in your classes often means redesigning existing activities to give them purpose and context.

Interview classmates about their favorite free-time activities. We'll use this to create an infographic and then interview our ePals. Finally, you'll compare our class' favorite free-time activities to those of your ePals.

FIGURE 5.4.
Sample Task
Source: Blouwolff & Ritz, 2019.

As you consider the types of learning experiences you use with your students, keep asking yourself, *Why are students doing this?* If your answer is "to practice language," you will want to dig deeper to find a more meaningful and authentic purpose. Table 5.3 summarizes the differences between exercises, activities, and tasks.

TABLE 5.3. DISTINCTIONS BETWEEN EXERCISES, ACTIVITIES, AND TASKS			
Type of Learning Experience	**Expression or Interpretation of Meaning?**	**Communicative Purpose?**	**Summary Statement**
Exercise	No	No	Not Communicative
Activity	Yes	No	Partially Communicative
Task	Yes	Yes	Fully Communicative

Source: Summarized from VanPatten, 2017, p. 84.

The SCRAP Framework

Coming up with an authentic purpose for a task can be achieved with the help of a structure called the SCRAP Framework (Pijanowski, 2016). SCRAP stands for Situation, Challenge, Role, Audience, and Product/Performance. Table 5.4 walks through the SCRAP Framework and provides examples for interpersonal and presentational communication. SCRAP asks you to create an authentic, real-world scenario that includes a purpose for communicating. Instead of just practicing asking questions, for example, the interpersonal task described in Table 5.4 gives students a purpose for asking questions: They are volunteering at a local library, and one of the patrons who comes in does not speak English. The student needs to ask the patron what they need and provide assistance. You can use the SCRAP Framework both to craft authentic, real-world purposes for tasks and to write performance assessments.

TABLE 5.4. SCRAP FRAMEWORK AND EXAMPLES

SCRAP Framework	Question to Consider	Interpersonal Example	Presentational Example
S: Situation	What is the situation?	At the public library	Traveling to Mexico with your family
C: Challenge	What challenge will students face in this situation?	There are some patrons who do not speak English	When you arrive at the airport, your luggage has been lost
R: Role	What role or roles will students take?	You are a library volunteer *or* You are the library patron (Two students work together, each taking a different role.)	You are the only person in your family who speaks any Spanish
A: Audience	Who is the audience?	Library patrons *or* Volunteers	Airport personnel
P: Product/ Performance	What product will students develop or what performance will students demonstrate?	*Interpersonal Performance Task Frame:* You volunteer every Saturday morning at the public library. You're stacking books near the reception area when a family comes in and asks the librarian for help. The librarian gives a blank look since the question was asked in Chinese. You have been studying Mandarin for a few years now and decide to go over to offer help. Greet the family, find out what they are looking for, and see how you can help. (One student will take the role of library volunteer, and the other will take the role of a family member.)	*Presentational Performance Task Frame:* You have finally convinced your parents to take your family on a trip to Mexico! Everyone is really excited, but your parents have made clear that they will be counting on you to help since you are the only person in your family who speaks Spanish. After a long flight, you finally arrive. You wait and wait and wait for your bags to come out in baggage claim, but they are nowhere to be found. With your parents nudging you, it's already time to put your Spanish skills to the test. You take a minute to rehearse what you will say, then walk up to the nearest airport employee to explain what has happened.

To build a learner-centered classroom culture where interaction in the target language is the norm, you can shift the way you talk to and ask questions of students, establish student target-language use expectations through fun and engaging strategies, and re-design classroom learning experiences to keep the focus on tasks that involve meaningful communication. In addition, teachers can embed interpersonal strategies in authentic tasks.

Interpersonal Strategies

Keeping the focus on interaction in a learner-centered classroom means that you are regularly engaging students in interpersonal communication tasks. Remember, though, that having students *speak* in the target language is not necessarily interpersonal communication. Oftentimes, student target-language use in our classes is actually limited to *presentational* communication. The classic example is a role play in which students are asked to prepare a dialogue between two people: a waiter and a customer, for example. If your students are working to *write* the dialogue and then present it to the class—either having memorized it or reading from the script they wrote—then this is presentational communication, *not* true interaction or interpersonal communication. Before reading the interpersonal strategies below, consider the ways in which your students currently speak in the target language in your classes. Would you categorize their speech as presentational or interpersonal? Ask yourself: *Are my students speaking spontaneously? Do they need to listen in order to respond? Or are they reading from something they have written or memorized?* Also ask yourself whether you will use these strategies as part of an *activity* or part of a *communicative task*. The strategies we share here can easily be adapted to any language or level and fit well with a range of interpersonal tasks. When using these strategies, make it a goal to incorporate multiple interpersonal communicative tasks in each and every class.

Turn and Talk/Think, Pair, Share

The easiest interpersonal strategies to build into any language class—Turn and Talks (simply: turn and talk to your partner) and Think, Pair, Shares (same as a Turn and Talk, but asking students to first quietly think and jot down some notes)—require no preparation and can be used at multiple points during any given class period. For a warm-up, you can ask students to turn to a partner and share what they did over the weekend while you are taking attendance or handing out papers. During a lesson, you can interject this strategy at any point, for example to ask students to make observations about an image or come up with a list of questions about a given topic. Students benefit from having someone to bounce ideas off of before presenting their ideas to the class. At the end of class, students can be asked to turn to a partner and reflect on what they learned in class and share takeaways.

Questioning

Asking questions is an important interpersonal function, but one that can be incredibly challenging for learners. At the Novice level, learners are more likely to produce questions as memorized chunks. Intermediate-level learners can be expected to produce their own (sometimes messy) questions. Advanced learners will have more control over question formation. As preparation for any interpersonal task, learners will benefit from a focus on questions they can use. This can be built into a conversation or partner interview as a strategy to support learners, and you can adjust the level of scaffolding as appropriate for your level of learners. Novice- and Intermediate-level learners can brainstorm with you to come up with questions on the topic while you write these down for the whole class to use in their conversation. Even though the questions learners come up with are either memorized chunks or simple questions (sometimes only a question word), it is important to give them the chance to generate the questions on their own after they have some familiarity with the topic and the types of questions they can ask. Alternatively, learners can work in pairs to generate as many questions as they can on the topic, using a timer to make the strategy feel more game-like. These are then shared out with the whole class as you write them down, not explicitly correcting any errors but rather just modeling accurate forms. After a group brainstorm, you can then put learners in pairs or small groups so they can use the questions they generated to have a conversation. Advanced or pre-Advanced learners will also benefit from a group brainstorm to help them form more complex questions to use.

Information Gaps

Information Gaps are designed so that each student has different information. In order to find out what the others know, the students must engage in discussion. For example, students A and B are given information about two different tourist destinations. They must ask each other questions about the different destinations to determine which one they would like to travel to together. This can be adapted to any number of topics or formats, such as using two different images, two different menus, two different school schedules, and so on.

Four Corners

Four Corners is an excellent way for students to engage in interpersonal discussion while also incorporating movement. The teacher has a set of questions with four possible answers and has posted small signs in each corner of the room with the letter corresponding to the answer (A, B, C, D). Each student walks to the corner of the room with the sign that represents their answer to the question. Once they are in their corners, students discuss their reason for choosing this answer with each other. For example, a teacher asks what students' favorite sport is, giving four possible responses. Once they are in their groups, students ask each other why they chose the sport as their favorite and what they like about it.

Speed Dating/Inside-Outside Circle

Speed Dating or Inside-Outside Circle (outlined in Figures 5.5 and 5.6) are great ways to get your students speaking interpersonally and interacting with lots of their classmates. It also supports student movement, but in an organized way. Depending on the classroom space, students can form two large circles (Inside-Outside Circle) or form two rows (Speed Dating). One circle or one row stays in place while the other rotates whenever you ask students to move. You can provide students with a discussion prompt or give them a question to ask their partner. Students talk for between 30 seconds and 2 minutes, depending on their proficiency level. The teacher then calls out for students to switch partners, and the rotating row moves one step forward to meet their new partner. They then discuss the same prompt or question again. As the teacher, you can either walk around and listen in on students as they discuss or join and participate in the discussion.

Philosophical Chairs

With Intermediate or Advanced groups, Philosophical Chairs is a way to help students take a position on a topic and defend it with evidence. Students will have first learned about the topic through various authentic resources. Then, when students come to class,

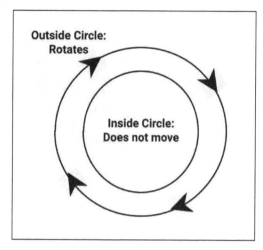

FIGURE 5.5.
Set-up for Inside-Outside Circle

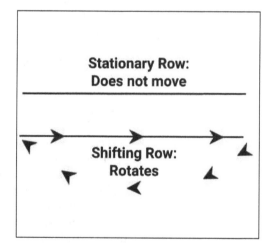

FIGURE 5.6.
Set-up for Speed Dating

the classroom desks or chairs are set up in a U-shape. Students are presented with the topic in the form of a statement, for example, "All students should learn coding in school." Students who are in agreement with the statement will sit on one side of the U and those who are opposed will sit directly across from them. If students are undecided, they sit in the middle of the U-shape. After taking their seats, students are encouraged to explain why those chose their position and provide evidence. The goal is for students to convince those on the other side or those who are undecided to change their minds. If any students do change their minds, they get up and move to a different place in the room. (*Classroom Close-Up 5.2* highlights this strategy in practice.)

Tech Zoom

Whatever your learning environment (in-person, hybrid, or remote), technology can support interaction in a learner-centered classroom. With a focus on the five interpersonal strategies we presented above, in this section we will look at how to integrate technology and adapt the strategies for different learning environments.

- Turn and Talk/Think, Pair, Share

  For hybrid or distance learning, Turn and Talks or Think, Pair, Shares can be used during synchronous class meetings on platforms such as Zoom, GoogleMeet, or Microsoft Teams. Although not quite as instantaneous as turning to a partner in a physical classroom, the breakout room feature in each of these platforms can replicate a quick partner discussion. Depending on the platform you use, you may be able to set a timer so that students have only 1 or 2 minutes for the partner discussion and are then quickly moved to another partner or back to the main session. Since you cannot easily monitor student discussions in breakout rooms, consider providing a question or prompt for students to refer to, as well as asking students to share out with the whole class. In-person learning can also take advantage of technology to support interpersonal communication beyond the school day, using Web tools such as Flipgrid, Padlet, or Classkick, where students can record themselves, listen to their peers, and then record a response. These types of interpersonal activities make a great replacement for traditional homework assignments!

- Information Gaps

  Information Gap activities can easily integrate technology, whether in-person, hybrid, or remote. Tools such as Seesaw and Classkick allow teachers to create interactive activity slides that include authentic resources or other information. Teachers can create two versions of the activity slide so that there is different information for two groups of students (student A and student B), pairing students so that each is matched with a student from the other group. Both Seesaw and Classkick allow students to record themselves on the activity slide. For in-person classes, this feature can be used during class time as a formative assessment check. For hybrid or remote learning, students can meet either in breakout groups or independently on another virtual platform and record their interaction.

- Four Corners

  While replicating Four Corners in a hybrid or remote environment may seem daunting, it can be achieved. Instead of posting signs to indicate the four corners of a classroom, teachers can have their students either hold up between 1 and 4 fingers to indicate their answer, or they can teach them the first four letters of the alphabet in American Sign Language (ASL) and have them show the letter (A, B, C, D) or stand up and do a different movement (jumping or running in place, for example) for the response they choose (Blouwolff, 2020). You can also use Google Jamboard, having students add their names to the Jamboard, then dragging them to the corner that matches their response. Students can then be moved to breakout rooms that match their response, or the teacher can ask students to discuss their answers.

- Speed Dating/Inside-Outside Circle
  Like Turn and Talks or Think, Pair, Shares, this strategy can be used with the support of the breakout room feature in whatever class meeting platform you may be using. Students are given the prompt or question, and then paired randomly with a partner for between 30 seconds and 2 minutes. Students are then moved automatically to a new partner for discussion. Since students cannot see the prompt or question written on the board, as they would be able to in a classroom, make sure they have access to it for reference, such as by providing a link to a GoogleDoc or GoogleSlide that they can have open while they talk.

- Philosophical Chairs
  Rather than setting up your classroom desks so that they are in a U-shape for this strategy, if you are meeting virtually with your class, you can create a Google Jamboard slide with two sides: Pro and Con (Byrne, 2020). The topic statement can be placed in the middle, along with an "undecided" section. When students join the Jamboard, they create a Post-it note with their name, which they can move from one side to another to indicate their stance on the issue. As you will see in *Classroom Close-Up 5.2*, you may also want to add a box on the Jamboard that says, "I would like to speak." Students can then pull their name to this box when they are ready to add to the discussion. Alternatively, Parlay Ideas allows you to create a virtual roundtable. You will need to set up a class account and invite your students to join. Then, you can run the discussion synchronously (over Zoom, GoogleMeet, or another platform) or asynchronously using the chat feature. For in-person instruction, this site can allow for discussion on the topic to occur before or after a Philosophical Chairs debate in class, providing an opportunity for students to extend their thinking and practice using the target language and structures. The site will also track student engagement, making it easier to know how much each student is participating.

Now that we have looked at how to rethink teacher talk and questions, establish target-language use expectations, use the SCRAP Framework, and employ numerous strategies for engaging students in interpersonal communication, we will walk through two *Classroom Close-Ups* that show how teachers of two different languages working with students at two different proficiency levels apply these features to their own teaching. In *Classroom Close-Up 5.2*, we will also show how the teacher engages students in a hybrid or distance learning environment.

Classroom Close-Ups
Classroom Close-Up 5.1: Let's Eat!
This classroom example was shared by Sheng-Chu Lu, Mandarin teacher at the Pingree School, South Hamilton, MA.

COURSE OVERVIEW	
Course Name	Chinese 3
Course Proficiency Target	Intermediate Low
LESSON OVERVIEW	
Unit Theme	Let's Eat!
Lesson Learning Outcome	I can ask and answer questions about what I like and don't like to eat and explain why.

Core Vocabulary and Forms	General Food Items:
	· 炒饭 (fried rice)
	· 饺子 (dumplings)
	· 青菜 (vegetables)
	· 茶 (tea)
	Food Items from Su Chang's Restaurant Selected by Students:
	· 蟹角 (crab rangoon)
	· 葱油饼 (scallion pancake)
	· 锅贴 (Peking ravioli)
	· 酸辣汤 (hot and sour soup)
	· 春卷 (spring rolls)
	· 左公鸡 (General Gau chicken,)
	Cooking Methods:
	· 炸 (fry)
	· 煎 (grill)
	· 清蒸 (steam)
	· 炒 (stir fry)
	Words to Describe Food:
	· 健康 (healthy)
	· 酸 (sour)
	· 辣 (spicy)
	· 甜 (sweet)
	· 油 (oily)
	· 清淡 (light)
	· 好吃 (delicious)
	Sentence Structures:
	· 不但...而且 (not only... but also)
	· 每...都 (every...all)
	· 比 (structure for comparing two things)
	· 最 (the most, -est)
	· 比较 (by comparison/relatively)
Materials and Resources	Menu from Su Chang's Restaurant (https://www.suchangspeabody.com/appetizers) Index cards
Lesson Length	60 minutes

LEARNING SEQUENCE

Focus of Learning	Students view the question *What do you like to eat and why?* as they come into the classroom.	Time: 1 min
Preview of Learning	The teacher asks one of the students to read the objective and agenda for the day.	Time: 1 min

Learning Episode 1		
Primetime 1	1. The teacher shows slides with images of Chinese dishes. The students turn to their partner and take turns asking if they like the dish or not and why. Then, they switch roles.	*Time:* 10 min
	2. Students are given a copy of a menu from a local Chinese restaurant along with an index card. The students read the menu and write down their favorite food item on the index card.	
	3. Students will ask the favorite food items of as many students as they can. The teacher models the dialogue for the class with a student.	
Downtime	4. The students then stand up and walk around the class asking their classmates what their favorite food is. Students record answers on their index cards.	*Time:* 5 min
Primetime 2	5. When the students return to their seats, they share their findings to determine what the class's favorite dish is.	*Time:* 5 min
Brain Break	The students take a minute to stretch out.	*Time:* 1 min
Learning Episode 2		
Primetime 1	6. The teacher explains the Four Corners activity and models with one or two students how to discuss whether food is healthy or not.	*Time:* 5 min
Downtime	7. Students move to the corner of the room that matches their response and discuss their reason why with their partner.	*Time:* 5 min
Primetime 2	8. While students are still in their corners, the teacher asks for students to share out.	*Time:* 5 min
Brain Break	Students have a minute to return to their seats, sharpen pencils, or chat.	*Time:* 1 min
Learning Episode 3		
Primetime 1	9. The teacher shows the Interpersonal Task frame and asks one of the students to read it to the class. Students are given copies of two different lunch menus from a school in China.	*Time:* 5 min
	10. The teacher models a possible conversation with a student.	
Downtime	11. Students are assigned pairs and begin the Interpersonal Task. Students may be asked to record their conversation.	*Time:* 5 min
Primetime 2	12. A few groups are asked to present their conversation for the whole class.	*Time:* 5 min
Celebration of Learning	The teacher returns students' attention to the learning goal and asks for a thumbs-up/thumbs-down self-reflection.	*Time:* 1 min

In this lesson for an Intermediate Low Mandarin class, students have already learned the vocabulary and target structures earlier in the unit and are now working to apply their learning through authentic interaction. The teacher begins class by greeting students in Mandarin and asking a student to read the objective and agenda, shown in Figure 5.7

𝓛earning Outcome: **I can ask and answer questions about what I like and don't like to eat and explain why.**
我可以问和回答有关喜欢和不喜欢吃的东西的问题，也可以解释为什么。

Agenda:

1. Our Class's Favorite Dish from Su Chang's Restaurant
2. Four Corners: Is General Gau's chicken healthy?
3. Information Gap: School Lunch Menus

FIGURE 5.7.
Lesson Objective and Agenda

The teacher begins a warm-up activity to review key vocabulary and structures. The teacher shows slides with images of Chinese dishes and text and asks students if they like them and why (Figures 5.8 and 5.9 show two of these slides). The teacher asks students to do a Turn and Talk where one student will ask the question on the slide (*Do you like beef with mushrooms? Why?*) and the partner will answer (*I like beef with mushrooms because... or I do not like beef with mushrooms because...*). Students switch roles with each slide so that they both get turns asking and answering questions.

你喜欢...

蘑菇牛肉?

为什么?

FIGURE 5.8.
Warm-Up Discussion Slide, Example 1

Translation
Do you like...
beef with mushrooms?
Why?

你喜欢...

蝦炒飯?

为什么?

FIGURE 5.9.
Warm-Up Discussion Slide, Example 2

Translation
Do you like...
shrimp fried rice?
Why?

The teacher then begins the next activity. Focusing on a local Chinese restaurant—Su Chang's restaurant—the teacher gives each student a copy of the menu (found online at https://www.suchangspeabody.com; the teacher has removed the English translations from the website, but no other modifications have been made) along with one index card per student. Students are given a few minutes to read the menu quietly and then write their favorite food item on the index card. The teacher then explains that the students will stand up and ask as many classmates as possible what their favorite food item is and why. Students will note the favorite item on the other side of their index card. Before beginning, the teacher models the activity with a student, demonstrating how students can ask *What's your favorite dish? Why?* (你最喜欢的一道菜是什么？为什么？) The teacher then instructs students to stand and begin asking each other about their favorite dish. The teacher circulates while students speak. After approximately 5-10 minutes (or when it appears that most students have had a chance to speak to each other), the teacher asks students to return to their seats. The teacher asks what items were the favorite and makes a tally on the board. In this example, the class's favorite item was General Gau's chicken, shown in Figure 5.10.

我们班最喜欢速晨餐厅的一道菜是什么?

左公雞

FIGURE 5.10.
The Class's Favorite Dish

Translation
What is our class's favorite dish from Su Chang's restaurant?
General Gau's chicken

After a brief brain break, the teacher transitions the class to the next activity, which will ask students to explain whether they think the favorite dish is healthy or not, and why. Using the Four Corners strategy, the teacher asks students to give their opinion as to whether General Gau's chicken is healthy by going to one corner of the classroom. The teacher has prepared ahead signs for each corner of the classroom, which state Strongly Agree, Agree, Disagree, Strongly Disagree. Figure 5.11 shows the directions for this activity. The teacher models a possible conversation with one or two students before asking students to move to their corner of choice, asking for some examples of possible reasons why the food could be healthy or unhealthy. Once students are in their corners, they are asked to explain to each other why they think the dish is healthy or unhealthy. After students have a few minutes to speak in groups, the teacher asks for a few share-outs from each group.

很同意

左公鸡健康吗?

不同意

同意

很不同意

FIGURE 5.11.
Four Corners Activity

Translation
Title: Is General Gau's chicken healthy?
Upper Left: Strongly agree
Lower Left: Agree
Upper Right: Disagree
Lower Right: Strongly disagree

The teacher now prepares students for their interpersonal speaking task. Using the SCRAP Framework, the teacher has written a task frame that will engage students in an Information Gap task. The teacher has found two school lunch menus from two different schools in China, which have been labeled A and B. Students will work in pairs, with one student given the A school lunch menu and their partner given the B school lunch menu. The teacher asks a student to read the task frame to the class, shown in Figure 5.12. The task frame is written in English, since this is not a focus of the content of the lesson.

学校餐厅的午餐是什么？

You and a friend are both spending a semester in Beijing during your senior year in high school, living with different families and attending high schools near each other. Each of your schools puts out the school lunch menu every Friday, and you and your friend have enjoyed comparing school menus and trying new food each week. You're chatting with your friend over ZOOM, and decide to ask about this upcoming week's menu. Ask them about their menu for the week, and find out what they are looking forward (and not looking forward) to eating. (Your partner should also ask about your lunch menu and what you want and do not want to eat and why.)

FIGURE 5.12.
Interpersonal Task Frame

Translation
Title: What is the school lunch in the cafeteria?

Before students begin working on the task in pairs, the teacher models a possible conversation with a student, shown in Figure 5.13.

对话示范

A: 星期二的午餐是什么？
B: 星期二的午餐是猪肉饺子。 你喜欢猪肉饺子吗？
A: 我最喜欢猪肉饺子了，但是我只喜欢清蒸的猪肉饺子，不喜欢煎的猪肉饺子。
B: 为什么？
A: 因为清蒸的不但健康，而且好吃。我常常去中国餐厅吃饺子。
B: 我也喜欢饺子。星期二的开胃菜是什么？
A: 星期二的开胃菜是春卷。
B: 我不喜欢春卷，因为春卷是炸的，很不健康。

FIGURE 5.13.
Sample Model Conversation for Interpersonal Task

Translation:
Title: Model conversation.
A: What's lunch on Tuesday?
B: Tuesday's lunch is pork dumplings. Do you like pork dumplings?
A: I like pork dumplings the most, but I only like steamed pork dumplings,
*   I don't like grilled pork dumplings.*
B: Why?
A: Because steamed dumplings are not only healthy but also delicious.
*   I often go to Chinese restaurant to eat dumplings.*
B: I also like dumplings. What's the appetizer on Tuesday?
A: The appetizer on Tuesday is spring rolls.
B: I don't like spring rolls, because they are fried, very unhealthy.

Students are then put in pairs and begin the interpersonal task. The teacher can choose to ask students to audio or video record the conversations, or have a few students present their conversation to the whole class. Students are given approximately 10 minutes to complete the interpersonal task. Before closing the class, the teacher returns to the learning outcome and asks students to reflect on their attainment of the goal by giving a thumbs-up/thumbs-down, shown in Figure 5.14

I can ask and answer questions about what I like and don't like to eat and explain why.

我可以问和回答有关喜欢和不喜欢吃的东西的问题，也可以解释为什么。

FIGURE 5.14.
Lesson Closing Slide

Classroom Close-Up 5.2: Volunteering Abroad
This classroom example was shared by Katrina Griffin, German teacher at North County High School, Glen Burnie, MD.

COURSE OVERVIEW	
Course Name	German 4
Course Proficiency Target	Intermediate Mid
LESSON OVERVIEW	
Unit Theme	Engagement Abroad
Lesson Learning Outcome	I can debate the pros and cons of volunteering in another country.
Core Vocabulary and Forms	• Phrases for expressing opinions, and agreement and disagreement, asking for more information, incorporating others into the discussion (basic expressions required for the Philosophical Chairs activity) • Vocabulary relating to volunteering and volunteering abroad

Materials and Resources	• Debate Cards
	 • Students should bring previous notes and research related to this topic
	 • Prepared Jamboard slides
	 • Authentic resources from:
	   • https://www.polgar-stuewe.de/wp-content/uploads/2016/10/freiwilligenarbeit-ausland-motive.jpg
	   • https://www.freiwilligenarbeit.de/freiwilligenarbeit-umfrage-2019.html

Lesson Length	5 minutes	
LEARNING SEQUENCE		
Focus of Learning	Students view the learning objective and agenda as they join class.	*Time:* 1 min
Preview of Learning	The teacher goes over the day's learning objective and agenda.	*Time:* 1 min
Learning Episode 1		
Primetime 1	1. Students are given a link to open a Google Jamboard. Students have 5 minutes to read the two infographics and add notes on one of the Jamboard slides. 2. The teacher explains the Philosophical Chairs activity and students are invited to add their name to the Jamboard slide to indicate their position (for/against) on the topic. Students are additionally reminded of the Debate Cards scaffold they have previously been given to use in this activity, which is also included on one of the Jamboard slides.	*Time:* 8 min
Downtime	3. The Philosophical Chairs activity begins. As students move their names into the box indicating they would like to speak, the teacher calls on students, trying to balance between those who are for or against the topic.	*Time:* 30 min
Primetime 2	4. Students are asked to add final thoughts to one of the Jamboard slides as the activity concludes.	*Time:* 4 min
Celebration of Learning	The teacher returns student attention to the learning outcome and asks students to reflect.	*Time:* 1 min

This lesson culminates in an interpersonal speaking task on the topic of working and volunteering abroad. Prior to this lesson, students have read, viewed, and listened to numerous authentic resources on this topic and have compiled their own notes from these various sources, which they are told to bring to class today. Students have additionally been practicing with expressions that enable their participation in a debate. In this lesson, students will read two short additional authentic resources, and then participate in a class-wide debate using the Philosophical Chairs strategy. Students are assessed in this activity for their knowledge of the content and their ability to discuss that content and make meaning with peers. This lesson can be taught in person or virtually over Zoom or GoogleMeet; this description presents the lesson as it was taught over Zoom, with notes about in-person adaptations.

The teacher opens class by greeting students and going over the day's learning outcome and agenda, shown in Figure 5.15.

> ### *Objectiv:*
> I can debate the pros and cons of volunteering in another country.
>
> ### *Agenda:*
>
> 1. Infografiken
> 2. Philosophische Stühle
>   a. *Pro:* Man soll sich im Ausland engagieren.
>   b. *Kontra:* Man soll sich nicht im Ausland engagieren.

FIGURE 5.15.
Objective and Agenda Slide

Translation
Objective: I can debate the pros and cons of volunteering in another country.
Agenda:
1. Infographics
2. Philosophical Chairs
*   a. For: One should get involved abroad.*
*   b. Against: One should not get involved abroad.*

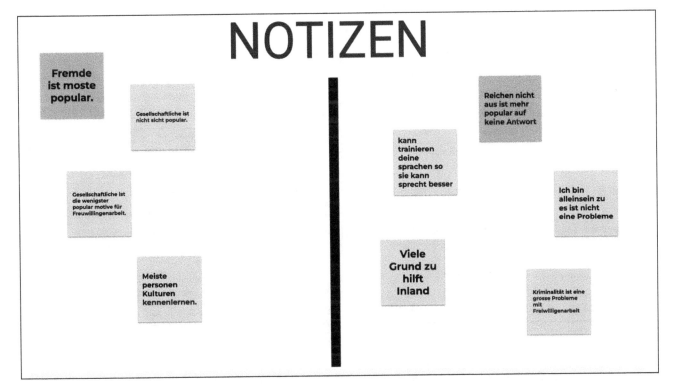

FIGURE 5.16.
Sample Student Notes Recorded on Google Jamboard

Translation
Title: Notes

Left-Hand Column, clockwise starting top right:
- *Foreigners is the most popular*
- *Corporate is not so popular*
- *Corporate is the least popular reason for volunteering abroad*
- *For most people, learning about culture*

Right-Hand Column, clockwise starting top right:
- *Can train your languages so you can speak better*
- *Reaching out is more popular*
- *I am alone, this is not a problem*
- *Many reasons for help domestically*
- *Criminality is a big problem with volunteer work abroad*

The teacher then begins by sharing a link to Google Jamboard where students begin by looking at two new authentic resources (short infographics) on the topic of volunteer work abroad. Students are asked to read these infographics silently and make notes in their own notebooks as well as on the Google Jamboard slides, looking in particular for information that can support their opinion on the topic of volunteering abroad. Sample student notes are shown in Figure 5.16.

The teacher then reviews the expectations for the Philosophical Chairs procedure. Students are reminded that they have access to debate cards as a scaffold for speaking (shown in Figure 5.17). Students have received these previously, but the teacher additionally includes them as one of the Google Jamboard slides for easy access. (The teacher may choose to include these with or without English translations, depending on the level of the class and their comfort using these expressions.)

My Opinion		**Follow-up Questions**	
I think that...	*Ich finde, dass...*	Can you explain that again?	*Kannst du das nochmal erklären?*
My opinion is that...	*Ich bin der Meinung, dass...*	I didn't understand that.	*Ich verstehe das nicht.*
I'm sure that...	*Ich bin mir sicher, dass*	What do you mean by that?	*Wie meinst du das?*
It's clear to me that...	*Für mich ist es klar, dass...*	Did I understand you correctly?	*Habe ich das richtig verstanden?*
		(So) you think...	*Du denkst,...*
		Do you really mean that...?	*Meinst du wirklich, dass...?*
For		**Against**	
An argument for that is...	*Ein Argument dafür ist...*	An argument against it is...	*Ein Argument dagegen ist...*
What I find positive is...	*Positiv finde ich...*	What I find negative is...	*Negativ finde ich...*
It is good/great/important that...	*Es ist gut/toll/wichtig, dass...*	It is bad/unfair/not nice that...	*Es ist schlecht/unfair/nicht schön, dass...*
An important reason is...	*Ein wichtiger Grund ist...*		
An advantage is...	*Ein Vorteil ist, dass...*	A disadvantage is that...	*Ein Nachteil ist, dass...*
To Agree		**To Disagree**	
Yes, I think that also.	*Ja, das finde ich auch.*	No, I don't agree.	*Nein, das finde ich nicht.*
You're right!	*Du hast schon recht.*	That isn't correct.	*Das stimmt doch nicht.*
Exactly right!	*Genau! Stimmt!*	That's nonsense.	*Das ist Quatsch.*
That is right.	*Das ist richtig.*	I can't understand that.	*Das kann ich nicht verstehen.*
I can understand that.	*Das kann ich gut verstehen.*	I'm of a different opinion.	*Ich bin die andere Ansicht.*
Interrupting Openers		**Integrating Others**	
Excuse me.	*Entschuldigung.*	What do you mean?	*Was meinst du?*
Sorry.	*Es tut mir Leid.*	What do you think?	*Was denkst du?*
May I cut in for a minute?	*Darf ich kurz unterbrechen?*	Do you share that opinion?	*Bist du auch der Meinung?*

FIGURE 5.17.
Debate Cards

Source: Adapted by Katrina Griffin from Dengler, Rusch & Shurig (2017, p. 196).

The teacher then begins the Philosophical Chairs activity. Students begin by indicating on the Google Jamboard slide (shown in Figure 5.18) whether they are for or against engaging in volunteer work abroad. Students create a Post-it note in Google Jamboard with their first name, and then move it to either side of the slide to indicate their position. Students can also move their name to a space on the slide to show they are undecided or not sure of their opinion. If this lesson were conducted in the classroom, students would move their chairs to different sides of the classroom. When students are ready to speak, they move the Post-it with their name to the *"Ich will sprechen"* [I want to speak] box on the slide (or raise their hand in class). The teacher calls on students to speak one at a time, trying to alternate between students who are in favor of and against the question.

FIGURE 5.18.
Philosophical Chairs Debate Participation Slide from Google Jamboard Translation

Title: Philosophical Chairs

Left-hand column:

- *For: I am in favor.*
- *One should get involved abroad.*

Middle:

- *Undecided/No idea*
- *I want to speak.*

Right-hand column:

- *Against: I am against it.*
- *One should not get involved abroad.*

The teacher has additionally provided students with a back-channel slide in Google Jamboard where they can write down questions and important information they want to remember and use in the debate, shown in Figure 5.19.

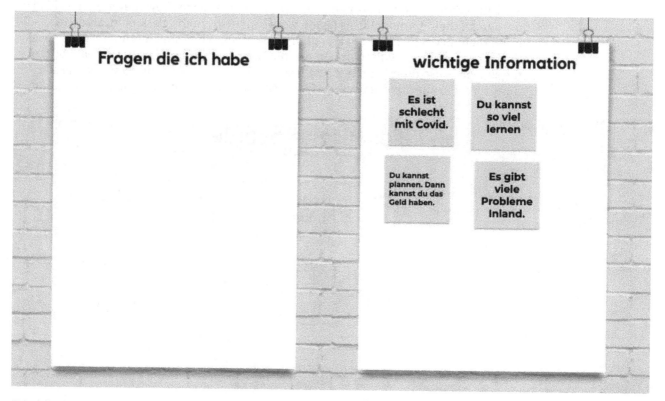

FIGURE 5.19.
Back-Channel Slide in Google Jamboard

Translation

Left: Questions that I have

Right: Important Information

- *This is hard with COVID.*
- *You can learn so much.*
- *You can plan. Then can you make money.*
- *There are a lot of domestic problems.*

The Philosophical Chairs debate continues for approximately 30 minutes, with every student being given a chance to speak multiple times. The debate requires students to use information from their notes and the two infographics they read at the beginning of class, explaining their perspective by drawing on factual information. Students may decide to change their opinion during the debate, moving their name from one part of the slide to the other.

When the conversation is coming to a close, the teacher asks students to write some final thoughts on a Google Jamboard slide (shown in Figure 5.19). For an in-person class, the teacher would ask students to write their final thoughts on an index card to hand in as they leave class. The teacher closes the class by asking students to write their final thoughts, and then returns their attention to the learning outcome and asks them to reflect.

During the Philosophical Chairs debate, the teacher serves as a discussion facilitator and also notes student participation in the debate. Each student will be given an assessment grade using the rubric shown in Figure 5.20.

Interpersonal Conversation Grading Rubric

Name: _____   Punkte_____ / 25

	5	4	3	2	1
Exchange	Maintains the exchange with a series of responses that are clearly appropriate within the context of the task.	Maintains the exchange with a series of responses that are generally appropriate within the context of the task.	Maintains the exchange with a series of responses that are somewhat appropriate within the context of the task.	Partially maintains the exchange with a series of responses that are minimally appropriate within the context of the task.	Unsuccessfully attempts to maintain the exchange with a series of responses that are inappropriate within the context of the task.
Task Completion	Provides required information (e.g., responses to questions, statement of support and opinion) with frequent elaboration.	Provides most required information (e.g., responses to questions, statement of support and opinion) with some elaboration.	Provides most required information (e.g., responses to questions, statement of support and opinion).	Provides some required information (e.g., responses to questions, statement of support and opinion) with some elaboration.	Provides little required information (e.g., responses to questions, statement of support and opinion) with some elaboration.
Language Usage	Fully understandable with ease and clarity of expression; occasional errors do not impede comprehension.	Fully understandable and some errors which do not impede comprehension.	Generally understandable with errors that may impede comprehension.	Partially understandable with errors that force interpretation and cause confusion to the reader.	Barely understandable with frequent or significant errors that impede comprehension.
Vocabulary	Varied and appropriate vocabulary.	Varied and generally appropriate vocabulary.	Appropriate but basic vocabulary.	Limited vocabulary.	Very few vocabulary resources.
Grammar, Syntax, and Usage	Very few grammar and syntax errors.	General control of grammar and syntax.	Some control of grammar and syntax.	Limited control of grammar and syntax.	Limited or no control of grammar syntax and usage.

Feedback:

_____

_____

_____

_____

FIGURE 5.20.
Interpersonal Grading Rubric

Reflection and Next Steps

In this chapter, we have examined how to change teacher talk in order to encourage student talk. We started by considering how teachers interact with their students. A common pattern of interaction with students follows IRE (Initiate-Respond-Evaluate), which places an emphasis on accuracy and tells students that *how* they say something is more important than *what* they say. By shifting the pattern of interaction to IRF (Initiate-Respond-Feedback), teachers can encourage more meaningful communication with and among their students. We also looked at the types of questions teachers ask students. If those questions only require one-word responses, then students will not be encouraged or challenged to expand beyond the Novice level. Incorporating more open-ended questions and ensuring variety in the types of questions asked will lead to more meaningful student output and better interaction with students. Establishing a target-language use expectation—regardless of the language or level—can be a transformative practice. This can be achieved through fun and engaging Responsibility Training strategies. In this chapter, we have also examined how to move from exercises to activities to tasks that require an expression or interpretation of meaning and a communicative purpose. The SCRAP Framework can serve as a guide for developing one's own communicative tasks. Finally, we looked at a number of specific interpersonal strategies to engage students, as well as how those strategies can be adapted for different learning environments. Our two *Classroom Close-Up* examples showed how teachers of two different languages and levels applied these various principles and strategies to their own classes.

Before moving on, take some time to reflect and assess your own practice. Consider how you are applying or would like to apply the practices and strategies discussed in this chapter. Where are your strengths? Where would you like to grow your practice? And what actions will you take to move forward? This one-point rubric is designed to help you reflect and assess your own teaching on building a learner-centered, interactive classroom.

One-Point Rubric: Creating a Learner-Centered, Interactive Classroom

GLOW *Where are my strengths related to this practice?*	CRITERIA *What should I be looking for in my own teaching?*	GROW *Where do I need to grow or expand my practice?*	TAKE ACTION *What steps will I take to move my practice forward?*
	I primarily use IRF (Initiate-Respond-Feedback) when interacting with my students.		
	When I ask questions of my students, I vary the question type to allow for more open-ended responses.		
	I have an established target-language use expectation in my classes for all students and all levels. If my students are resistant to using the target-language, I incorporate an engaging strategy to encourage them to do so.		

	I incorporate multiple opportunities for students to engage in Interpersonal (interactive) Communication in each and every class meeting.		
	I do not use drill-based exercises in my classes.		
	I primarily use tasks when designing learning experiences for my classes, and am able to redesign existing class activities to add a communicative purpose.		
	I can use the SCRAP Framework to design communicative tasks that are real-world, authentic, and meaningful for my students.		
	My students and I use the target language 90% or more of lesson time. I do not translate text or ask students to translate as one of their activities.		
	I use a communicative learning outcome, which is shared with students. All activities used reflect steps toward attainment of the student learning outcome.		

Level Up Your Learning

- **Grahn, L. (2021).** *Designing performance tasks.* **GrahnForLang. https://www. grahnforlang.com/designing-performance-tasks.html**
  Leslie Grahn's website is chock full of incredible resources, including a page dedicated entirely to performance tasks and the SCRAP Framework. You will find examples for each element of SCRAP, along with sample performance task frames (please note, however, that all the task frames provided are in the presentational mode of communication).

- **STARTALK. (2017, August 15).** *Keeping students in the target language* **[Video]. You-tube. www.youtube.com/watch?v=wW91LHV_IXc**
  This 23-minute video walks through specific strategies for supporting students in maintaining target-language use, aligning with the STARTALK Principles for Effective Teaching and Learning and the Teacher Effectiveness for Language Learning (TELL) Project.

Chapter 5 References

Blouwolff, R. (2020, July). *'Some things never change:' 90%+ target language in the remote classroom* [Conference workshop]. Massachusetts Foreign Language Association (MaFLA) Classroom Collaborative, online.

Blouwolff, R., & Ritz, C. (2019, February 7). *High-leverage teaching practices: A how-to boot camp.* [Conference workshop]. Northeast Conference of the Teaching of Foreign Languages, New York, NY, United States.

Byrne, R. (2020). *Create an online philosophical chairs activity with Jamboard.* Free Technology for Teachers. https://www.freetech4teachers.com/2020/09/create-online-philosophical-chairs.html

Clementi, D., & Terrill, L. (2017). *The keys to planning: Effective curriculum, lesson, and unit design* (2nd ed.). ACTFL.

Dengler, S., Rusch, P., & Shurig, C. (2017). *Portfolio Deutsch: Teacher's manual, level 3.* Ernst Klett Sprachen.

Gass, S. M. (2013). *Second language acquisition: An introductory course* (4th ed.). Routledge.

Glisan, E. W., & Donato, R. (2017). *Enacting the work of language instruction: High-leverage teaching practices.* ACTFL.

Grahn, L. (2021). *Designing performance tasks.* GrahnForLang. https://www.grahnforlang.com/designing-performance-tasks.html

Grahn, L., & McAlpine, D. (2017). *The keys to strategies for language instruction.* ACTFL.

Jones, F. (2014). *Tools for teaching* (3rd ed.). Frederic H. Jones & Associates.

Krashen, S. (1985). *The input hypothesis.* Longman.

Lightbown, P. M., & Spada, N. (2013). *How languages are learned* (4th ed.). Oxford University Press.

Pijanowski, L. (2016). *Authentic performance tasks: Strategies to improve learning and literacy.* International Center for Leadership in Education. http://handouts16.modelschoolsconference.com/files/upload/APT_MSC_LP_Handout.pdf

Shrum, J. L., & Glisan, E. W. (2016). *Teacher's handbook: Contextualized language instruction* (5th ed.). Heinle Cengage Learning.

STARTALK. (2017, August 15). *Keeping students in the target language* [Video]. Youtube. www.youtube.com/watch?v=wW91LHV_IXc

VanPatten, B. (2017). *While we're on the topic: BVP on language, acquisition, and classroom practice.* ACTFL.

Wong, W., & VanPatten, B. (2003). The evidence is IN: Drills are OUT. *Foreign Language Annals, 36*(3), 403–423. https://doi.org/10.1111/j.1944-9720.2003.tb02123.x

CHAPTER 6

Interaction for All Learners

Have you ever come up with what you thought was a great interactive discussion for your students, sent them off into small groups to talk, and then been stunned when they either reverted entirely into English or just sat there not saying a word? What went wrong? While you might be tempted to lay the blame on your students and assume that they just do not have the natural ability or motivation to learn another language, you should instead carefully consider what happened *before* you sent them off into groups. Were they fully prepared to engage in this discussion? Had language been carefully modeled for them so that they had a clear understanding of how to use it in context? Was the discussion task appropriate for their proficiency level and did it include needed scaffolds? Considering all of these questions can help you unpack how to ensure that *all learners*—each and every one—can successfully engage in interactive interpersonal communication.

To help you understand what students are ready to do with language, let's look briefly at sociocultural theory and what is called the Zone of Proximal Development (Lantolf, Thorne, & Poehner, 2015). In a nutshell, sociocultural theory maintains that people learn and develop through social interaction. Through participation in both informal (such as family) and formal (such as schooling) activities, they develop stronger ability to "regulate" the use of various skills (Lantolf, Thorne, & Poehner, 2015). Children are not born with an innate ability to cook, for example, but as they grow up, they observe their parents or other community members cooking. They may begin to cook simple items for themselves as others watch and guide them. What they cook may become more complex as they grow older, and they may rely on family recipes or cooking shows for guidance on what ingredients go together and how to cook them. Children develop more and more control or "regulation" over their ability to cook as they grow thanks to interaction with their community. The same thing happens in the world language classroom. Students observe the teacher using the target language, access resources and support materials, and slowly develop greater control over their own ability to use the language.

Sociocultural theory also holds that learners can be given support to push beyond their independent learning level into what is called their Zone of Proximal Development (ZPD). The ZPD is what learners are able to do *with support*. ZPD is different from comprehensible input ($i + 1$). Comprehensible input focuses on providing language input to learners that is slightly more challenging than what they are likely to *understand* independently. ZPD, on the other hand, focuses on what the learner *can do* with the language if given certain supports. For example, a Novice learner may need the support of a word bank or sentence frame to help them discuss a particular topic, such as cooking. The word bank or sentence frame *scaffolds* their learning, enabling them to push beyond their independent level within their ZPD. Learners at different levels will need different kinds and amounts of support. Novice learners will be unable to use language at the Superior level no matter what support they are given, because Superior language proficiency is not within a Novice speaker's ZPD.

Learners also need to build up gradually to independent levels, being supported not only with concrete scaffolds such as word banks and sentence frames, but also with careful modeling and planning of instruction. Before students can successfully engage in an independent interpersonal discussion using all of the vocabulary and language structures you want them to use, they first need to have sufficient experience with input to effectively use the language.

So how can you gradually prepare students to engage in independent interpersonal interactions? What supports and scaffolds can you use to enable them to stretch beyond their independent level and into their ZPD? In this chapter, we will look closely at the Gradual Release of Responsibility (GRR) Model with a particular focus on how it can be used to prepare students for interaction. We will also look at numerous scaffolds that can be adapted for any language or learning task, and we will explore how to tier learning tasks for different levels of student readiness.

The Gradual Release of Responsibility Model

The Gradual Release of Responsibility (GRR) Model (Fisher & Frey, 2008) provides a framework for carefully structuring and preparing students for independent work. This framework includes four phases, each intended to move students toward increased independence and responsibility for the learning task while simultaneously decreasing reliance on the teacher. Before students are asked to do independent speaking tasks, they first need carefully structured support and guidance that move them toward independence step by step. This begins with focused instruction and modeling from the teacher and then moves to guided instruction and collaborative learning, before ending with independent student work. While this model can be used to support students in any kind of learning activity, we will focus here on preparing them for interactive speaking tasks.

Focus Lesson: "I do it."

The first step in the GRR Model is a teacher-led focus lesson in which the teacher models the learning task and uses think-alouds that enable students to "hear" how the teacher might approach the task. A teacher who is preparing students to engage in an interpersonal speaking task, for example, may want to model how to brainstorm questions that could be asked by the students, model phrases or expressions that could be used in the conversation, or do a think-aloud on how they might use a graphic organizer during the interpersonal task. Teachers of younger students might use storybook characters to model interactions or songs with call and response.

Guided Instruction: "We do it."

In the next phase of the GRR Model, the "teacher uses questions, prompts, and cues to facilitate student understanding," beginning the process of "releasing responsibility to students while providing instructional scaffolds to ensure that students are successful" (Frey & Fisher, 2013). To prepare students for an interpersonal task, this phase may involve the teacher asking students questions as a whole class that they may be asked in the interpersonal conversation. The teacher may ask a student to model a conversation with the teacher, then ask the class what was effective, what else could have been said in the conversation, and so on. Guided instruction can occur either through whole class or small-group instruction.

Collaborative Learning: "You do it together."

Students are now given additional responsibility and independence to work in small groups or pairs to apply their understanding with appropriate scaffolds and supports. The teacher serves as a resource and monitors student work. For an interpersonal speaking task, students may be asked to work in pairs to engage in the task, again using scaffold supports.

Independent Work: "You do it alone."

In the final phase of the model, students are expected to demonstrate their independent ability to engage in the task. It should be noted that students may not be ready for this phase within one class session, and teachers may cycle through the first three phases numerous times before students are adequately prepared to be successful with independent work. The teacher may also choose to use this phase as a formative check for learning. In an interpersonal speaking task, this phase may occur when students are ready to engage in the task without the need for the scaffolds that had been used earlier in instruction, or students may be asked to participate in an interpersonal task at home using a digital platform.

While the GRR Model is presented in a linear fashion, oftentimes teachers may shift back and forth between phases depending on the needs of their students. Table 6.1 presents a summary of the GRR Model along with an example from a Spanish classroom.

TABLE 6.1. THE GRADUAL RELEASE OF RESPONSIBILITY MODEL WITH EXAMPLE

Step	Description	Example
I do it.	*Focus lesson* The teacher models the learning task with direct instruction and the use of think-alouds.	*Learning Outcome: I can ask and answer questions about my preferences regarding air travel.* Using a graphic organizer, the teacher uses a think-aloud to brainstorm ideas regarding which seat on an airplane different travelers would prefer (saying, for example, "On an airplane, you can sit in the center, aisle, or window seat. I like to sit in the window seat."). The teacher models questions and answers related to this topic.
We do it.	*Guided instruction* The teacher guides students to complete the learning task using scaffolds, known as guided practice.	The teacher asks students the same types of questions about where other types of travelers, such as members of their family or friends, would like to sit on an airplane. The teacher provides prompts as needed.
You do it together.	*Collaborative* Students work collaboratively to complete the learning task using scaffolds in small groups or pairs.	Using the graphic organizer the teacher previously presented, students now work in pairs to ask each other questions about a third type of traveler.
You do it alone.	*Independent* Students work independently to complete the learning task.	At home, students are given an independent assignment. The teacher has recorded questions about seat preference, and students must record their answer orally.

Scaffolding Student Target-Language Use

As with the GRR Model, scaffolds are an instructional tool that can be applied across any area of learning. In fact, beyond supporting student language use, "research has shown gains in reading comprehension, written recalls, many aspects of the writing process, and factual and conceptual comprehension through instruction incorporating scaffolded supports" (Mariage, Winn, & Dabo, 2019, p. 198). In this section, we will highlight some commonly used scaffolds that can support interpersonal communication. These scaffolds can be adapted to meet the needs of the speaking task.

Think-Alouds

Think-alouds are a simple strategy to make your thinking visible to students. Essentially, as you walk students through how to approach a question, fill out a graphic organizer, or solve a problem, you say out loud what you are thinking as you go. This enables students to understand your thought process, which will support them in moving toward independent work.

Modeling

As discussed in earlier chapters, teacher target-language use is a crucial source of language input for your students. Through your speaking, students are exposed to model language, and you can be deliberate in what you say and how you say it. Think about how you might introduce vocabulary such as descriptive adjectives, for example. Rather than giving students a list of adjectives and going over them one by one, you can instead present the vocabulary in a way that pairs *lexical items* with *grammatical structures*. In Figures 6.1 and 6.2, a French teacher is introducing adjectives (the lexical items) with a simple question *(What is he like?)* and response *(He is...)*. This small shift in how the vocabulary is presented models clearly to students how they can use the vocabulary in context.

Modeling can also be used when a teacher partners with a student to demonstrate how to interact on a particular topic. If the teacher wants students to work in pairs to ask each other what they did over the weekend, for example, the teacher can invite one student to have an abbreviated conversation with them first as a model for the rest of the class. The teacher may say, "So, Michelle, what did you do this weekend?" and the student responds, "Went to my friend's." The teacher continues the conversation model, asking, "Oh really, what did you do at your friend's house?" Modeling this conversation in front of the class will help learners get a clear picture of the type of conversation they can engage in, while also reminding them of key vocabulary and structures they know and how they can use them in context.

FIGURE 6.1.
Vocabulary in Context, Sample 1

Translation
What is he like?
He is tall.

FIGURE 6.2.
Vocabulary in Context, Sample 2

Translation
And him, what is he like?
He is short.

Word Walls or Word Banks

As students are developing and beginning to use new vocabulary or phrases, having access to these words through an in-class Word Wall or a printed Word Bank can help them use the vocabulary or structures in context when they speak. In general, we encourage teachers not to provide literal translations of words when using Word Walls or Word Banks. Try using images or sample sentences instead. Figure 6.3 shows a Word Bank for breakfast food items. A teacher may use this with a class when they are still building familiarity with the key vocabulary. For example, if students are put in pairs to discuss what they typically eat for breakfast, the teacher may have them use the Word Bank as a scaffold while they are still learning the vocabulary.

FIGURE 6.3.
Sample Word Bank

Translation (left to right, top to bottom)
bread, cereal, donut, pancakes, bagel with cream cheese, scrambled eggs, bacon, French toast, hot chocolate

Sentence Starters

Sentence starters are particularly useful when students are just beginning to use new constructions or phrases in the language. A starter helps get them going in using the construction, while still giving them space to provide their own content. Figure 6.4 shows a sentence starter in which students are supported in learning how to say what foods they do and do not like.

Me gusta _____

No me gusta _____

Yo prefiero _____

No prefiero _____

Yo quiero _____

No quiero _____

FIGURE 6.4.
Sample Sentence Starter

Translation
I like_____
I don't like _____
I prefer_____
I don't prefer _____
I want _____
I don't want_____

Sentence Frames

Like sentence starters, sentence frames are excellent tools for supporting students in using new constructions or phrases. These typically include more complex sentences with two clauses. Again, students are left room to provide their own content. Figure 6.5 shows a sentence frame in which students make comparisons.

_____ es más _____ que_____

_____ es menos _____ que _____

_____ es mejor que _____ porque....

_____ es peor que _____ porque....

_____ es tan _____ como _____ porque....

FIGURE 6.5.
Sample Sentence Frame

Translation
_____ is more _____ than _____
_____ is less _____ than _____
_____ is better than _____ because...
_____ is worse than _____ because...
_____is as _____ as _____ because...

Graphic Organizers

Graphic organizers are excellent tools to help students prepare for an interactive speaking task. Graphic organizers can be used in any number of ways, and there are likely an infinite number of them. You can use these tools when students are completing an interpretive listening or reading task, and then have students use them as notes as part of an interpersonal speaking task. Students can use graphic organizers to generate questions on the topic, help them make comparisons or determine cause and effect, help organize how they would interact in a conversation, and much more. Figures 6.6 through 6.12 depict some sample graphic organizers that can easily be adapted to most topics and to any language and level.

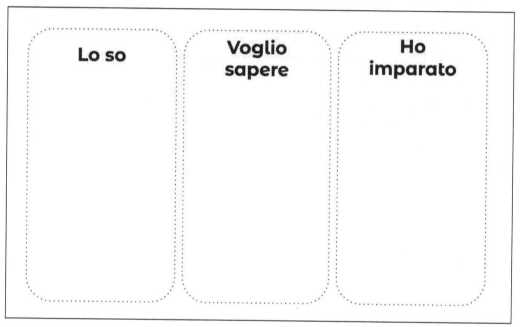

FIGURE 6.6.
Know, Want to Know, Learned (KWL) Chart (Italian)

Translation (left to right) I know, I want to know, I learned

FIGURE 6.7.
See, Think, Wonder (STW) Chart (Swedish)

Translation (left to right) I see, I think, I wonder

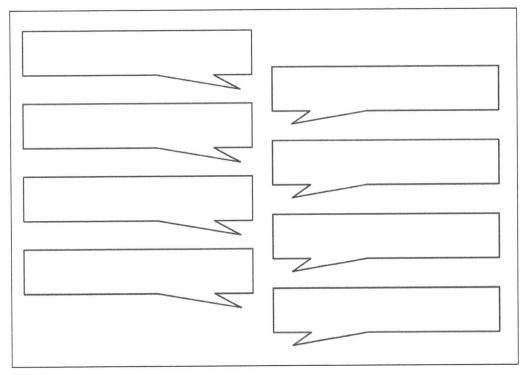

FIGURE 6.8.
Conversation Organizer

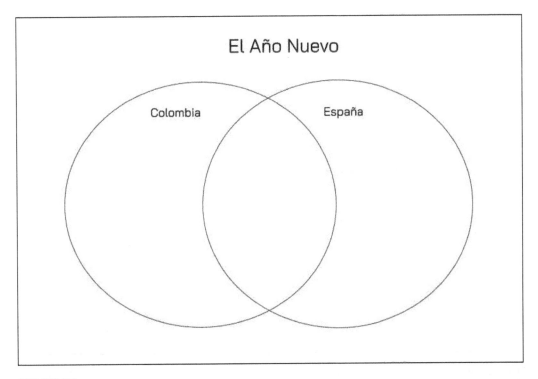

FIGURE 6.9.
Venn Diagram (Spanish)

Translation
The new year
[Left circle] Colombia
[Right circle] Spain

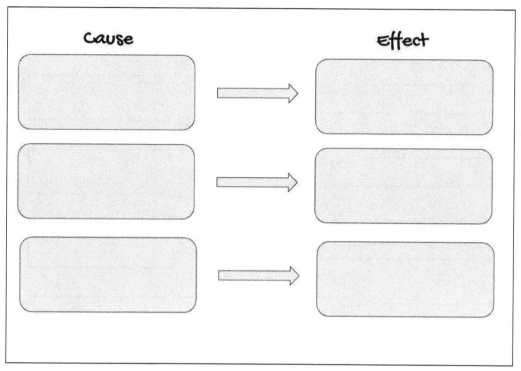

FIGURE 6.10.
Cause and Effect Chart

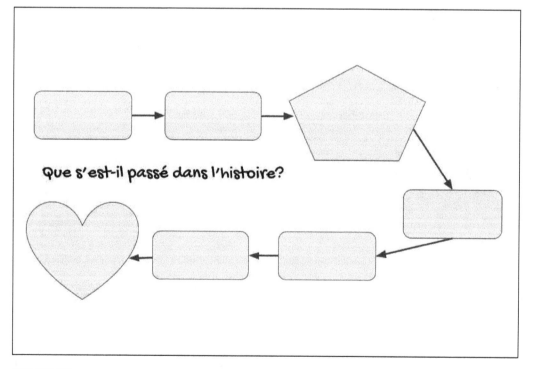

FIGURE 6.11.
Flow Chart (French)

Translation
What happened in the story?

Tema: La comida rápida		
	Colombia	Estados Unidos
Producto		
Práctica		
Perspectiva		

FIGURE 6.12.
T-Chart (Spanish)

Translation
Theme: Fast Food
Left column: Product, Practice, Perspective
Second row: Colombia, United States

Tiering Tasks

At any given point in time in your class, different students are ready for different tasks. Some may be ready to move to independent work, while others require more scaffolds to complete the same task successfully. How do you support these different levels of readiness? Enter tiering! Tiering is a way to design tasks or assessments that address "different levels of difficulty, but [are] focused on the same key learning goals" (Tomlinson & Strickland, 2005, p. 10). Student readiness can be defined as "the current knowledge, understanding, and skill level a student has to a particular sequence of learning" (Tomlinson & Strickland, 2005, p. 6). For any one student, the readiness level may change as learning progresses and for different units of learning. Tiering your tasks means that you create at least two modifications of the same task to support these different readiness levels. While it may feel daunting to have to create multiple versions of the same task, with some practice developing the different tiers can be quickly accomplished. Here, we will walk you through how to design a task with three tier levels: Support Level, On Level, and Challenge Level.

The first step in designing your tiered task is to develop the On Level assignment. Next, you determine the additional scaffolds students need for the Support Level and include them in the task. Finally, you develop a Challenge Level task. This level may be more open-ended than the On Level task or may have removed any scaffolds that were included for the On Level version. Figures 6.13, 6.14, and 6.15 show samples of Support Level, On Level, and Challenge Level tiers for a French class that is discussing how to address bullying. Students have been reading and learning about bullying and how to respond effectively and are now working in small groups. As you will notice, the Support Level includes statements about what to do when bullying occurs. Students must determine if the statements are true or false, followed by an explanation pulled from the authentic resource. The On Level task asks students to write their own statements of what to do when bullying occurs but provides sample sentence starters and a word bank. The Challenge Level task also asks students to write their own statements of what to do when bullying occurs, but rather than include sentence starters and a word bank, it asks students to reflect on why students are bullied in a more open-ended response. (A special thank you to Khadija Tlaiti, graduate student and pre-service French teacher, for sharing these examples.)

Group A

Harcèlement Scolaire: Que faire?

Vrai ou faux? Si c'est faux, corrige:

	Vrai	Faux	Correction
Si je reçois une photo ou un humiliante d' un camarade de classe, je peux circuler		✓	Je dois supprimer la photo
Si je vois quelqu'un se faire intimider, je fais semblant de rien			
Pour se protéger du harcèlement, il ne faut jamais publier des photos ou information privée sur internet.			
Parler à un adulte n'est pas la solution pour l'harcèlement			
Si je suis témoin, je peux aller voir un adulte pour signaler les faits.			
Montrer à l'harceleur que ce qu'il fait n'est pas acceptable : se taire c'est l'encourager.			
N'utilise pas la violence. Cela ne fera qu'aggraver la situation			
Menacer, insulter, se moquer de quelqu'un est inacceptable			

FIGURE 6.13.
Support Level Sample Task

Translation
School Bullying: What to do?
True or false. If it's false, correct:
- *If I receive a humiliating photo of a classmate, I can circulate it. — Correction: I should delete the photo.*
- *If I see someone being intimidated, I act like nothing is happening.*
- *To protect yourself from bullying, you should never publish any photos or private information on the internet.*
- *Talking to an adult is not the solution to bullying.*
- *If I am a witness, I can go see an adult to let them know the facts.*
- *Show the bully that what he's doing is unacceptable: being quiet is a sign of encouragement.*
- *Don't use violence. That only aggravates the situation.*
- *Threatening, insulting, and making fun of someone is unacceptable.*

Groupe B

Harcèlement Scolaire: Que faire?

Si tu es victime	Si tu es témoin

Exemples de phrases:

• Tu regardes • Tu rigoles • Tu ne t'en occupes pas
• Tu interviens • Tu vas parler à des adultes • Tu soutiens

Vocabulaire:

Porter plainte, signaler une agression, soutenir, participer, rire, se moquer, humiliation, isolement

FIGURE 6.14.
On Level Sample Task

Translation
School Bullying: What to do?
(Left-Hand Column): If you are a victim (Right-Hand Column): If you are a witness
Example of sentences: • You look • You laugh • You don't worry about it • You intervene
• You go talk to adults • You support
Vocabulary: • lodge a complaint • report an assault • to support • to participate • to laugh
• to make fun of • humiliation • isolation

Groupe C

Harcèlement Scolaire: Que faire?

Si tu es victime	Si tu es témoin

À votre avis:

Pour quelle raison penses-tu qu'un élève est harcelé?

_____

_____

_____

FIGURE 6.15.
Challenge Level Sample Task

Translation
School Bullying: What to do?
(Left-Hand Column): If you are a victim
(Right-Hand Column): If you are a witness
In your opinion: For what reason do you think students are bullied?

Tech Zoom

How can you effectively use technology and the GRR Model, scaffolds, and tiering in different learning environments? The good news is that you already have many of the tools you need from earlier *Tech Zoom* sections of this book. For I Do, you can use video recording tools to develop short videos in which you model instruction. We Do can be achieved when meeting synchronously with students on Zoom or Google Meet, or for asynchronous remote or in-person classes by creating a student-paced activity using tools such as Nearpod or Pear Deck. You Do It Together and You Do It Alone can incorporate any number of tools where students show their learning, such as Flipgrid, Vocaroo, Google Slides, and more. In this section, we will highlight a few additional tools that can help transform scaffolds and tiered tasks in the digital world.

- Virtual Word Walls as Background: Virtual word walls can easily be made for any lesson or proficiency level. Virtual word walls may be as simple as providing students with a Google Doc with the key words, or you can make a virtual background to use on Zoom or another platform that will show the key words in your video frame. Figure 6.16 shows a Spanish teacher using a virtual word wall background to support students in using transition words.

FIGURE 6.16.
Word Wall as Virtual Background

Translation
Title: Transitions
Starting bottom left, ending bottom right:
• in the first place • again • in the same way • as you can see • in the beginning • at the same time • additionally
• what's more • in summary • in the second place • most of the time • meanwhile • the other part • in conclusion • to start
• to summarize • finally • at last • next

- Digital Graphic Organizers: Any of the graphic organizers we highlighted in this chapter can easily be created in Google Slides, Google Docs, Jamboard, or another digital platform that allows for student collaboration or independent work. If you are putting students in breakout groups to work collaboratively, consider using the Grid View in Google Slides so that you can see the progress of each group at the same time.

- Digital Tiered Tasks: If you are using tiered tasks for your learners, you can either assign the tier level you feel is appropriate for them or let them choose for themselves. Using a breakout room choice board (Park, n.d.), you can ask students to click on the level they feel would work best before they join a breakout room to work. Figure 6.17 shows a breakout room choice board for a tiered task; each door is linked to a Google Doc at a different level, and students click on the door for the level they would like.

Choose a task level that you'd like to work on during our break-out...

FIGURE 6.17.
Breakout Room Choice Board
Source: Adapted from Park, n.d.

Now that we have looked at the Gradual Release of Responsibility (GRR) model, as well as numerous scaffolds to support student target-language use and interaction, we will walk through two *Classroom Close-Ups* that show how teachers of two different languages working with students at two different proficiency levels apply these to their own teaching. In *Classroom Close-Up 6.2*, we will also show how the teacher adapts the model for a hybrid or distance learning environment.

Classroom Close-Ups
Classroom Close-Up 6.1: The story of kǒng róng ràng lí
This classroom example was shared by Yingmin He, Mandarin Chinese teacher at the Josiah Quincy Upper School, Boston, MA.

COURSE OVERVIEW	
Course Name	Mandarin 6th Grade
Course Proficiency Target	Novice Mid-High
LESSON OVERVIEW	
Unit Theme	Family
Lesson Learning Outcome	I can retell the story of "kǒng róng ràng lí (孔融让梨)" by using simple sentences with some details.

Core Vocabulary and Forms	• Family vocabulary • Elements of storytelling	
Materials and Resources	Video: https://www.youtube.com/watch?v=9WloCebSKMA	
Lesson Length	50 minutes	

LEARNING SEQUENCE		
Focus of Learning	The teacher asks students if they have siblings and if they are older or younger. The teacher asks students if they had one pear, whether they would share it with their sibling.	*Time:* 5 min
Preview of Learning	The teacher shares the learning outcome and goes over the agenda.	*Time:* 1 min
Learning Episode 1		
Primetime 1	1. The teacher shows the students the video of the story. Students write down the vocabulary that they understand as well as new words they may not. 2. The teacher plays the video a second time, and students are then asked to share vocabulary. The teacher clarifies any vocabulary that was not understood. 3. The teacher projects a graphic organizer and models how to use it with the class (I Do It). The teacher then invites students to suggest items to add to the graphic organizer (We Do It).	*Time:* 10 min
Downtime	4. Students may choose Tier A, B, or C of the graphic organizer and work in small groups to complete it (You Do It Together).	*Time:* 5 min
Primetime 2	5. Students share out examples of what they have recorded for each of the categories on the graphic organizer.	*Time:* 5 min
Brain Break	Students stretch in place.	*Time:* 1 min
Learning Episode 2		
Primetime 1	6. The teacher uses a think-aloud to model how to retell the story using the five elements from the graphic organizer (I Do It). 7. The teacher then begins to retell the story again, this time asking for students to add elements of the story (We Do It).	*Time:* 5 min
Downtime	8. Students return to their small groups to retell the story. Students take turns telling the story, with one student as the storyteller and the other as the prompter, who will check to see if all five elements are included. Students record the story (You Do It Together).	*Time:* 10 min

Primetime 2	9. One or two groups are asked to retell the story for the whole class.	*Time:* 5 min
Check for Learning	The teacher asks the students to turn in the recording of the story via email.	*Time:* 1 min
Celebration of Learning	The teacher calls the students' attention back to the learning outcome and asks for feedback.	*Time:* 2 min

This lesson is part of a unit on family, and students have previously learned names for different family members as well as elements of a story. In this lesson, students will be hearing a cultural story about some brothers and will be asked to use simple language to retell the story focusing on particular elements of storytelling.

The teacher begins class by greeting students in Mandarin and engaging them in a short warm-up, asking them if they have brothers or sisters (using the slide shown in Figure 6.18). The teacher asks students who have brothers and sisters to raise their hands. Individual students may be called on to say how many brothers and sisters they have and whether they are older or younger. The teacher then asks students, "If you only had one pear, would you give it to your brother or sister?" This question is intended to be intriguing for students and hook them in, connecting as well to the story they are about to hear. Students are asked to share out whether they would share the pear or not.

FIGURE 6.18.
Warm-Up Question Slide

Translation
Do you have brothers or sisters?

FIGURE 6.19.
Learning Outcome Slide

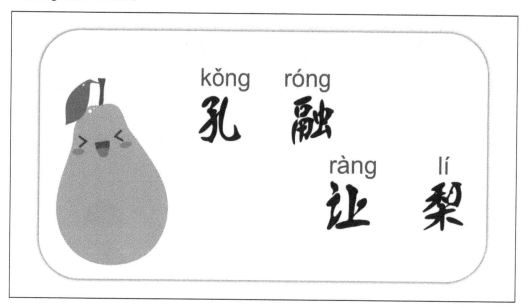

FIGURE 6.20.
Title of the Story Slide

The teacher then shows the students the learning outcome for the lesson using the slide shown in Figure 6.19 and explains that they will be listening to a story about some brothers who were given some pears. The teacher also introduces the title of the story using the slide shown in Figure 6.20.

The teacher tells the class that they will now hear the story and plays the video (www.youtube.com/watch?v=9WloCebSKMA). Students are asked to jot down key words they hear using pinyin (a Roman alphabet system used to support learners' use of Mandarin Chinese characters), noting both words they understand and those they hear but do not understand. The teacher then plays the video a second time to allow students to add to and edit their lists. Students then compare lists with a partner. Afterward, the teacher asks the students to share key words with the whole group and helps clarify any unknown vocabulary.

After a brain break, the teacher begins preparing students to retell the story, projecting a graphic organizer. The graphic organizer has been prepared at three different tier levels: A (shown in Figure 6.21), B (shown in Figure 6.22), and C (shown in Figure 6.23). To model how to use the graphic organizer, the teacher uses the tier B organizer (Figure 6.22), which includes cues for five story elements: character, setting, problem, solution, ending. The teacher models how to fill in the graphic organizer by thinking aloud while writing a few notes.

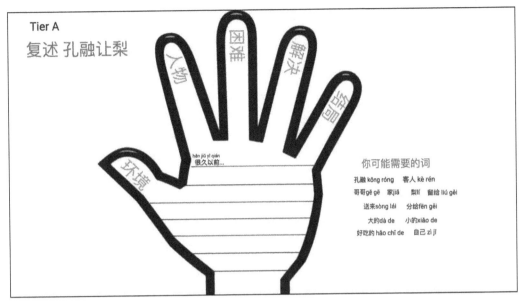

FIGURE 6.21.
Tier A Graphic Organizer (Support Level)

Translation:
Tier A - Retelling the story of kǒng róng ràng lí
Words in each finger, from thumb to pinky (left to right):
      • setting • character • problem • solution • ending
Text in the Hand:
      Long, long ago...
Word Bank (top to bottom, left to right): Words you might need
kǒng róng, guests, brother, home, leave it to, sent, distribute, big, small, delicious, oneself

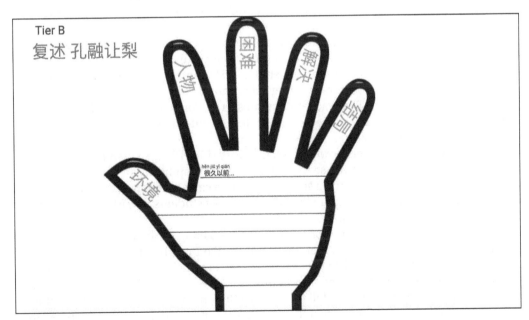

FIGURE 6.22.
Tier B Graphic Organizer (On Level)

Translation:
Tier B - Retelling the story of kǒng róng ràng lí
Words in each finger, from thumb to pinky (left to right):
      • setting • character • problem • solution • ending
Text in the Hand:
      Long, long ago...

Tier C	孔融让梨
hěn jiǔ yǐ qián 很久以前...	

FIGURE 6.23.
Tier C Graphic Organizer (Challenge Level)

Translation:
Tier C
Title: kǒng róng ràng lí
Text: Long, long ago...

The teacher then shifts to the We Do It stage, inviting students to share notes they might include in the graphic organizer. The teacher writes down a few notes on the projected graphic organizer as students speak. The teacher wants to model clearly how students can fill out the graphic organizer, while being careful not to fill it out completely together as a class.

Moving to the You Do It Together stage, the teacher asks students to take a copy of the graphic organizer, choosing tier A, B, or C for themselves. (Alternatively, the teacher could decide which level to give to each student.) Students are then placed in small groups of two or three based on the tier they have chosen and asked to complete the graphic organizer together. The teacher circulates as students work to provide support. The teacher calls the class back together after a few minutes and asks for a few share outs in each of the five categories.

The teacher now models how to retell the story (I Do It), again using a think-aloud strategy to show students how to use the notes from the graphic organizer to recount what happens in the story and make sure they include each of the five categories. After doing this, the teacher may additionally choose to show students a written version of how the story was retold, shown in Figure 6.24.

The teacher then starts the story over, this time asking students from the class to contribute details and add pieces of the narrative (We Do It Together). The teacher prompts students to add something about the characters, the setting, the problem and solution presented in the story, and the ending.

Students are now ready to retell the story in their own words (You Do It Together). They return to their small groups to tell each other the story. Students are instructed to take a role in their group, either being the storyteller or the prompter. The storyteller retells the story, while the prompter checks to see if each of the five elements is included and prompts the storyteller to include any that are missing. Students then swap roles so that each one has a turn to tell the story. The teacher may choose to have students record themselves and turn in the recording. The teacher may ask one or two groups to tell the story for the whole class.

At the end of the class time, the teacher returns students' attention to the learning outcome and asks for feedback.

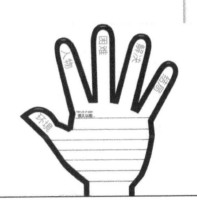

kǒng róng   ràng   lí
孔融让梨

hěn jiǔ yǐ qián ，   yī wèi kè rén dào kǒng róng jiā zuò kè 。 kè rén sòng
很久以前，一位客人到孔融家做客。客人送

gěi tā mén hěn duō hǎo chī de lí 。 mā mā jiào kǒng róng bǎ lí fēn gěi
给他们很多好吃的梨。妈妈叫孔融把梨分给

gē gē dì dì 。 kǒng róng bǎ dà de dū gěi le gē gē ，   dì dì ，
哥哥弟弟。孔融把大的都给了哥哥，弟弟，

zì jǐ zhǐ liú xià le zuì xiǎo de 。 mā mā zhī dào hòu hěn gāo xīng ，
自己只留下了最小的。妈妈知道后很高兴，

ràng hái zǐ mén xiàng kǒng róng xué xí 。
让孩子们向孔融学习。

FIGURE 6.24.
Teacher Model of Retelling the Story

Translation
A long time ago, a guest visited Kong Rong's family and gave them a lot of delicious pears.
Mother asked KongRong to distribute the pears to his siblings. KongRong gave those big pears
to his elder brother and younger brother, leaving only the smaller pears to himself. After knowing
this, the mother was very happy and asked the children to learn from Kong Rong.

Classroom Close-Up 6.2: Les Jeux Olympiques
This classroom example was shared by Nicole Russo, a graduate student in the Master's
of Teaching (M.A.T.) program in Modern Foreign Language Education (French) at the
Boston University Wheelock College of Education and Human Development, Boston, MA.

COURSE OVERVIEW	
Course Name	French 3, High School
Course Proficiency Target	Intermediate Low
LESSON OVERVIEW	
Unit Theme	Les Jeux Olympiques (The Olympic Games)
Lesson Learning Outcome	I can give my opinion on how the Olympic Games impact a host city.
Core Vocabulary and Forms	• Expressing opinions • Vocabulary related to hosting the Olympics

Materials and Resources	• Article from https://www.france24.com/fr/20150728-boston-renonce-candidature-jo-2024-jeux-olympiques-paris-los-angeles-etats-unis	
	• Video: "Accueillir les Jeux olympiques: est-ce vraiment une bonne affaire?" from https://www.youtube.com/watch?v=7XBD51yE74I	
	• Video: "Allez, allez" from https://www.youtube.com/watch?v=6jkYPZ6_8po	
Lesson Length	65 minutes	

LEARNING SEQUENCE		
Focus of Learning	The teacher posts a question to the students regarding whether or not they would like Boston to host the Olympics. They talk in groups for a few minutes and share out after the breakout groups.	*Time:* 5 min
Preview of Learning	The teacher shares the lesson objective and agenda with the class.	*Time:* 1 min

Learning Episode 1		
Primetime 1	1. The teacher posts a headline and the first paragraph from an article about Boston removing its candidacy to host the Olympics, which students read and discuss in a teacher-led discussion.	*Time:* 5 min
Downtime	2. Students are put in breakout groups for a Turn and Talk to discuss why a city would not want to host the Olympics.	*Time:* 5 min
Primetime 2	3. Students share out reasons they have generated from the Turn and Talk.	*Time:* 5 min
Brain Break	Students take a quick stretch break.	*Time:* 1 min

Learning Episode 2		
Primetime 1	4. The teacher then shows students screenshots taken from a video on hosting the Olympics.	*Time:* 8 min
	5. Students make observations about each screenshot in a whole class discussion, while also taking notes on an I See, I Think, I Wonder graphic organizer.	
	6. The teacher shows the video for the first time, and students add additional ideas to their graphic organizer.	
Downtime	7. Students are put in breakout groups to discuss what they learned and recorded on their graphic organizer.	*Time:* 5 min
Primetime 2	8. A few students are asked to share out when the class returns to the main session.	*Time:* 2 min
Brain Break	The teacher plays a dance video to allow the students to get some movement in.	*Time:* 1 min

Learning Episode 3		
Primetime 1	9. The students watch the video about the Olympics a second time using a new graphic organizer. They will now identify cost and economic concerns of countries when hosting the Olympics. 10. Students are asked to share some of the concerns they identified.	*Time:* 8 min
Downtime	11. The teacher then shares a series of Tweets sharing personal opinions on whether France should or should not host the Olympics. The class reads these together. 12. The teacher reads the Interpersonal Task frame.	*Time:* 7 min
Primetime 2	13. Students are placed in pairs in breakout groups, with one student taking a "for" position and the other an "against" position. Students have access to a word bank to support the discussion. Students debate whether a city should host the Olympics or not and record their conversation.	*Time:* 10 min
Check for Learning	Students are asked to write an example of one positive and one negative impact of hosting the Olympics in the chat box.	*Time:* 1 min
Celebration of Learning	The teacher returns students' attention to the learning outcome and asks for a thumbs-up/thumbs-down self-assessment.	*Time:* 1 min

This lesson is part of a unit on the Olympics, which Paris will be hosting in 2024. In earlier lessons, students have learned about the history of the Olympics, sports vocabulary related to the Olympics, and personal preferences and opinions related to sports. This lesson asks students to consider the pros and cons of hosting the Olympics, a topic of particular relevance to these Boston-area students because Boston withdrew its name for consideration as a host city in 2015. The lesson is taught synchronously over Zoom, though it could easily be adapted for in-person learning, and is designed using the Interactive Model.

The teacher begins the class by greeting students and showing a warm-up discussion question, depicted in Figure 6.25. Since the class is meeting virtually, the teacher puts students in breakout groups with two or three people per group for a virtual Turn and Talk. As soon as students are in their breakout groups, the teacher immediately closes the groups, giving students 60 seconds to discuss before returning to the main room.

After students return from the Turn and Talk, the teacher asks a few of them to share their responses with the whole class. The teacher then shares the lesson objective and agenda, shown in Figure 6.26.

Échauffement...

Aimerais-tu que Boston accueille les J.O.?

FIGURE 6.25.
Warm-Up Slide

Translation
Warm-Up...
Would you like Boston to host the Olympic Games?

Objectif:
I can give my opinion on how the Olympic games impact a host city.

Agenda:

1. Discussion en groupes
2. Vidéo:
   Accueillir les Jeux Olympiques: Est-ce vraiment une bonne affaire?
3. Débat

FIGURE 6.26.
Lesson Objective and Agenda Slide

Translation
Objective: I can give my opinion on how the Olympic games impact a host city.
Agenda:
1. Discussion in groups
2. Video: Hosting the Olympic Games: Is it really a good investment?
3. Debate

Preparation Phase

The teacher then shows the headline and first paragraph from the article *"Boston renonce à sa candidature aux JO-2024"* [Boston removes its candidacy from the 2024 Olympic Games] (France24, 2015). The class reads the headline and the short first paragraph together, and the teacher then engages students in a second short Turn and Talk using breakout rooms, asking them why a city might *not* want to host the Olympics. Students share out some reasons when they return to the main session. The teacher has prepared a series of slides using screenshots from the video *"Accueillir les Jeux olympiques: est-ce vraiment une bonne affaire?"* [Hosting the Olympic Games: Is it really a good investment?] (https://www.youtube.com/watch?v=7XBD51yE74I). As the teacher shows each screenshot, students engage in a discussion regarding what they see and what they would like to learn more about. This discussion is intended to activate prior knowledge, preview key vocabulary, and anticipate what students will encounter when they view the video. As students view the screenshots and engage in the whole class discussion, they fill out an adaptation of a See, Think, Wonder chart, shown in Figure 6.27.

FIGURE 6.27.
See, Think, Wonder Chart

Translation
(Left to Right) I see… I think… I wonder…

Comprehension Phase, Part 1

The teacher now plays the video, which is just over four minutes in length, for the first time. Students watch the video and add to their See, Think, Wonder Chart with new information, new ideas, and new questions they have. After the video ends, the teacher again puts students in groups of two or three to discuss what they have learned from it. When students return to the main group, the teacher asks for a few share outs.

The teacher incorporates a short brain and body break at this point, playing a short dance video, "#AllezAllez" (https://www.youtube.com/watch?v=6jkYPZ6_8po). Students have been learning the dance moves from this video in earlier class sessions, and the teacher uses it as a way for students to stand and be active during their virtual class.

Comprehension Phase, Part 2

After the break, the teacher plays the video on the Olympic Games a second time. This time, students use a graphic organizer that the teacher has adapted specifically for this authentic resource, shown in Figure 6.28. Students are asked to take notes on the economic impact of hosting the Olympic Games, noting issues of cost and consequences for host cities, and are told that they will use the information from the video to engage in a debate on the pros and cons of serving as a host city.

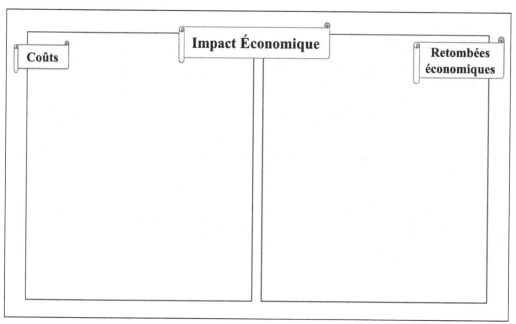

FIGURE 6.28.
Note-Taking Graphic Organizer

Translation
(Left to Right) Costs, Economic Impact, Economic Consequences

After watching the video a second time and taking notes, students share out some of their takeaways with the whole class. The teacher then asks students to read a series of Tweets that express opinions for or against hosting the Olympics, such as the following (translations are provided here, but not for students):

- "Les #JO2024 à Paris, une catastrophe écologique en Seine-Saint-Denis. Des collectifs dénoncent une accélération des projets de destruction, de pollution, d'expulsion et de spéculation." (Isabelle, 2020)
  - *The #JO2024 in Paris, an ecological catastrophe in Seine-Saint-Denis. Groups denounce an acceleration of destructive projects, pollution, evictions and gambling.*

- "Très heureux pour Paris et pour la France. Bravo et merci à toute l'équipe #Paris2024" (Delanoë, 2017)
  - *Very happy for Paris and for France. Bravo and thank you to the entire team #Paris2024*

- "Pour fêter les Jeux à #Paris2024 la Tour Eiffel sera éteinte ce soir pour commencer à économiser les 6 milliards d'€ qu'ils vont coûter" (Ripisylve, 2017)
  - *To celebrate the Games in #Paris2024 the [lights of the] Eiffel Tower will be turned off tonight to start to save the 6 billion euros that it is going to cost.*

Interpretation/Discussion Phase
The teacher has previously told students that they will be participating in a debate in which they will use the information from the authentic video and Tweets. Students are now shown the interpersonal task frame depicted in Figure 6.29. They are asked to add *"pour"* (for) or *"contre"* (against) before their name in Zoom. The teacher then pairs students, with one person "for" hosting the Olympics and the other "against." If the number of "fors" and "againsts" is not even, the teacher may change some students to the other side, so students are told to be prepared to argue either way.

Débat:

You are having a conversation with your friend who lives in Paris about the 2024 Olympics. They are explaining to you why it was a bad decision for the city to host, but you disagree. Each person will discuss the positive and negative impacts of the Olympics, based on their viewpoint, and try to find at least one point you can both agree on.

FIGURE 6.29.
Authentic Task Frame for the Debate

Translation
Title: Debate

Expressions Utiles...

Être en accord:
- Je suis d'accord.
- Tu as raison./Vous avez raison.
- Tout à fait.

Être en accord: avec réserves
- Peut-être.
- C'est possible.
- C'est peut-être le cas.

Être en accord: en étant concilliant
- C'est vrai, mais…
- Tu dis que/Vous dîtes que… mais
- Le seul problème, c'est que...

Être en désaccord:
- Je ne suis pas d'accord.
- Je ne trouve pas que…
- Non, ce n'est pas vrai…
- Tu te trompes./Vous vous trompez.

Être en désaccord: légèrement
- Pas vraiment.
- Ce n'est pas sûr.

Être en désaccord: fortement
- Mais pas du tout.
- C'est parfaitement faux.
- Tu exagères./Vous exagérez.

FIGURE 6.30.
Useful Expression Word Bank

Translation
Title: Useful expressions
Left-Hand Column:
To be in agreement:
- *I agree.*
- *You are right. (informal/formal)*
- *Completely.*

To be in agreement: with reservation
- *Maybe.*
- *It's possible.*
- *It's possibly the case.*

To be in agreement: conciliatory
- *It's true, but...*
- *You say that (informal/formal)...but*
- *The only problem is that...*

Right-Hand Column:
To disagree:
- *I do not agree.*
- *I don't find that...*
- *No, it's not true...*
- *You are wrong. (informal/formal)*

To lightly disagree:
- *Not really.*
- *That's not definite.*

To strongly disagree:
- *But not at all.*
- *That's completely false.*
- *You're exaggerating. (informal/formal)*

Students are instructed to use the graphic organizers they completed while watching the video and the information from the Tweets as they debate. They are also given a word bank of common expressions to use when engaging in a debate, shown in Figure 6.30. These expressions are not new to students, but the teacher includes them as a scaffold here because students are still developing their language skills in this area. Students have 8-10 minutes to engage in the debate, using Vocaroo to record their conversation. They receive a link to their recording from Vocaroo, which they must email to the teacher to "hand it in."

After students return from their breakout groups, the teacher turns their attention to the learning outcome and asks for a thumbs-up/thumbs-down self-assessment, shown in Figure 6.31. The teacher additionally asks students to post an example of a positive and negative impact of being a host city for the Olympics using the chat function in Zoom. If this lesson were conducted in person, the teacher could ask students to write this down on an index card as an exit ticket.

I can give my opinion on how the Olympic games impact a host city.

Dernier mot...
Écris un exemple d'impact positif
et d'impact négatif des Jeux
Olympiques sur une ville-hôte.

FIGURE 6.31.
Exit Ticket and Check-In on Learning Outcome Slide

Translation
The last word...
Write an example of a positive and negative impact of the Olympic Games on a host city.

Reflection and Next Steps

In this chapter, we have looked at the Gradual Release of Responsibility (GRR) Model, which is a way to carefully move students toward independent work. We have also explored a number of scaffolds for supporting student work, with a particular eye on interpersonal speaking tasks. Scaffolds from modeling to sentence starters to a range of graphic organizers can all be employed to support learners in successfully engaging in interaction in the target language. We also looked at how to use scaffolds within a tiered task, incorporating more scaffolds for Support Level tasks and fewer for On Level or Challenge Level tasks. Finally, we considered how to leverage technology for in-person, remote, or hybrid learning environments and walked through two classroom examples to show how two teachers have approached supporting all learners in interactive interpersonal communication.

Before moving on, take some time to reflect and assess your own practice. Consider how you are applying or would like to apply the practices and strategies discussed in this chapter. Where are your strengths? Where would you like to grow your practice? What actions will you take to move forward? This one-point rubric is designed to help you reflect and assess your own teaching on supporting interaction for all learners.

One-Point Rubric: Interaction for All Learners

GLOW *Where are my strengths related to this practice?*	CRITERIA *What should I be looking for in my own teaching?*	GROW *Where do I need to grow or expand my practice?*	TAKE ACTION *What steps will I take to move my practice forward?*
	I can use the GRR Model to carefully prepare students for interpersonal speaking tasks.		
	I can use a range of scaffolds to support students during interpersonal speaking tasks.		
	I can develop tiered tasks that provide different levels of scaffolding to meet the needs of all my learners		
	My students and I use the target language 90% or more of lesson time. I do not translate text or ask students to translate as one of their activities.		
	I use a communicative learning outcome, which is shared with students. All activities used reflect steps toward attainment of the student learning outcome.		

Level Up Your Learning

- **Fisher, D., & Frey, N. (2013).** *Better learning through structured teaching: A framework for the gradual release of responsibility, 2nd ed.* **ASCD**
  For a deep dive into the Gradual Release of Responsibility model, check out this book by Fisher & Frey. They walk through the model in detail, with clear examples and rationale.

- **ACTFL. (n.d.). Graphic organizers for language learning: CARLA graphic organizers. https://www.actfl.org/learn/graphic-organizers-language-learning**
  On this page of the ACTFL website, you will find numerous editable graphic organizers which you can copy or download either as Google Docs or Microsoft Word docs. The graphic organizers are categorized by mode of communication and skill or type of knowledge, making it easy to scan for ones that fit your needs.

- **Grahn, L. (n.d.).** *Tiering tasks and text.* **Grahnforlang. https://www.grahnforlang. com/tiering-tasks-and-text.html**
  For more information on how to tier, you will want to explore the tiering page on Leslie Grahn's website. You will find videos and reading material, as well as additional examples of tiered tasks (and tiered texts, which were not discussed in this chapter).

Chapter 6 References

ACTFL. (n.d.). Graphic organizers for language learning: CARLA graphic organizers. https://www.actfl.org/learn/graphic-organizers-language-learning

Delanoë, B. [@BertrandDelanoe]. (2017, September 13). Très heureux pour Paris et pour la France. Bravo et merci à toute l'équipe #Paris2024 [Tweet]. https://twitter.com/BertrandDelanoe/status/908024723564646405

Fisher, D., & Frey, N. (2008). *Better learning through structured teaching: A framework for the gradual release of responsibility.* ASCD.

France24. (2015, July 28). *Boston renonce à sa candidature aux JO-2024.* https://www.france24.com/fr/20150728-boston-renonce-candidature-jo-2024-jeux-olympiques-paris-los-angeles-etats-unis

Frey, N., & Fisher, D. (2013). *Gradual Release of Responsibility instructional framework.* ASCD. https://pdo.ascd.org/lmscourses/pd13oc005/media/formativeassessmentandccswithelaliteracymod_3-reading3.pdf

Grahn, L. (n.d.). *Tiering tasks and text.* Grahnforlang. https://www.grahnforlang.com/tiering-tasks-and-text.html

Isabelle. [@ZabouF]. (2020, December 12). Les #JO2024 à Paris, une catastrophe écologique en Seine-Saint-Denis. Des collectifs dénoncent une accélération des projets de destruction, de pollution, d'expulsion et de spéculation. [Tweet]. https://twitter.com/ZabouF/status/1337741008965132288

Lantolf, J. P., Thorne, S. L., & Poehner, M. E. (2015). Sociocultural theory and second language development. In B. VanPatten & J. Williams (Eds.), *Theories in second language acquisition* (pp. 207–226). Routledge.

Mariage, T., Winn, J., & Dabo, A. (2019). Provide scaffolded supports. In J. McLeskey, L. Maheady, B. Billingsley, M. T. Brownelle, & T. J. Lewis (Eds.), *High leverage practices for inclusive classrooms* (pp. 197–214). Routledge.

Park, E. (n.d.). *Free resources.* Mrs. Park. https://www.mrspark.org/free

Ripisylve. [@Ripisylve]. (2017, September 13). Pour fêter les Jeux à #Paris2024 la Tour Eiffel sera éteinte ce soir pour commencer à économiser les 6 milliards d'€ qu'ils vont coûter. [Tweet]. https://twitter.com/Ripisylve/status/908027467880857601

Tomlinson, C. A., & Strickland, C. A. (2005). *Differentiation in practice: A resource guide for differentiating curriculum, grades 9-12.* ASCD.

CHAPTER 7

Critical Perspectives: Input and Interaction About What?

Throughout this book, we have been focusing on how to create and sustain a classroom environment in which students are immersed in the target language, through both teacher target-language use and the use of authentic materials, as well as how learners can be engaged in using the target language to interact in meaningful contexts and with appropriate supports. Teaching for proficiency means developing student language proficiency in line with the ACTFL Proficiency Guidelines (ACTFL, 2012), using pedagogical practices that focus on what students can do with language, and building curriculum around the World-Readiness Standards for Learning Languages (National Standards Collaborative Board, 2015). While the primary focus of this book has been centered on the first C of the World-Readiness Standards—Communication—the connection to the other Cs should be emphasized: students will be communicating about Culture and making Comparisons and Connections to other disciplines while they engage with target-language Communities. A focus on input and interaction in a proficiency-based classroom, therefore, should be viewed as part of a foundation of instructional practices needed to integrate all five Cs of the World-Readiness Standards.

But neither the use of proficiency-based instructional practices nor the integration of the World-Readiness Standards dictates the specific content focus for a curriculum. The beauty of world language education is that teachers may adapt content to the needs of their own learners as well as focus on topics of current interest and importance in the world. A unit on health and well-being, for example, can focus on any number of culturally relevant historical or contemporary issues or events, such as health and social distancing measures during the COVID-19 pandemic. When school buildings in the United States were first shut down at the beginning of the pandemic, Erica Saldívar García and Melanie Manuel (2020) developed one such unit that centered on using trauma-informed principles while engaging students in a culturally relevant and authentic context through the Mexican character *Susana Distancia* (a play on words, meaning both the name of the character and *Your Healthy Distance*). In emphasizing students' social and emotional well-being and focusing on an important current event, the unit drew on authentic resources to provide meaningful language input for learners and engaged students in authentic interpersonal conversations through the use of breakout rooms during synchronous remote class time.

Teachers may also choose to focus curricular content on issues of social justice, helping to equip learners with both world language skills and tools for critical engagement in their society. Glynn, Wesley, and Wassell (2014) provide many examples of such units, including ones that engage students in reflecting on questions of identity, stereotypes, privilege, standards of beauty, climate justice, and more. In each of these units, students investigate Culture, make Comparisons, Connect to other disciplines, and engage with their Community while using the target language to Communicate. Learners interpret authentic resources and receive language input from their teacher, while also engaging in interpersonal discussions about the content of the unit.

With strong proficiency-based instructional practices and in alignment with the World-Readiness Standards, teachers can focus curriculum on issues of social justice, cultural competence, and supporting learners' social and emotional well-being. Through careful planning and the use of various comprehensible input strategies, they can eliminate the need to switch into English, which pauses the development of students' language proficiency. Rather, they can use effective proficiency-based practices to continue providing learners with target-language input and engaging them in interpersonal interactions while furthering their cultural knowledge, encouraging critical engagement in social justice issues, and supporting a sense of emotional well-being in their classrooms.

In this chapter, we will explore culturally responsive and sustaining pedagogy as we consider how to integrate culture into course work. We will then look at teaching for social justice and the Social Justice Standards (Teaching Tolerance, 2018), discussing how the many strategies and models outlined in this book can support a focus on issues of social justice. We will also look at Social Emotional Learning (SEL) and consider how it can be integrated in teaching rather than treated as an add-on. We will pull these different considerations together as we use the NCSSFL-ACTFL Can-Do Statements (ACTFL, 2017), using Intercultural Communicative Competence (ICC) to identify what learners at different proficiency levels are able to do when they investigate and communicate about these important topics.

Culturally Responsive and Sustaining Pedagogy

Culturally responsive pedagogy affirms the many diverse backgrounds of learners, viewing them as assets in the classroom. Culturally sustaining pedagogy goes further to build communities where students' cultural backgrounds are sustained, rather than eradicated. Culture is at the heart of what teachers do in the world language classroom, and they must ensure that their practices respond to and sustain the cultural backgrounds of their learners while also connecting them to the many cultures where the target language is spoken. The classroom's cultural focus should serve as both a mirror of the students and a window into other cultures (Style, 1996). Learners must be able to see themselves in the curriculum, while also exploring other cultures.

Sondra Nieto (2010) cautions, however, that, "[c]ulture is complex and intricate [and] it cannot be reduced to holidays, foods, or dances, although these are of course elements of culture" (p. 9). Nor should teachers simply add "some books about people of color, [have] a classroom Kwanzaa celebration, or [post] 'diverse' images" to make material more "culturally relevant" (Ladson-Billings, 2014, p. 82). Rather, teachers need to reflect carefully on their own biases as educators and the bias intrinsic in the curricular materials they use with their learners, taking a more critical view of culture that resists homogeneity and embraces multiculturalism. In the words of Sondra Nieto (2010):

> If culture is thought of in a sentimental way then it becomes little more than a yearning for the past that never existed, or an idealized, sanitized version of what exists in reality. The result may be an unadulterated, essentialized 'culture on a pedestal' that bears little resemblance to the messy and contradictory culture of real life. The problem of viewing some aspects of culture as indispensable attributes that must be shared by all people within a particular group springs from a romanticized and uncritical understanding of culture. (p. 9)

A culturally responsive, sustaining, and critical pedagogy in the world language classroom challenges teachers to "not only simply [celebrate] cultural differences, but also [name] and [challenge] social inequities in relation to race, class, gender, sexual orientation, religion, and other social identities" (Martell & Stevens, 2021, p. 45).

Input and Interaction While Engaging in Topics of Social Justice

Teaching for social justice provides an opportunity to engage students in critical investigations of culture, while connecting those investigations to significant and highly relevant issues. Rather than learning lists of words for food, for example, learners can instead investigate issues of global hunger. The traditional clothing unit or household chore unit can be transformed to engage students with questions of gender identity. A unit on daily routines can instead investigate how learners around the world access education. The issues you choose to focus on will reflect your target language, the level and age of your learners, and the issues' interest and relevance for your students. The Social

Justice Standards (Teaching Tolerance, 2018) identify four domains in teaching for social justice: Identity, Diversity, Justice, and Action. The anchor standards and domains are shown in full in Box 7.1. Teachers can use these standards to help focus curriculum and instruction, complementing the World-Readiness Standards for Learning Languages.

BOX 7.1. SOCIAL JUSTICE STANDARDS: ANCHOR STANDARDS AND DOMAINS

Identity

1. Students will develop positive social identities based on their membership in multiple groups in society.

2. Students will develop language and historical and cultural knowledge that affirm and accurately describe their membership in multiple identity groups.

3. Students will recognize that people's multiple identities interact and create unique and complex individuals.

4. Students will express pride, confidence and healthy self-esteem without denying the value and dignity of other people.

5. Students will recognize traits of the dominant culture, their home culture and other cultures and understand how they negotiate their own identity in multiple spaces.

Diversity

6. Students will express comfort with people who are both similar to and different from them and engage respectfully with all people.

7. Students will develop language and knowledge to accurately and respectfully describe how people (including themselves) are both similar to and different from each other and others in their identity groups.

8. Students will respectfully express curiosity about the history and lived experiences of others and will exchange ideas and beliefs in an open-minded way.

9. Students will respond to diversity by building empathy, respect, understanding and connection.

10. Students will examine diversity in social, cultural, political and historical contexts rather than in ways that are superficial or oversimplified.

Justice

11. Students will recognize stereotypes and relate to people as individuals rather than representatives of groups.

12. Students will recognize unfairness on the individual level (e.g., biased speech) and injustice at the institutional or systemic level (e.g., discrimination).

13. Students will analyze the harmful impact of bias and injustice on the world, historically and today.

14. Students will recognize that power and privilege influence relationships on interpersonal, intergroup and institutional levels and consider how they have been affected by those dynamics.

15. Students will identify figures, groups, events and a variety of strategies and philosophies relevant to the history of social justice around the world.

Action

16. Students will express empathy when people are excluded or mistreated because of their identities and concern when they themselves experience bias.

17. Students will recognize their own responsibility to stand up to exclusion, prejudice and injustice.

18. Students will speak up with courage and respect when they or someone else has been hurt or wronged by bias.

19. Students will make principled decisions about when and how to take a stand against bias and injustice in their everyday lives and will do so despite negative peer or group pressure.

20. Students will plan and carry out collective action against bias and injustice in the world and will evaluate what strategies are most effective.

A common misperception is that Novice-level learners will not be able to engage in issues of social justice due to their limited language skills. However, as demonstrated throughout this book, with careful planning learners at all proficiency levels can interpret authentic material (input) and engage in meaningful, if simple, discussion (interaction).

Consider first how to provide input when addressing topics of social justice. As shown in Chapter 3, teachers can select an authentic resource for any proficiency level by considering both linguistic factors (such as vocabulary and target structures) and non-linguistic factors (such as background knowledge, visual support, and organization). The same criteria apply when selecting authentic resources to engage students in topics of social justice. Teachers may even choose images that contain little if any text in the target language, but are culturally authentic. For example, Figure 7.1 depicts an image used by a German teacher to introduce learners to student activism on climate change: *Alles Fürs Klima* [All for the Climate]. The image contains little text but is visually rich. The teacher can use the target language to describe the image, introducing simple vocabulary and structures on this topic and using the many comprehensible input strategies that were presented in Chapter 2.

FIGURE 7.1.
Authentic Image: All for the Climate (#AlleFürsKlima) Protest

When the teacher is ready to shift learners to interaction on this topic, careful modeling of language use, appropriate scaffolds, and the use of interpersonal strategies will help ensure successful interaction (refer to Chapters 5 and 6 for more details). The teacher must also consider the language that learners will use to communicate on the topic. Novice-level learners, for example, will be unable to make a hypothesis about how this protest will impact global policies on addressing climate change (a Superior-level skill), nor will they be able to narrate what happened at this particular protest (an Advanced-level skill). If learners are asked to engage in interaction at a skill level that is far beyond their capability (that is, their Zone of Proximal Development), they will quickly revert to English. However, with scaffolding and support, Novice-level learners can provide simple descriptions of the students in the picture, they can ask each other simple questions, and they can make simple statements about the importance of addressing climate change (all of which are Novice High/Intermediate-level skills that can be reached after teacher modeling and with scaffolds). For example, Spanish students could use present tense + infinitive to make sentences such as *"Debo usar menos agua"* [I should use less water] or *"Tenemos que cuidar el planeta"* [We have to take care of the planet]. Teachers should think carefully about the type of language they want their learners to use when interacting and then model that language extensively when providing language input.

Social-Emotional Learning

Social-emotional Learning (SEL)—defined as a "set of social, emotional, behavioral, and character skills that support success in school, the workplace, relationships, and the community" (Frey, Fisher, & Smith, 2019, p. 2)—has long been viewed as an add-on to education. Teachers may consider SEL as something they need to do *on top of* teaching academic content. In the world language classroom, this may result in teachers pausing the use of the target language to engage students in discussion on SEL topics. However, a focus on developing learners' social and emotional skills can easily be integrated into world language teaching and learning.

The Collaborative for Academic, Social, and Emotional Learning (CASEL) has developed a framework of competencies to describe effective social and emotional behavior:

- Self-Awareness: The abilities to understand one's own emotions, thoughts, and values and how they influence behavior across contexts.

- Self-Management: The abilities to manage one's emotions, thoughts, and behaviors effectively in different situations and to achieve goals and aspirations.

- Social Awareness: The abilities to understand the perspectives of and empathize with others, including those from diverse backgrounds, cultures, and contexts.

- Relationship Skills: The abilities to establish and maintain healthy and supportive relationships and to effectively navigate settings with diverse individuals and groups.

- Responsible Decision-Making: The abilities to make caring and constructive choices about personal behavior and social interactions across diverse situations.
(CASEL, 2021)

To integrate SEL into your world language courses, consider starting with two practices: integrating explicit SEL language in goal-setting and encouraging student self-reflection on SEL. Consider the Social Awareness competency as you think about what this might look like in a world language classroom. As learners engage in interaction in the language, they develop an understanding of cultural differences and learn how to respectfully navigate those differences while using the target language. For most world language teachers, helping learners develop social awareness as they use the target language is nothing new. However, making it *explicit* as part of instruction is. You can begin to build a focus on SEL by integrating learning outcomes that explicitly state a social-emotional learning goal. For example, in a lesson in which learners will engage in an interpersonal task on the topic of daily routines, you can add an SEL focus to your learning outcome:

- I can ask and answer questions about my daily routine.

- I can ask and answer questions about my daily routine *while demonstrating awareness of and respect for cultural differences.*

Making these goals explicit means that you are intentionally focusing on them in your classes. You can then ask learners to reflect on their own social-emotional development through weekly reflection journals, reflection prompts at the end of assessments, or pauses at the end of each class while students consider how they have demonstrated attainment of the learning outcome.

Intercultural Communicative Competence

Culturally responsive and sustaining pedagogy, a focus on social justice themes, and social-emotional learning can all be reflected in the important world language practice of developing students' Intercultural Communicative Competence (ICC). ICC is different from Cultural Competence, which, as defined by proponents of culturally responsive and sustaining pedagogy, is the ability to "appreciate and celebrate [one's own] cultures of origin while gaining knowledge and fluency in at least one other culture" (Ladson-Billings, 2014, p. 75). ICC is also different from Intercultural Competence, which includes the following five competencies:

1. Knowledge: Knowledge of social groups and their products and practices in one's own and in one's interlocutor's country or region and of the general processes of societal and individual interaction.

2. Skills of interpreting and relating: Ability to interpret a document or event from another culture, to explain it and relate it to documents or events from one's own culture.

3. Skills of discovery and interaction: Ability to acquire new knowledge of a culture and cultural practices, and ability to operate knowledge, attitudes, and skills under the constraints of real-time communication and interaction.

4. Attitudes: Curiosity and openness; readiness to suspend disbelief about other cultures and belief about one's own culture.

5. Critical cultural awareness: Ability to evaluate perspectives, practices, and products in one's own and other cultures and countries, both critically and on the basis of explicit criteria.
(Wagner, Cardetti, & Byram, 2019, p. 20)

To demonstrate Intercultural *Communicative* Competence, an activity must involve learners developing all of the above competencies *while communicating in the target language*. This distinction reinforces the vital importance of giving learners comprehensible input and engaging them in meaningful interaction in the target language at all levels of language instruction.

But what does ICC look like for learners at different proficiency levels? The NCSSFL-ACTFL Can-Do Statements (ACTFL, 2017) provide performance descriptors for different proficiency levels and ICC, as shown in Figure 7.2. These descriptors are grouped into two overarching categories: Investigate and Interact. When students investigate cultural products and practices to understand perspectives, they are reading, listening to, and viewing authentic materials, receiving critical input in the target language. When students interact with others in and from another culture—although this may be a simulated practice during class time—they must use the target language in authentic, interpersonal discussions. Language input and interaction should not be divorced from cultural exploration, critical investigation of topics of social justice, or social-emotional learning. In the world language classroom, with the use of the strategies and models explored in this book, the target language becomes the medium through which students engage in these important areas.

NOVICE

INVESTIGATE	PROFICIENCY BENCHMARK		
	In my own and other cultures *I can* identify products and practices to help me understand perspectives.		
Investigate Products And Practices To Understand Cultural Perspectives		PERFORMANCE INDICATORS	
	PRODUCTS	In my own and other cultures *I can* identify some typical products related to familiar everyday life.	
	PRACTICES	In my own and other cultures *I can* identify some typical practices related to familiar everyday life.	

INTERACT	PROFICIENCY BENCHMARK		
	I can interact at a survival level in some familiar everyday contexts.		
Interact With Others In And From Another Culture		PERFORMANCE INDICATORS	
	LANGUAGE	*I can* communicate with others from the target culture in familiar everyday situations, using memorized language and showing basic cultural awareness.	
	BEHAVIOR	*I can* use appropriate rehearsed behaviors and recognize some obviously inappropriate behaviors in familiar everyday situations.	

INTERMEDIATE

INVESTIGATE	PROFICIENCY BENCHMARK		
Investigate Products And Practices To Understand Cultural Perspectives	In my own and other cultures **I can** make comparisons between products and practices to help me understand perspectives.		
	PERFORMANCE INDICATORS		
	PRODUCTS	In my own and other cultures **I can** compare products related to everyday life and personal interests or studies.	
	PRACTICES	In my own and other cultures **I can** compare practices related to everyday life and personal interests or studies.	

INTERACT	PROFICIENCY BENCHMARK		
Interact With Others In And From Another Culture	**I can** interact at a functional level in some familiar contexts.		
	PERFORMANCE INDICATORS		
	LANGUAGE	**I can** converse with peers from the target culture in familiar situations at school, work, or play, and show interest in basic cultural similarities and differences.	
	BEHAVIOR	**I can** recognize that significant differences in behaviors exist among cultures, use appropriate learned behaviors and avoid major social blunders.	

ADVANCED

INVESTIGATE	PROFICIENCY BENCHMARK		
Investigate Products And Practices To Understand Cultural Perspectives	In my own and other cultures **I can** explain some diversity among products and practices and how it relates to perspectives.		
	PERFORMANCE INDICATORS		
	PRODUCTS	In my own and other cultures **I can** explain how a variety of products of public and personal interest are related to perspectives.	
	PRACTICES	In my own and other cultures **I can** explain how a variety of practices within familiar and social situations are related to perspectives.	

INTERACT	PROFICIENCY BENCHMARK		
Interact With Others In And From Another Culture	**I can** interact at a competent level in familiar and some unfamiliar contexts.		
	PERFORMANCE INDICATORS		
	LANGUAGE	**I can** converse comfortably with others from the target culture in familiar and some unfamiliar situations and show some understanding of cultural differences.	
	BEHAVIOR	**I can** demonstrate awareness of subtle differences among cultural behaviors and adjust my behavior accordingly in familiar and some unfamiliar situations.	

FIGURE 7.2.
The NCSSFL-ACTFL Can-Do Statements for Intercultural Communicative Competence
Source: ACTFL, 2017.

Table 7.1 provides examples of learning outcomes for ICC at the three major proficiency levels and shows the types of authentic resources that may be appropriate, along with possible communicative tasks and sample learner discourse. A common topic for Novices, for example, is a focus on food. To better integrate topics of social justice and develop learners' ICC, you can shift the focus slightly to the sustainability of different food items commonly eaten in the target culture. Novice-level learners can use simple language structures and vocabulary to identify food-related cultural products and practices and interact on a simple level. An infographic that shows the amount of water needed to produce different types of food, for example, may be appropriate for Novices assuming it is visually rich and clearly organized. Students can use what they learn from the infographic to ask a partner simple questions in the target language, such as *"Qu'est-*

ce que tu aimes manger?" [What do you like to eat?]. If the partner responds that they like to eat hamburgers, the student may ask, *"Il faut combien de litres d'eau pour produire un hamburger?"* [How many litres of water are needed to produce a *hamburger*?]. The question structures learners use in this sample discourse will be chunks of language supported by sentence frames or sentence starters, with learners manipulating only the key vocabulary words (food words and numbers). So if the partner responded instead that they liked to eat pizza, the student's question would become, *"Il faut combien de litres d'eau pour produire une pizza?"* [How many litres of water are needed to produce a *pizza*?]. With careful planning and consideration of the target structures and key vocabulary, learners at all proficiency levels can focus on issues of social justice while developing their Intercultural Communicative Competence.

TABLE 7.1. SAMPLE ICC LEARNING OUTCOMES, AUTHENTIC RESOURCES, AND COMMUNICATIVE TASKS FOR DIFFERENT PROFICIENCY LEVELS

Learner Proficiency Level	ICC Learning Outcome	Sample Authentic Resource	Communicative Task	Sample Learner Discourse
Novice	I can identify sustainable food practices common in the target culture.	Infographic from the target culture showing the amount of water needed to produce common types of food.	Learners use a graphic organizer to take notes on the kinds of food and how sustainable they are while reading the infographic. Learners then ask their partners which kinds of food they like to eat and how sustainable each kind of food is.	Do you like hamburgers? *Yes, I do.* How much water does it take to produce a hamburger? *It takes 660 gallons of water.*
Intermediate	I can compare access to education for women and girls in different target cultures.	One short article and one short news report focusing on two different target cultures and describing access to education for women and girls.	Learners are broken into two groups, with one group reading the article and the other watching the news report. Learners are then paired with someone from the other group to compare when they learned, collecting their information in a graphic organizer.	In ____ culture, all women and girls can access education. However, in ____ culture, women and girls have less access to education because...
Advanced	I can explain causes for immigration connected to climate change.	Magazine article discussing patterns of immigration in the target culture due to climate change.	After reading the article, learners are broken into groups to discuss what happens for an immigrant before, during, and after a climate event that prompts their immigration.	As a result of the ____ climate event in ____ culture, thousands of people began immigrating to other areas. During their immigration, they experienced ____. After arriving in ____, they experienced ____.

Tech Zoom

As you consider the critical perspectives discussed in this chapter, this *Tech Zoom* section will provide some digital resources to support you along the way. We focus here on professional learning, in the forms of special interest groups, online learning, and virtual communities where you can connect with others who are interested in this work. We acknowledge that the list of groups here will change and grow over the years (as they should!), so the resources listed here will likely change.

- ACTFL Special Interest Groups (SIGs): As an ACTFL member, you can join various special interest groups to connect with world language educators and build professional communities in your areas of interest. While there are many different SIGs, two that connect to this chapter focus on teaching for social justice and the teaching of culture. Follow this link to find out more: https://www.actfl.org/connect/special-interest-groups
  - ACTFL Critical and Social Justice Approaches SIG: Promotes and supports critical and social justice approaches in language instruction.
  - ACTFL Teaching and Learning of Culture SIG: Encourages a better understanding of the teaching of culture and its place in the world language curriculum.

- Learning for Justice Professional Development: The Learning for Justice website provides information on workshops, self-guided learning, webinars, podcasts, and more. Although not specifically geared toward world language education, it provides an excellent place to begin your journey towards teaching for social justice. https://www.learningforjustice.org/professional-development

- Facebook Groups/Pages:
  - Courageous Dialogues with Chinese Educators Facebook (FB) Page: A "group of K-16 Chinese heritage educators and non-heritage Chinese language and culture teachers promoting courageous dialogues among teachers' communities and in the curriculum." https://www.facebook.com/CourageousChinese
  - Incorporating Afro-Latino Culture in Spanish Classrooms FB Group: A group that "demonstrates ideas, perspectives, news, and pictures of how diverse Latinos are." https://www.facebook.com/groups/2024151774569280/
  - Teaching for Intercultural Competence FB Group: "A place for teachers to share and discuss teaching methods, resources, tools, and practices to help our students develop Intercultural Competence." https://www.facebook.com/groups/TeachingforICC

Now that we have looked at culturally relevant and sustaining pedagogy, input, and interaction when teaching for social justice, integrating social-emotional learning, and Intercultural Communicative Competence, we are going to walk through two *Classroom Close-Ups* that show how teachers of two different languages working with students at two different proficiency levels apply these topics to their own teaching. In *Classroom Close-Up 7.2*, we will also show how the teacher adapts the model for a hybrid or distance learning environment.

Classroom Close-Ups

Classroom Close-Up 7.1: ¡Empiezo la escuela!

This classroom example was shared by Bárbara Barnett, K-5 Department Head for World Language Classical and Modern Languages at Wellesley Public Schools, Wellesley, MA.

COURSE OVERVIEW	
Course Name	First-Grade Spanish (second year of language, Foreign Languages in Elementary School [FLES]
Course Proficiency Target	Novice Mid

In this first-grade FLES program, the year-long theme is *Somos iguales y somos diferentes* [We are all the same, we are all different.]. There are seven elementary schools in this school district, and all teachers use the same lesson plans, including materials, across schools. There are four first-grade units of study:

- *Yo empiezo la escuela* [I start school]
- *Yo describo mi mundo* [I describe my world]
- *Tengo hambre* [I'm hungry]
- *Mi comunidad* [My community]

FIGURE 7.3.
Good Listening Friend, Sample 1
Translation
I listen with my whole body.
Left-Hand Column: Focused eyes, Attentive ears, Quiet mouth, Upright body
Right-Hand Column: Calm hands, Still feet, Considerate heart, Thinking head

This program has intentionally investigated and attempted to address bias in its curriculum materials, including in the visuals used with students. For example, the teachers reevaluated using a popular elementary school character, Listening Larry, who helps children learn how to be good listeners. Upon reviewing this character for bias using a framework from Sadker (n.d.), the program realized that Listening Larry was not inclusive of the different genders and ethnicities of its children. Ten new characters were therefore created, including the two shown in Figures 7.3 and 7.4, that could be rotated by teachers to show a broader representation of children.

Additionally, throughout the year students use an *Escalera de español* [Spanish Ladder] that encourages them to expand their language use (see Figure 7.5). This ladder is purposefully set in Spain because one of the yearly thematic questions for first grade is, How are we connected to Spain?

FIGURE 7.4.
Good Listening Friend, Sample 2
Translation
I listen with my whole body.
Left-Hand Column: Focused eyes, Attentive ears, Quiet mouth, Upright body
Right-Hand Column: Calm hands, Still feet, Considerate heart, Thinking head

FIGURE 7.5.
The Escalera de español

Translation
My Spanish Ladder
What is your name?
Question? - And you? What is your name?
Sentence - My name is Antonio Luis.
Word - Antonio Luis.
Don't know yet (in English) - I don't know.

This classroom example presents a two-day learning sequence, with each class lasting 25 minutes.

LESSON OVERVIEW: DAY 1	
Unit Theme	*¡Empiezo la escuela!* (I start school!)
Lesson Learning Outcome	I can recognize body parts in Spanish to construct a fictional character. I can describe the whole-body listening characteristics in Spanish of a fictional character.
Core Vocabulary and Forms	Eight body parts in Spanish: *los ojos, los oídos, la boca, las manos, los pies, el cuerpo, la cabeza,* and *el corazón.* [eyes, ears, mouth, hands, feet, body, head, and heart]
Materials and Resources	• Song /Video: *"Pongo una mano aquí"* by Atención, Atención • Song: *"Hay un amigo en mí"* • Mystery box • Visual of *la cabeza* [head] for the mystery box • Ratoncito Pérez puppet • Magnetic whiteboard (mounted on teacher's traveling cart) • Manipulatives: Laminated soccer ball outline and body parts, each with a magnet • Visual/Poster: *"Escucho con todo mi cuerpo"* [I listen with my whole body] • Visual/Poster: *"Mi escalera de español: España"* [My Spanish Ladder: Spain] • Visual/Poster: *"Habla con tu compañero"* [Talk to your partner]
Social Justice Standards	*Identity K-2.3:* I know that all my group identities are part of me—but that I am always ALL me. *Diversity K-2.6:* I like being around people who are like me and different from me, and I can be friendly to everyone.
Social-Emotional Learning Standards	Relationship Skills Self-Management
Lesson Length	25 minutes

LEARNING SEQUENCE		
Focus of Learning	Students sing *"Pongo una mano aquí"* [Put a hand here] to signal the beginning of class and to review two words for body parts (*mano* and *pie*: hand and foot) as they move to the meaning of the words.	*Time:* 1 min
Preview of Learning	The teacher reviews the learning outcome and the lesson agenda.	*Time:* 1 min

Learning Episode 1		
Primetime 1	1. The teacher presents a mystery box and asks students what could be inside. The teacher gives hints using Spanish and whole language. 2. Students are invited to talk with a partner about what they think is in the mystery box. Students are reminded of using whole-body listening to be a good listening partner.	*Time:* 2 min
Downtime	3. Students Turn and Talk, discussing what they think is in the mystery box.	*Time:* 2 min
Primetime 2	4. The teacher asks students to share what they think is in the mystery box and explain why they think that. 5. The teacher uses a hand puppet to ask students for any updates on their lost teeth. The teacher models and explains how the hand puppet is being a good listener by using whole-body listening.	*Time:* 6 min
Brain Break	Students are asked to stand and stretch.	*Time:* 1 min
Learning Episode 2		
Primetime 1	6. The teacher reminds students of the recent story they read (*Teo viaja por España*) and asks them what a popular sport in Spain is. Students should respond by saying *fútbol* [soccer]. 7. The teacher explains that the class will build together a *muñeco de fútbol* [soccer character] and hands out magnetic body parts. A soccer ball outline is placed on a magnetic whiteboard.	*Time:* 2 min
Downtime	8. The teacher engages students by asking many questions about the soccer character's body parts and where students would like to place them on the character. Students stand to place the body parts on the soccer character. 9. When the character is completed, the teacher asks more questions of the class, such as how many legs it has, how many eyes, and why the heart is red and yellow and why that is important.	*Time:* 6 min
Primetime 2	10. Students are asked to briefly close their eyes. The teacher quickly rearranges some of the body parts on the soccer doll. 11. When students open their eyes, the teacher asks if the doll is different and in what way. 12. The teacher closes by reminding students of the year-long theme (we are all the same, we are all different).	*Time:* 2 min
Check for Learning	Students' attention is returned to the learning outcome and students are asked for a thumbs-up/thumbs-down self-assessment.	*Time:* 1 min
Celebration of Learning	Students sing the Spanish song *"Hay un amigo en mí"* [You've got a friend in me].	*Time:* 1 min

Opening Routine

The teacher begins class with an opening routine in which students stand and sing *"Pongo una mano aquí"* [Put your hand here], a song that students are already familiar with. Students stand and sing along with the song, following the actions. The teacher then shares the learning outcome and reviews the agenda.

First Learning Episode

The teacher shows learners a mystery box and asks them what they think is inside. The teacher uses Spanish to give hints, such as: *Soy una parte del cuerpo muy importante. Yo pienso mucho. En mí, yo llevo dos ojos, una nariz, una boca y dos oídos (orejas). ¿Quién soy?* [I think a lot. In me, I carry two eyes, a nose, a mouth, and two ears. What am I?]

The teacher invites students to Turn and Talk with a partner. Students have been working on being good listening partners using whole-body listening. The teacher shows students a visual and reminds them how to be good listeners to their partner. Figure 7.6 shows the visual reminder steps of a productive Turn and Talk, including facing a partner and talking turns. Students are reminded to use Spanish when they speak.

FIGURE 7.6.
Turn and Talk

Translation
Hi Julie. How are you?
Hi Roberto. I am fine, thank you. And you?

After students speak to their partner in Spanish, the teacher asks guided questions for ideas on what might be in the mystery box. As students share, the teacher refers to the *Escalera de español* [the Spanish Ladder] and reminds students to *sube, sube la escalera* [climb, climb the ladder] as they speak. After students have correctly guessed the mystery box item, the teacher uses a hand puppet—el Ratoncito Pérez—to invite them to share any updates on their lost teeth (an important topic for children of this age). The teacher uses popsicle sticks to call on learners equitably and also reminds students how the puppet is being a good listener by using whole-body listening, saying for example that the puppet has *ojos fijos* [focused eyes], *oídos atentos* [attentive ears], *boca callada* [quiet mouth], *cuerpo derecho* [upright body], *manos tranquilas* [calm hands], *corazón considerado* [considerate heart], and *cabeza pensando* [thinking head]. This provides another opportunity to use the target vocabulary in context and model self-management and relationship skills.

Second Learning Episode

After a quick stretch break, the teacher begins the second learning episode. Students have recently read the book *Teo viaja por España* [Teo travels through Spain], and the teacher reminds them of the story and asks them what one of the most popular sports in Spain is. When students call out *fútbol* [soccer], the teacher says yes and reminds them that *fútbol* is different from *fútbol americano* [American football]. The teacher then quickly transitions to the next activity: the class will make a *muñeco de fútbol* [a soccer character] by building a character together. The teacher places the outline of their character—a large soccer ball—on the magnetic whiteboard, which is mounted to their traveling cart (Spanish FLES teachers at all schools in this district push into students' classrooms). This visual and students' manipulatives are printed on cardstock paper and laminated, and magnet dots have been added to the back. (In a remote learning environment, this activity can be completed using Seesaw or Google Jamboard.)

The teacher begins by looking at the soccer ball outline and asking, *Pero… ¿Dónde están los ojos, los oídos (orejas), la boca, las manos, las piernas y los pies, la cabeza y el corazón del muñeco?* [But… where are the eyes, ears, mouth, hands, legs and feet, head and heart of the doll?] The teacher clearly sets the expectation for this activity and gives each student a different body part; the visual has multiple versions of each body part, thus ensuring that everyone is included. The teacher begins to build the *muñeco de fútbol* by asking students, *¿Dónde está la cabeza? El muñeco tiene una cabeza que está pensando.* [Where is the head? The character has a head that is thinking.] A student who has the head will then stand and come up to the magnetic whiteboard, placing the head on the outline. This continues as the teacher asks about different parts of the body, using the chunks of language that describe whole-body listening. Figure 7.7 shows the soccer ball character outline and body parts, and Figure 7.8 shows a possible finished character.

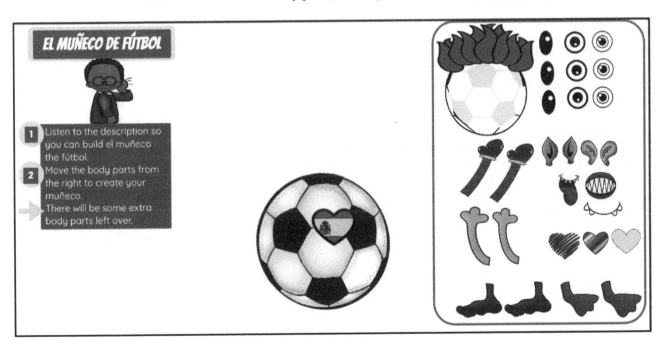

FIGURE 7.7.
Muñeco de fútbol Outline and Body Parts

After the character is completed, the teacher leads the class in a discussion, asking questions such as these:

- *¿Cuántos ojos tiene el muñeco de fútbol?* [How many eyes does the soccer character have?]

- *¿Cuántas bocas tiene el muñeco?* [How many mouths does the character have?]

- *El muñeco ya tenía un corazón muy bonito, de color rojo y amarillo. ¿Por qué crees que es especial ese corazón?* [The character already has a beautiful heart that is red and yellow. Why do you think this heart is special?]

The teacher reminds students to *sube, sube la escalera* as they hear a full detailed description of the character. The teacher uses humanizing characteristics to describe the soccer character, such as *El muñeco de fútbol es mi amigo. Está muy contento. Escucha muy bien con un cuerpo derecho, una cabeza pensando, tres manos tranquilas, cuatro piernas y pies quietos, seis ojos fijos, dos bocas calladas y dos oídos atentos. ¡Wow! El muñeco de fútbol es muy especial.* [The soccer character is my friend. He is very happy. He listens well with an upright body, a thinking head, three calm hands, four calm legs and feet, six focused eyes, two quiet mouths and two attentive ears. Wow! The soccer character is very special!]

Students are now asked to close their eyes momentarily. While their eyes are shut, the teacher quickly rearranges some of the soccer character's body parts. When students open their eyes, the teacher asks some questions to see if students notice the changes. Students may say, for example, *"Tiene tres piernas!"* [He has three legs!] The teacher reminds students to *sube, sube la escalera* as the expectation is set to answer using a complete thought. The teacher concludes this learning episode by explaining to students that we may not have six eyes or four legs like the soccer character, but we are all people and have a lot in common. We may all be different in certain ways, but we should always be kind to each other. The teacher emphasizes the first-grade theme: *Somos iguales y somos diferentes* [We are all the same and we are all different].

Closing Routine

The teacher then returns to the learning outcome and asks students for a thumbs-up/thumbs-down check on whether they feel they achieved the goal. The teacher closes class by asking students to stand and sing a song they have previously learned: *Hay un amigo en mí* [You've got a friend in me].

FIGURE 7.8.
Muñeco de fútbol, Sample Completed Character

LESSON OVERVIEW: DAY 2	
Unit Theme	*¡Empiezo la escuela!* (I start school!)
Lesson Learning Outcome	I can recognize body parts in Spanish to construct a fictional character. I can describe the whole-body listening characteristics in Spanish of a fictional character.
Core Vocabulary and Forms	• Eight body parts in Spanish: *los ojos, los oídos, la boca, las manos, los pies, el cuerpo, la cabeza,* and *el corazón.* [eyes, ears, mouth, hands, feet, body, head, and heart]
Materials and Resources	• Song/Video: *"Pongo una mano aquí"* by Atención, Atención • Song: *"Hay un amigo en mí"* • Presentation: *¿Qué prefieres?* [What do you prefer?] • Visual/Poster: *"Habla con tu compañero"* [Talk to your partner] • Visual/Poster: *"Mi escalera de español: España"* [My Spanish Ladder: Spain] • Worksheet *"Nuestro amiguito peludo"* [Our furry little friend] • SMART Board/Screen • Clipboards • Pencils (with erasers)
Social Justice Standards	*Identity K-2.3:* I know that all my group identities are part of me—but that I am always ALL me. *Diversity K-2.6:* I like being around people who are like me and different from me, and I can be friendly to everyone.
Social-Emotional Learning Standards	Relationship Skills Self-Management
Lesson Length	25 minutes

LEARNING SEQUENCE		
Focus of Learning	Students sing *"Pongo una mano aquí"* [Put a hand here] to signal the beginning of class and to review two words for body parts (*mano* and *pie*: hand and foot) as they move to the meaning of the words.	*Time:* 1 min
Preview of Learning	The teacher reviews the learning outcome and the lesson agenda.	*Time:* 1 min

Learning Episode 1			
Primetime 1	1.	The teacher reminds students what it means to be a good listener and to climb the proficiency ladder when they speak.	*Time:* 5 min
	2.	The teacher invites students to participate in the *¿Qué prefieres?* [What do you prefer?] ritual and routine in which students express their preface in response to the prompt presented. For today's presentation, the prompt shows sentence frames and images supporting the question *¿Qué prefieres, tener pelo morado o dientes coloridos?* [Do you prefer to have purple hair or multi-colored teeth?] The teacher instructs students to climb up their Spanish ladder of proficiency as they discuss their preference for purple hair or colorful teeth with their partner. The teacher reminds students to only use the Spanish that they know and to use the strategies they have learned to express their thoughts even if they don't know a word.	
Downtime	3.	The teacher reminds students of the *Muñeco de fútbol* [soccer character] they collaboratively built during the previous class and what he looked like. The teacher then explains that students will work with a partner to draw a new character: *Nuestro amiguito peludo* [our furry friend].	*Time:* 8 min
	4.	The teacher hands out a worksheet with the outline of the character and puts students in pairs. The teacher instructs students to go to the back of the worksheet and goes over the Can-Do Statements of the activity by using an equitable calling system to call on a volunteer to read out loud the statements.	
	5.	The teacher describes the character (e.g., Our furry little friend has five still feet) while students take turns drawing what they hear on their shared worksheet. (In a remote learning environment, this activity can be completed using GoogleJamboard.) The teacher checks for comprehension as students draw.	
Primetime 2	6.	The teacher now explains that students will ask each other to describe what they drew. The teacher provides a model question and sentence starter to scaffold the students' conversations.	*Time:* 8 min
	7.	In the same pairs, students take turns asking each other what their character looks like and then describing the character.	
	8.	The teacher asks students to hold up their drawings and look around. Because each drawing will be different, the teacher reminds students that even though we heard the same description, our interpretations are different due to our different experiences. The teacher connects back to the year-long theme (we are all the same, we are all different).	
Check for Learning		Students' attention is returned to the learning outcome and students are asked for a thumbs-up/thumbs-down self-assessment.	*Time:* 1 min
Celebration of Learning		Students will sing the Spanish song *"Hay un amigo en mí"* [You've got a friend in me].	*Time:* 1 min

FIGURE 7.9.
Visual support: What would you prefer?

Translation
What do you prefer?
[Left] I prefer to have
[Top] purple hair
[Right] because
[Bottom] different colored teeth

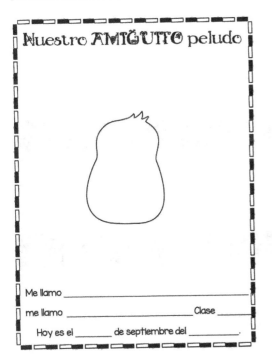

FIGURE 7.10.
Nuestro amiguito peludo Worksheet

Translation
Our furry little friend.
My name is ____ and my name is ____.
Class ____.
Today is the ____ of September ____.

Opening Routine

On the second day, the teacher once again opens class with the song *"Pongo una mano aquí"* [Put your hand here]. The teacher then shares the learning outcome and reviews the agenda.

Main Learning Episode

Students are reminded of what it means to be a good listener and to always try to climb the proficiency ladder when they speak. The teacher activates today's learning with the *¿Qué prefieres?* [What do you prefer?] routine where students see a prompt supported by images and then are asked to converse with their partner. They must ask each other if they prefer one item over the other and must justify their answer only using the Spanish that they know. These questions are usually silly in nature and do not necessarily connect to the theme of the lesson. They are intended to connect with students' interests and to spark creativity with the language.

After posing the question, the teacher gives students a sentence frame to guide their responses: *Prefiero tener... porque...* [I prefer to have ... because...]. They may also choose to provide a visual short word bank as an additional support. For today's lesson, the teacher asks students, *¿Prefieres tener pelo morado o dientes coloridos?* [Would you prefer to have purple hair or different colored teeth?] The teacher uses the shared Google Slide Presentation to provide visual support and reinforce the sentence structure and target vocabulary, as shown in Figure 7.9. Throughout this conversation, the teacher will reference the visuals in *Habla con tu compañero* (Figure 7.6) and *Mi escalera de español* (Figure 7.5).

The teacher then reminds students of the *Muñeco de fútbol* [soccer character] they created during the previous lesson, recalling what he looked like. The teacher explains that students will now work with a partner to collaboratively draw the missing body parts that they hear for a new friend, *nuestro amiguito peludo* [our furry little friend] (shown in Figure 7.10). The teacher hands out the worksheet and puts students in pairs because they will be drawing on the same sheet of paper. (In a remote learning environment, this activity can be completed using Google Jamboard.) Students will listen to the description of the *amiguito peludo* and take turns drawing the missing body parts. The teacher says, for example:

- *Nuestro amiguito peludo tiene cinco pies quietos.* [Our furry little friend has five still feet.]

- *Nuestro amiguito peludo tiene un mano tranquila.* [Our furry little friend has one calm hand.]

- *Nuestro amiguito peludo tiene dos cabezas pensando.* [Our furry little friend has two thinking heads.]

- *Nuestro amiguito peludo tiene seis ojos fijos.* [Our furry little friend has six focused eyes.]

After checking for comprehension, the teacher explains that students will now describe to their partner what their new friend looks like. The teacher reminds students of a simple question—*¿Cómo es nuestro amiguito peludo?* [What is our furry little friend like?]—and the sentence starter, *Tiene...* [He has...]

as a scaffold support for this interaction. One partner then begins the conversation by asking what the *amiguito peludo* is like, and the other responds. Students then switch roles. After a few minutes, the teacher invites students to show their drawings to the rest of the class and to silently look at everyone's work. The teacher holds a discussion about whether the drawings are the same or different. The teacher reminds students that even though they all heard the same description, our interpretations look different. Connecting to the unit theme, the teacher reinforces that no matter what we look like on the outside, we are all special on the inside. Students heard the same description of *nuestro amiguito peludo*, but their interpretation and experiences made it "look" different.

Closing Routine
The teacher then returns to the learning outcome and asks students for a thumbs-up/thumbs-down reflection on whether they feel they achieved the goal. The teacher closes class by asking students to stand and sing a song they have previously learned: *"Hay un amigo en mí"* [You've got a friend in me].

The images used in this lesson (Figures 7.3-7.10) were either created by Bárbara Barnett or purchased by her on TeachersPayTeachers.com from the following vendors:
- A Sketchy Guy
- Educlips
- Jax & Jake
- Kate Hadfield Designs

Classroom Close-Up 7.2: Examining Social Hierarchy Through Tableware
This classroom example was shared by Ikuko Yoshida, Japanese professor at Bennington College, Bennington, VT.

COURSE OVERVIEW	
Course Name	Modernizing the Nation: From the Edo Period to the Meiji Period
Course Proficiency Target	Intermediate Low
LESSON OVERVIEW	
Unit Theme	*Daily Living*
Lesson Learning Outcome	I can discuss how tableware is a reflection of social status.
Core Vocabulary and Forms	• Colors • Materials • Designs • Number • Shape • Items in a kitchen
Materials and Resources	• Images • 360 Augmented Reality Headsets (one per student) • 360 Video on the Edo period: https://youtu.be/mj7vtke81h8 • 360 Virtual Exhibit - Japanese Museum: https://www.edo-tokyo-museum.or.jp/panorama/en/

Social Justice Standards	*Diversity 9-12.7*	
	I have the language and knowledge to accurately and respectfully describe how people (including myself) are both similar to and different from each other and others in their identity groups.	
	Diversity 9-12.10	
	I understand that diversity includes the impact of unequal power relations on the development of group identities and cultures.	
Lesson Length	55 minutes	

LEARNING SEQUENCE		
Focus of Learning	Students view images of chopsticks with question prompts and discuss with a partner.	*Time:* 3 min
Preview of Learning	The teacher goes over the objective and agenda.	*Time:* 1 min
Learning Episode 1		
Primetime 1	1. The teacher asks for share-outs from the focus of learning activity. 2. Students do a short Turn and Talk to ask their partner about their own use of chopsticks. The teacher surveys students to ask for them to share. 3. Using a graphic organizer, students brainstorm key vocabulary in pairs. They then share out with the whole class.	*Time:* 7 min
Downtime	4. The teacher leads students in a whole-class discussion on the societal perspectives of different kinds of chopsticks, as well as other kinds of tableware, such as teapots.	*Time:* 10 min
Primetime 2	5. The teacher presents three images of three different kinds of chopsticks and puts students in small groups to make observations and discuss which country the chopsticks are used in. Students are asked to share their observations with the whole class.	*Time:* 5 min
Brain Break	Stretch break.	*Time:* 1 min
Learning Episode 2		
Primetime 1	6. The teacher shares two authentic resources (a video and a virtual museum tour). Students use their AR headsets to view the video and the museum tour. Students take notes on the tableware using a Venn diagram graphic organizer.	*Time:* 10 min
Downtime	7. Students work in small groups to discuss what they learned in the authentic resources. Students are provided with sentence starters and discussion prompts.	*Time:* 6 min

Primetime 2	8. Students share out to the whole-class. 9. The teacher leads a whole class discussion around social status and tableware using images. The teacher connects the discussion to American tableware as well.	*Time:* 10 min
Check for Learning	As an exit ticket, the teacher projects four new images of chopsticks and has students write who the chopsticks would belong to.	*Time:* 1 min
Celebration of Learning	The teacher returns to the learning outcome and asks for feedback.	*Time:* 1 min

In this Intermediate-Low course, students practice linguistic skills while also developing a deeper understanding of Japanese history and society. Early in the course, students learn about the Edo Period, a time which was marked by Japan's isolation from the outside world. Then they compare this with the Meiji Period when Japan was influenced by Western culture. By analyzing different cultural products—such as chopsticks or houses—students reflect on how one event in history can have reverberations both within Japan and throughout the world and examine how drastic social and cultural changes have formed the foundation of modern Japanese society. This lesson utilizes a variety of images to help students with limited linguistic skills understand unfamiliar objects and obtain a deeper understanding of the content.

The class is 1 hour and 50 minutes long and meets twice a week, but the lesson presented here is for half of a class. The class additionally uses Augmented Reality (AR) to explore cultural products. Each student has access to an AR headset such as a Google Cardboard 3D headset. In order to use the headset, each student must have a smartphone to attach it to.

As students join the class, they view images of chopsticks with some discussion questions, shown in Figure 7.11. Students discuss briefly with their partner as class begins. In a remote class, students post responses in the chat.

The teacher begins class by reviewing the learning outcome and agenda, seen in Figure 7.12. The teacher then asks students to share their comments from the warm-up discussion. The teacher may also bring chopsticks to class to show the students in addition to the photos.

The teacher asks students to Turn and Talk with a partner to ask them about their own use of chopsticks (in a remote class, students are placed in breakout rooms). After a few minutes of discussion, the teacher surveys the students to see what exposure to chopsticks they have had. The teacher follows up by asking students to share their opinions about chopsticks or describe a time when they used them.

Before going into the historical context of chopsticks, the teacher reviews the vocabulary needed to describe and differentiate between the types of chopsticks students will encounter later in the lesson. Students work in pairs (by Turn and Talk in class or a breakout room in remote teaching) to brainstorm a list of vocabulary words with categories such as number, color, shape, or material and design, using the graphic organizer in Figure 7.13. The teacher can also have the students look at different chopsticks using Google Arts and Culture's AR app, which the students can download onto their phones. Seeing the chopsticks in AR allows the students to zoom in and see the chopsticks in more detail.

Students share out the vocabulary they have generated. The teacher then leads them in a discussion around the societal use of chopsticks, asking questions such as, *Which members of society might use which kind of chopsticks? How might this perspective be different for Japanese and Americans?* This discussion helps students acknowledge their cultural lens and articulate how it might differ from a Japanese perspective. The teacher uses images of other kinds of tableware, such as teapots, to expand the discussion (Figure 7.14).

パートナーに聞きましょう。

1. お箸を使いますか。

2. よくお箸を使いますか。（毎日・よく・たいてい・ときどき・あまり・ぜんぜん）

3. お箸でどんな食べ物を食べますか。

4. お箸のどんなところが好きですか。

FIGURE 7.11.
Background Knowledge Slide

Translation
Find out if your partner uses chopsticks.
1. Do you use chopsticks?
2. How often do you use them? (everyday/often/usually/sometimes/not much/never)
3. What kinds of foods do you eat with chopsticks?
4. What do you like about chopsticks?

学習課題

Objective: I can discuss how tableware is a reflection of social status.

1. お箸についてパートナーと話す
2. お箸やその他の物の特徴を描写する
3. お箸やその他の物を観察し、それらがどのアジアの国の物か認識する
4. 様々な日本人が使用するお箸を比較する
5. お箸が様々な人々どの様に使用されるか

Extension Activity: Describe how the houses in Yokohama reflect changes in Japanese society

FIGURE 7.12.
Objective and Agenda Slide

Translation
Objective: I can discuss how tableware is a reflection of social status.
1. Talk with my partner about chopsticks
2. Describe the characteristics of chopsticks and other objects
3. Observe an image and identify which Asian country the items are from
4. Compare and contrast the tableware between different individuals in Japanese society
5. Compare practices between Japan and their community
Extension Activity: Describe how the houses in Yokohama reflect changes in Japanese society

お箸を描写するための単語を確認しましょう。

数	
色	
形	
材料	
デザイン	

FIGURE 7.13.
Slide of Categorization Graphic Organizer

Identify the words you need to describe the chopsticks.
Number
Color
Shape
Material
Design

お箸と食器類

これらはどの様に使いますか。(使用目的)	
だれが使いますか。(性別, 年齢, 職業, 社会的地位など)	
いつ使いますか。(日時, 行事など)	

FIGURE 7.14.
Tableware Objects and Their Uses Slide

Translation
Chopsticks and other tableware...
What are these objects used for? (purpose)
Who uses them? (gender, age, occupation, social rank, etc.)
When do they use them? (time, date, occasions)

The teacher then shows students images of three different types of chopsticks (Figure 7.15) and asks them to discuss which chopsticks came from which country—Japan, China, or Korea—and explain why they think so. Students discuss in small groups. The purpose of this task is to show that although people in these three countries use chopsticks, the historical context behind each type is unique to that culture. For example, chopsticks with ivory were used in China because ivory came through the Silk Road.

どこの国の食器か見分けましょう。

a. この3つの食器の写真を見てください。この3つの写真に共通していることを探しましょう。
b. では、この3つの食器の写真を比べて、何が違いますか。
c. 日本の食器は、どれですか。
d. どうしてその食器は日本の食器だと思いますか。
e. 中国の食器はどれですか。
f. どうしてその食器は中国の食器だと思いますか。
g. 韓国の食器はどれですか。
h. どうしてその食器は韓国の食器だと思いますか。
i. ペアになって、自分の予想とパートナーの予想が同じか聞きましょう。

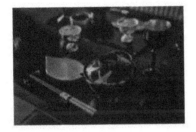  

FIGURE 7.15.
Chopsticks from Different Countries Slide

Translation
Identify which country this tableware is from.
    a. Look at the 3 images below. What are the similarities that you observe in these images?
    b. By contrasting and comparing the images, what are the differences?
    c. Which one is from Japan?
    d. Why do you think so?
    e. Which one is from China?
    f. Why do you think so?
    g. Which one is from Korea?
    h. Why do you think so?
    i. In pairs check your hypotheses to see if they match with your partner's ones.

After a short stretch break, the teacher uses two authentic resources to give students more information to inform the discussion. First, the teacher shows a video (https://youtu.be/mj7vtke81h8) of a house where a shogun (one of the military rulers who governed Japan from 1185 to 1868) used to live. While watching the video, students take notes using a Venn diagram graphic organizer, shown in Figure 7.16. Students are asked to pay close attention to the kitchen and take note of the utensils and other objects on the table. Next, the teacher asks students to visit the Edo-Tokyo Museum's virtual exhibit (https://www.edo-tokyo-museum.or.jp/panorama/en/) that shows a 360-degree view of a farmer's house from the Edo Period. The students observe the house and finish filling out the graphic organizer.

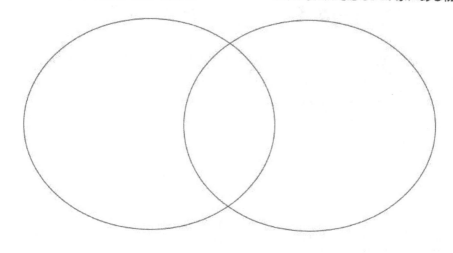

FIGURE 7.16.
Venn Diagram Graphic Organizer

Translation
Compare tableware between two houses from the Edo Period.
Farmer's house
Samurai's house

Working in small groups, students now use what they have learned from the video and the virtual museum visit to compare the two kitchens and the different kinds of tableware they saw being used in each. The teacher provides a list of sentence starters, transitions, and connecting words to scaffold the discussion (Figure 7.17). After a few minutes, the teacher asks a few students to share their observations with the class.

The teacher now leads the class in another discussion in which students use the knowledge from the authentic resources they have explored to discuss their understanding of the social hierarchy in Japan. The teacher presents relevant the images shown in Figure 7.18 and students discuss who each set of chopsticks would belong to and why. Students are asked to justify their answers and support them with details.

The teacher shifts the discussion to encourage students to reflect on their own culture, using images of table settings from American culture (Figure 7.19). The teacher asks, for example, if the tableware reflects social status in the students' culture as well. Students are asked who would use these table settings, when, and where.

The teacher closes this portion of the class by referring to the learning outcome and showing four new images of chopsticks. Students write on an index card (or post in the chat for a remote class) with a short explanation of the social status or country of origin of the chopsticks.

さむらいの家と農民・商人の家の
共通点と相違点を述べよう。

Sentence Starters
農民・商人の家は…。
武士の家は…。

Connectors
NounとNoun
Verbて、Verb
NounもVerb
――が、――。 Or ――――。しかし、――。
――から、――――。

Transitions
まず，
次に，
それから、そして、，
最後に，

FIGURE 7.17.
Discussion Prompt and Scaffolds

Translation
Describe how the houses are similar and different.

Sentence Starters	Connectors	Transitions
Farmer's house is…	*Noun, Noun*	*First*
Samurai's house is…	*Verb, verb*	*Then*
	Noun, verb	*Next*
	but	*Finally*
	or	
	however	
	from	

下のお箸は、だれのお箸だと思いますか。
それは、どうしてですか。

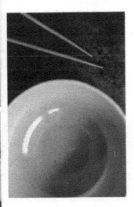

FIGURE 7.18.
Images of Chopsticks to Discuss Social Status

Translation
Identify who these chopsticks belong to and explain why.

ペアワーク

江戸時代の社会階級について勉強しましたが、今、自分が住んでいる地域社会と共通点・相違点があります か。それは、何ですか。

FIGURE 7.19.
Cultural Images of Tableware from American Culture

Translation
Pair Discussion
After learning about the hierarchy during the Edo Period in Japan, do you see any similarities/ differences to the society where you live now? How so?

Reflection and Next Steps

In this chapter, we explored culturally responsive and sustaining pedagogy to begin consideration of approaches to integrating culture in language courses. We also looked at teaching for social justice and the Social Justice Standards, discussing how the many strategies and models we have looked at in this book can support a focus on issues of social justice. Social-emotional learning (SEL) can also be integrated in teaching, rather than being considered an add-on. The NCSSFL-ACTFL Can-Do Statements focusing on Intercultural Communicative Competence (ICC) help us identify what learners of different proficiency levels are able to do when they investigate and interact on important topics. In our two *Classroom Close-Up* examples, we showed how teachers of two different languages and levels applied these important principles and perspectives in their own classes.

Before moving on, take some time to reflect and assess your own practice. Consider how you are applying or would like to apply the topics discussed in this chapter. Where are your strengths? Where would you like to grow your practice? What actions will you take to move forward? This one-point rubric is designed to help you reflect and assess your own teaching when considering the content of your instruction, using input and interaction strategies from throughout this book.

One-Point Rubric: *Considering Critical Perspectives and Input and Interaction*

GLOW *Where are my strengths related to this practice?*	CRITERIA *What should I be looking for in my own teaching?*	GROW *Where do I need to grow or expand my practice?*	TAKE ACTION *What steps will I take to move my practice forward?*
	I can define culturally relevant and culturally sustaining pedagogy and objectively critique how I am teaching culture in my classes.		
	I can summarize the Social Justice Standards and consider how to reframe some traditional topics to focus on issues of social justice in my classes.		
	I can explain CASEL's Framework for Social and Emotional Learning and identity and implement specific strategies to integrate social-emotional learning in my classes.		
	I can use strategies and models (discussed throughout this book) to maintain the target language and support student target-language use while focusing on social emotional learning and issues of social justice.		
	I can define Intercultural Communicative Competence (ICC) and use the NCSFSFL-ACTFL Can-Do Statements to describe what learners at different proficiency levels can do as they investigate and interact.		

Level Up Your Learning

- **Teaching Tolerance. (2018).** *Social justice standards: The teaching tolerance anti-bias framework.* **The Southern Poverty Law Center. https://www.learningforjustice.org/sites/default/files/2020-09/TT-Social-Justice-Standards-Anti-bias-framework-2020.pdf**
  The Social Justice Standards are available at no cost online. The four anchor domains discussed in this chapter each include a number of specific descriptors. These are broken down for various age groups to make them easily applicable to different educational levels.

- **CASEL. (2021).** *What is SEL?* **https://casel.org/what-is-sel/**
  If you would like to learn more about social-emotional learning, the CASEL framework is fully available online, along with numerous resources including webinars, program guides, research, and newsletters.

- **Reagan, T. G., & Osborn, T. A. (2021).** *World language education as critical pedagogy: The promise of social justice.* **Routledge.**

In addition to *Words and Actions: Teaching Languages Through the Lens of Social Justice* (Glynn, Wesley, & Wassell, 2014), this book provides an excellent entry point to teaching for social justice in world language education. Its aim is less practical than that of *Words and Actions,* but it provides much needed background and thought-provoking research and discussion to explore critical issues and demonstrate the importance of teaching for social justice in world language education.

Chapter 7 References

ACTFL. (2012). *ACTFL proficiency guidelines.* http://www.actfl.org/sites/default/files/pdfs/public/ACTFLProficiencyGuidelines2012_FINAL.pdf

ACTFL. (2017). *NCSSFL-ACTFL can-do statements: Performance indicators for language learners.* https://www.actfl.org/publications/guidelines-and-manuals/ncssfl-actfl-can-do-statements

CASEL. (2021). *What is SEL?* https://casel.org/what-is-sel/

Frey, N., Fisher, D., & Smith, D. (2019). *All learning is social and emotional: Helping students develop essential skills for the classroom and beyond.* ASCD.

Glynn, C., Wesley, P., & Wassell, B. (2014). *Words and actions: Teaching languages through the lens of social justice* (2nd ed.). ACTFL.

Ladson-Billings, G. (2014). Culturally relevant pedagogy 2.0: a.k.a the remix. *Harvard Educational Review, 84*(1), 74-84.

Martell, C. C., & Stevens, K. M. (2021). *Teaching history for justice: Centering activism in students' study of the past.* Teachers College Press.

National Standards Collaborative Board. (2015). *World-Readiness Standards for Learning Languages* (4th ed.). National Standards Collaborative Board

Nieto, S. (2010). *Language, culture, and teaching: Critical perspectives* (2nd ed.). Routledge.

Reagan, T. G., & Osborn, T. A. (2021). *World language education as critical pedagogy: The promise of social justice.* Routledge.

Sadker, D. (n.d.). Some practical ideas for confronting curricular bias. https://www.sadker.org/curricularbias.html

Saldívar García, E., & Manuel, M. (2020). Implementing trauma-informed principles in the remote Spanish classroom during the Coronavirus pandemic. *The Language Educator, 15*(3), 16-22.

Style, E. (1996). Curriculum as window and mirror. *Social Sciences Record.* http://www.nationalseedproject.org/images/documents/Curriculum_As_Window_and_Mirror.pdf

Teaching Tolerance. (2018). *Social justice standards: The teaching tolerance anti-bias framework.* Southern Poverty Law Center. https://www.learningforjustice.org/sites/default/files/2020-09/TT-Social-Justice-Standards-Anti-bias-framework-2020.pdf

Wagner, M., Cardetti, F., & Bryam, M. (2019). *Teaching intercultural citizenship across the curriculum: The role of language education.* ACTFL.

CHAPTER 8

Moving from Input to Interaction

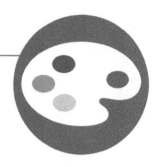

T hroughout this book, we have looked at numerous models and strategies to support a classroom where target-language use—through input and interaction—is the norm. Many of the models we have looked at, such as the Interactive Model for Interpretive Communication and the Gradual Release of Responsibility Model, can be used to effectively move students from receiving language input to producing language through interaction. In addition, many of the *Classroom Close-Ups* have integrated both language input and student interaction in one lesson. These chapters and lesson examples may have already given you a good idea of how to move students along the input-to-interaction continuum. In this final chapter, we will look more closely at learning sequences that move intentionally from input to interaction, and perhaps also to output in the presentational mode, which has not been the focus of this book. We will look at the Integrated Performance Assessment (IPA) and consider how to use it as a design framework for a unit or learning sequence. Our *Classroom Close-Ups* will walk you through how an elementary school teacher and a university lecturer each approach designing learning sequences. Careful planning and sequencing will support your learners in effectively moving from receiving input to engaging in meaningful interaction in the target language.

The IPA as a Design Framework

An Integrated Performance Assessment (IPA) is a sequence of assessments focused on each of the three modes of communication: interpretive, interpersonal, and presentational. Students engage in an interpretive assessment task in which they read or listen to an authentic resource and are assessed based on their comprehension and interpretation. Students then use what they have learned from the reading or listening resource to engage in an interpersonal task with a classmate. Finally, students create a product (presentational communication) that integrates learning from the interpretive and interpersonal assessment tasks (see Adair-Hauck, Glisan, & Troyan, 2013, for more information on the IPA). Figure 8.1 presents a graphic summary of the IPA framework.

While the IPA was designed as an assessment tool, it also provides a framework that can be used to design curriculum and instruction, moving students from input to interaction. IPAs are typically written first by crafting an authentic frame, similar to the SCRAP Framework described in Chapter 5. However, IPAs integrate all three modes of communication, as well as the 5 Cs from the World-Readiness Standards for Learning Languages. As you read the frame below, see if you can identify the 5 Cs and the three modes of communication:

> You will be studying abroad next fall in Argentina as part of an exchange program through your high school. You and your friend have been in touch with a student from the high school in Argentina, who is going to be your host. The student from Argentina has asked the two of you if you are interested in joining an interest group at their school working to promote gender equality through the use of gender-inclusive language. Argentina is known for using gender-inclusive language in certain arenas, but still has a lot of work to do. To prepare for joining this group, you will do some research on gender equality, gender stereotypes, and inclusive language in Spanish. First, you will be reviewing information about gender equality

I. Interpretive Communication Phase
Students listen to or read an authentic text (e.g., newspaper article, radio broadcast, etc.) and answer information as well as interpretive questions to assess comprehension. (T) provides ss with feedback on performance.

III. Presentational Communication Phase
Students engage in presentational communication by sharing their research/ideas/options. Sample presentational formats: speeches, drama skits, radio broadcasts, posters, brochures, essays, websites, etc.

II. Interpersonal Communication Phase
After receiving feedback regarding Interpretive Phase, ss engaged in interpersonal oral communication about a particular topic which relates to the interpretive text. This phase should be either audio- or videotaped.

FIGURE 8.1.
Integrated Performance Assessment: A Cyclical Approach
Source: Adair-Hauck, Glisan, & Troyan, 2013, p. 10.

and inclusive language in Spanish-speaking countries. Next, you will be sharing your ideas with your classmate in Argentina, to find out what each of you has learned, and will be comparing your ideas. Finally, you will be creating a social media campaign to use at the school in Argentina, once you arrive in the fall. In the social media campaign, you will be creating a hashtag, a short video, and multiple content posts to share with the school to promote the use of gender-inclusive language to help combat gender inequality and stereotypes.
(A special thank you to Spanish teacher Francesca Crutchfield-Stoker, who developed this frame for a second-year Spanish class.)

Were you able to identify the 5 Cs and the three modes?

- Communication
    - Interpretive: "First, you will be reviewing information about gender equality and inclusive language in Spanish-speaking countries."

    - Interpersonal: "Next, you will be sharing your ideas with your classmate in Argentina, to find out what each of you has learned, and will be comparing your ideas."

    - Presentational: "Finally, you will be creating a social media campaign to use at the school in Argentina, once you arrive in the fall. In the social media campaign, you will be creating a hashtag, a short video, and multiple content posts to share with the school to promote the usage of gender-inclusive language to help combat gender inequality and stereotypes."

- Cultures: Students will review information about gender equality and inclusive language in Spanish-speaking countries, with a particular focus on Argentina.

- Connections: Students will conduct research on gender equality and inclusive language in Spanish-speaking countries, which connects to Social Studies content.

- Comparisons: Students will compare their findings on different Spanish-speaking countries.

- Communities: Students will create a social media campaign, shared on the teacher's website or other online platforms.

This example demonstrates how the IPA frame can serve as the outline for an entire unit. Students begin with a focus on interpretive communication in which they explore authentic resources to build vocabulary and knowledge on the topic of gender equality and inclusivity. They then shift to a stronger focus on interpersonal communication, discussing and sharing findings from various resources with classmates. Finally, they focus on presentational communication by preparing their social media campaigns and getting feedback from the teacher and their classmates. You may choose to sequence an IPA so that interpersonal is the final mode rather than presentational, but this will depend on your goals for the unit and for your learners. The next section looks more closely at how an IPA frame can be used to build a learning sequence to move students from input to interaction.

Developing a Learning Sequence

Input: Interpretive Listening and Reading

Providing input and engaging students in interpretive communication should be the starting point for any unit or learning sequence design. As noted in previous chapters, the input that teachers provide through use of the target language and authentic resources is necessary for language acquisition. Learners need a substantial amount of target-language input in order to make sense of the language, build vocabulary, and recognize language patterns that will enable them to produce the language themselves. Using the IPA as a framework, you can design the first phase of a learning sequence with a strong emphasis on input.

However, focusing primarily on input at the beginning of a learning sequence does not mean that you should not also engage students in language production through interpersonal or presentational communication. As you saw in *Classroom Close-Up 2.1*, students can begin using the language on day one of a first-year class. Indeed, it would be an unusual class where students sat mute as they listened to the teacher or read and listened to authentic resources silently. Any lesson will likely involve more than one mode of communication, and students will both receive input and engage in interaction.

Interaction: Interpersonal Speaking and Listening

After students have received sufficient input, the primary focus of instruction shifts to engaging students in interpersonal interaction in which students use what they have learned from the authentic resources, as well as the vocabulary, grammar, and discourse patterns addressed in the learning sequence, to discuss what they have learned in meaningful ways. As demonstrated in Chapters 5 and 6, at this stage students will need scaffolding support, expectations for target-language use when working in pairs or small groups, and a focus on authentic communication. During this phase students may also continue exploring authentic resources for use in their discussions. Recall that the Interactive Model for Interpretive Communication discussed in Chapter 3 includes both engaging in reading or listening to an authentic resource (Comprehension Phase) and discussing it with classmates (Interpretation/Discussion Phase).

Output: Presentational Speaking and Writing

As the culminating component of the learning sequence, students then engage in presentational communication. According to the IPA Framework, students use their learning from the interpretive and interpersonal phases in the products they create for this final step. They may be asked to write a polished essay, short story, comic book, or any other creative written product that connects to the theme of the learning sequence, or to prepare a polished speaking product, such as a video, a short play that they write and act out, or a report that is presented to the class.

Figure 8.2 provides a graphic summary of how a learning sequence can intentionally move students from input (interpretive) to interaction (interpersonal) to output (presentational).

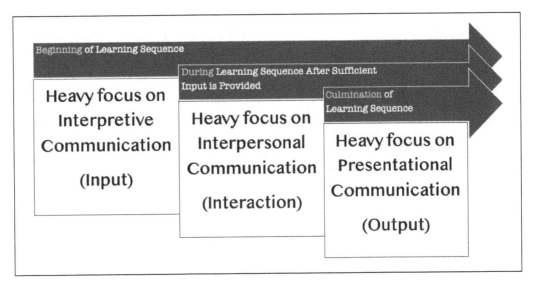

FIGURE 8.2.
Learning Sequence Guide

Tech Zoom

This *Tech Zoom* focuses on how to integrate technology to assess students, whatever learning model (in-person, hybrid, or remote) you may be using. Prior to the COVID-19 pandemic, it would be fair to say that the majority of assessments students took were on paper. Teachers would find themselves taking home big stacks of papers or tests to grade, along with some student audio samples. The pandemic has pushed teachers to adapt and find new ways to assess students virtually, and many have discovered that technology actually allows them to provide feedback to learners more effectively and efficiently. Here are a few platforms that can help make assessing and providing feedback across the three modes of communication easier than ever.

- Assessing Interpretive (Input)
  - Google Forms: If you are in a school district that uses Google, you already have access to this easy-to-use tool. You can build reading and listening assessments, and with quiz mode you can quickly score students' responses. There is also space to provide individualized feedback.

  - Edpuzzle: This platform can be used for listening assessments. Like Google Forms, it allows you to give students immediate feedback.

- Assessing Interpersonal (Interaction)
  - Formative: This tool can be used to integrate interpretive and interpersonal communication easily. You can upload a visual or an infographic for students to read, or an audio file for students to listen to, adding prompts for students to respond to. Students record their responses to the prompts after reading or listening to the authentic resource. While this is a simulation of a truly interpersonal interaction, this type of assignment can be easier to administer and mirrors how learners are assessed for interpersonal communication on the Advanced Placement language exams.

  - Extempore: This cloud-based platform allows teachers to create speaking prompts that students can respond to. You can leave either written or spoken feedback on student responses. Extempore is also a great way for students to see their progress throughout the year, since all the oral assessments are housed on the platform.

- Assessing Presentational (Output)
  - Kaizena and Mote: These tools allow you to leave feedback on students' work using voice comments. Leaving voice comments is often faster than writing

feedback, and students can hear your feedback in a more personalized way. You can also turn these tools into a more interactive format if you ask students to respond orally to your comments.

Now that we have looked at the IPA as a framework for designing a learning sequence to move students from input to interaction to output, we are going to walk through two *Classroom Close-Ups* that show how teachers of two different languages working with students of two different proficiency levels apply this framework in their own teaching. In *Classroom Close-Up 8.2*, we will also show how the teacher adapts the learning sequence for a hybrid or distance learning environment.

Classroom Close-Ups
Classroom Close-Up 8.1: Les dinosaures
This classroom example was shared by Allison Litten, French teacher at the Marion Cross School, Norwich, VT.

COURSE OVERVIEW	
Course Name	First-Grade French (second year of language, FLES program)
Course Proficiency Target	Novice Mid

LESSON OVERVIEW	
Unit Theme	*Les dinosaures (Dinosaurs)*
Day 1 Lesson Learning Outcome	I can identify different kinds of dinosaurs and their characteristics.
Day 2 Lesson Learning Outcome	I can compare and contrast dinosaurs based on size, eating habits, and movement.
Day 3 Lesson Learning Outcome	I can provide information about dinosaurs by asking and answering a few simple questions using a mixture of practiced or memorized words, phrases, and simple sentences.
Day 4 Lesson Learning Outcome	I can provide information about an authentic resource by asking and answering a few simple questions using a mixture of practiced or memorized words, phrases, and simple sentences.
Day 5 Lesson Learning Outcome	I can describe images using a mixture of practiced or memorized words, phrases, and simple sentences.
Day 6 Lesson Learning Outcome	I can draw images that relate to simple text to show my understanding of the written text.
Day 7 Lesson Learning Outcome	I can provide and request information about an authentic resource by asking and answering a few simple questions using a mixture of practiced or memorized words, phrases, and simple sentences.

Core Vocabulary and Forms	• Names of different dinosaurs
	• Action words
	• Adjectives of size
Materials and Resources	• Videos: "T'choupi à l'école - Papi au temps des dinosaures" https://www.youtube.com/watch?v=c6C2bh71skQ
	• Play food items
Lesson Length	Each class session is 30 minutes long.

FIGURE 8.3.
Slide Introducing Dinosaur, Sample 1

Translation
Pteranodon:
• He is big.
• He has two feet.
• He flies.

FIGURE 8.4.
Slide Introducing Dinosaur, Sample 2

Translation
Stegosaurus:
• He is enormous.
• He has four feet.
• He walks.

This lesson sequence takes place in a first-grade FLES (Foreign Languages in Elementary School) French program. Each class session is 30 minutes long. The teacher begins with a heavy emphasis on oral language input, using vocabulary in context and screenshots from an authentic video, then moves to more of an emphasis on written language input, and finally has students write and interact using the vocabulary and structures in context.

Day 1
The teacher begins by presenting the student learning outcome. Using body language, the teacher reviews vocabulary that students have previously learned, such as *jump, swim, run,* and *fly*. Students act out these actions when they hear them. The teacher then shows images of dinosaurs (Figures 8.3 and 8.4) and asks students simple yes/no questions about them: *Comment s'appelle ce dinosaure?* [What is this dinosaur called?] *Il a combien de pattes?* [How many feet does he have?] *Il est grand ou petit?* [Is he big or small?] *Il marche ou il vole?* [Does he walk or fly?]

The teacher then introduces a game: *What's in the box?* The teacher asks students, *Qu'est-ce qu'il y a dans le carton?* [What's in the box?] and pulls out different plastic food items. Students have previously learned food words, so this is a review and anticipates an important component of the story they will watch on the following day

Day 2
The teacher begins by presenting the student learning outcome, and then shows slides similar to those from Day 1. The teacher reviews the dinosaurs that were discussed on Day 1 and introduces a few new ones. The teacher again engages students in the *What's in the box?* game using different kinds of plastic food. The teacher has prepared slides with screenshots from the video *T'choupi à l'école - Papi au temps des dinosaures* (https://www.youtube.com/watch?v=c6C2bh71skQ) [T'choupi at school – Grandpa during the time of dinosaurs]. Using the screenshots, the teacher narrates the story from the video using comprehensible language. In this story, T'choupi's grandfather is coming to his class to speak about dinosaurs. The children have seen him looking through a box and talking to whatever is inside it, and they wonder whether there are baby dinosaurs in the box.

After narrating the story using the screenshots, the teacher plays the video for the first time, pausing frequently to ask simple questions, such as: *Comment s'appellent les amis de T'choupi?* [What are T'choupi's friends' names?] *Avec quels types de dinosaures jouent T'choupi et son ami?* [What kind of dinosaurs do T'choupi and his friend play with?] *Qu'est-ce qu'il y a dans le carton? Que pense T'choupi?* [What's in the box? What does T'choupi think?] *Qui pense qu'il a un vrai dinosaure dans le carton?* [Who thinks there is a real dinosaur in the box?] The teacher then plays the video a second time, this time without stopping.

Day 3

The focus today is to repeat and re-emphasize the language from the first two days. The teacher begins by presenting the student learning outcome and then playing the *What's in the box?* game, this time with different kinds of objects that students know, not just food. The teacher then introduces the video from Day 2 and plays it again. The teacher uses the same screenshots of the video that were used the day before to preview the video. This time, however, the teacher asks students questions about each screen shot, including yes/no, either/or, or who/what/where/when questions. The teacher may ask students to respond as a whole class, or Turn and Talk to their partner before sharing their response.

Day 4

The teacher now shifts to a focus on written language, first presenting the student learning outcome. The teacher has prepared a sentence to describe each screenshot from the video, such as: *T'choupi arrive à l'école avec des biscuits en forme de dinosaures!* [T'choupi arrives at school with biscuits in the shape of dinosaurs!] *Les herbivores mangent des plantes et les carnivores mangent les animaux.* [Herbivores eat plants and carnivores eat animals.] *Papi arrive à l'école avec deux cartons.* [Grandpa arrives at school with two boxes.] The teacher presents the slide with the written sentence first, reading it aloud to the class, then forwards the slide to make the corresponding image appear.

Day 5

The teacher reviews the sentences and images from Day 4 to start the class. The teacher then shows the images without the written sentences one by one, asking students to share what a sentence describing this image would be. The teacher continues showing images and asking students what is happening in each one, eliciting a simple sentence to describe the screenshot from the story.

Day 6

Today, the teacher begins by reviewing the Day 5 material, showing students the screenshots and asking for a simple sentence describing what is happening in each part of the story. The teacher then hands out a packet in which the written sentences from the story are printed along with a space for students to draw what is happening. Students draw images to match each sentence, as shown in Figures 8.5, 8.6, and 8.7. The packet serves as students' own version of the story.

Les herbivores mangent des plantes et les carnivores mangent les animaux.

FIGURE 8.5
Student Drawing, Sample 1

Translation
Herbivores eat plants and carnivores eat animals.

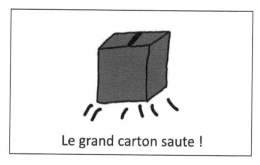

Le grand carton saute !

FIGURE 8.6
Student Drawing, Sample 1

Translation
The big box jumps!

Dans les cartons il y a des dinosaures mais pas les *vrai* dinosaures !

FIGURE 8.7.
Student Drawing, Sample 3

Translation
In the box there are dinosaurs but not real dinosaurs!

On the final day of this learning sequence, students engage in a book party in which they are asked to read the story from their packet and share the images they drew. This is done by putting students in pairs. Each student reads the story aloud and shows their drawings to the partner. After reading their stories, students ask each other questions about their stories by rolling a die and using the question word that matches the number they roll. Students have previously studied how to ask questions, so in this activity they are reusing knowledge from an earlier unit. The teacher provides question words and model questions as a scaffold for students (Figure 8.8).

Roll the die!
Ask a question about the story using the question word below that matches the number you roll!

1. **où**

   Où est T'choupi?

2. **qui**

   Qui est son ami?

3. **comment**

   Comment est le dinosaure?

4. **pourquoi (parce que)**

   Pourquoi Papi va à l'école?

5. **quoi**

   C'est quoi ça?

6. **À ton choix!**

FIGURE 8.8.
Question Word Scaffold

Translation
1. *where*
   Where is T'choupi?
2. *who*
   Who is his friend?
3. *how*
   What is the dinosaur like?

4. *why (because)*
   Why does Papi go to school?
5. *what*
   What is that?
6. *Your choice!*

Classroom Close-Up 8.2: What is good health?

This classroom example was shared by Borja Ruiz de Arbulo Alonso, Senior Lecturer in Spanish at the Boston University College of Arts and Sciences, Boston, MA.

COURSE OVERVIEW	
Course Name	Spanish for the Professions (300-level university course)
Course Proficiency Target	Advanced Low-Mid

LESSON OVERVIEW	
Unit Theme	Health Care
Day 1 (synchronous) Lesson Learning Outcome	I can describe what healthy elements are within my community using detailed ideas in connected paragraphs with clear organization and across all time frames.
Day 2 (synchronous) Lesson Learning Outcome	I can describe and elaborate on various ways to take care of mental health using concrete, well-connected examples.
Day 3 (asynchronous) Lesson Learning Outcome	I can react to and compare preferences and opinions about the impact of the environment on our mental health in detail.
Day 4 (synchronous) Lesson Learning Outcome	I can identify and describe major cardiovascular diseases using technical vocabulary in complete, connected sentences.
Day 5 (synchronous) Lesson Learning Outcome	I can identify and describe major neurological diseases using technical vocabulary in complete, connected sentences.
Day 6 (asynchronous) Lesson Learning Outcome	I can identify and describe major mental health disorders and their perception in society by using technical vocabulary in complete, connected sentences.
Core Vocabulary and Forms	• Vocabulary related to health and well-being • The verbs *estar, ser, tener,* and *haber* • *por* and *para* (two ways to say *for*)
Materials and Resources	Authentic materials: • https://cnnespanol.cnn.com/2020/09/22/esta-es-la-comunidad-mas-saludable-de-ee-uu-este-es-el-porque/ • https://www.infobae.com/america/tendencias-america/2020/10/10/no-hay-salud-fisica-sin-buena-salud-mental-la-reivindicacion-del-bienestar-emocional-en-tiempos-de-covid-19/ • https://www.nimh.nih.gov/health/publications/espanol/index.shtml • https://www.youtube.com/watch?v=OmLu1tZJyj0 • https://www.eluniverso.com/noticias/2020/09/28/nota/7993780/como-reconocer-enfermedades-cardiovasculares/ • https://medicoplus.com/neurologia/enfermedades-neurologicas-mas-comunes • https://www.youtube.com/watch?v=EOpLHOMyXng&t=6s
Lesson Length	Each class is 50 minutes long.

This example provides a 2-week learning sequence, with three class meetings per week, two of which are synchronous (meeting over Zoom or in person) and one asynchronous (with students given an independent learning task to complete on their own).

The first week of the sequence focuses on perceptions of health, what it means to be healthy, how people usually seek support for their health and well-being, and how the environment may influence health. The primary focus this week is on interpretive communication, with students reading numerous authentic articles and viewing authentic videos, including TedX Talks or YouTube videos on the topic. Students also engage in interpersonal communication during class time to discuss the authentic resources. They are expected to read or listen to material as homework beforehand, with the goal of having some familiarity with the theme prior to the class session. The bulk of the analytical work, however, is done during class time through interaction and discussion.

The second week of the learning sequence focuses on students identifying various major health threats (cardiovascular and neurological) as well as how to deliver care to less privileged communities.

Week 1, Day 1 (synchronous)

In this first class, students are presented with input related to elements of health in different communities. As a daily routine, the teacher uses images to open the class and begin discussion connected to the topic (see the example in Figure 8.9).

FIGURE 8.9.
Warm-Up Images for Class Discussion

Students have read an article about the healthiest community in the United States (https://cnnespanol.cnn.com/2020/09/22/esta-es-la-comunidad-mas-saludable-de-ee-uu-este-es-el-porque) prior to coming to class. Class time is used to break the article into smaller chunks for students to read more closely and discuss in detail. The teacher integrates regular pair and group work throughout the class session to discuss aspects of the reading, before shifting to focus on students' local community. Students are given discussion prompts (Figure 8.10) to consider how their local community supports health and well-being.

1. ¿Cómo es tu barrio de Boston en términos de salud? Explica por qué.
2. ¿Hay oportunidades para ser voluntario en tu barrio?
3. ¿Tiene la gente una titulación académica avanzada?
4. ¿Está ese barrio cerca de espacios verdes/ naturaleza?

FIGURE 8.10.
Discussion Prompts

Translation
1. *What is your Boston neighborhood like in terms of health? Explain why.*
2. *Are there volunteer opportunities in your neighborhood?*
3. *Do people in your neighborhood have advanced academic degrees?*
4. *Is your neighborhood close to green spaces/nature?*

Week 1, Day 2 (synchronous)

Having completed another reading on the topic prior to class, students again engage in deeper reading and discussion during class time. The teacher presents a few infographics (see example in Figure 8.11) to provide further information and details. Students are invited to use the authentic text they read prior to class and the in-class infographics to describe reasons why humans' health might suffer. Students additionally work in pairs to identify and elaborate on tips to improve mental health using concrete examples.

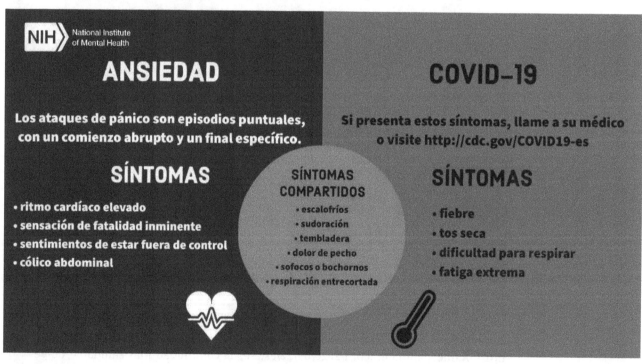

FIGURE 8.11.
Sample Infographic
Source: National Institute of Mental Health, n.d.

Week 1, Day 3 (asynchronous)

Working independently, students watch a TedX video on the impact of social media on mental health (https://www.youtube.com/watch?v=OmLu1tZJyj0). Students then use Flipgrid to record a response to the questions shown in Figure 8.12. Students must also listen to their peers' responses and reply to at least two classmates by offering similarities as well as contrasts to them. Students are given a sentence starter to use for this response (also shown in Figure 8.12).

---

1. ¿Usas redes sociales con frecuencia?
2. ¿Qué red social usas más? ¿Hay alguna más útil que otra?
3. ¿Cambian tus emociones cuando usas las redes sociales?
4. Responde a tus compañer@s, y ofrece un contraste...
    1. ¡Yo también! Sin embargo...
    2. ¡A mí también! Pero...

FIGURE 8.12.
FlipGrid Discussion Questions

Translation
1. Do you frequently use social media?
2. What social media platform do you use the most? Is one more useful than others?
3. Do your emotions change when you use social media?
4. Respond to your classmates and offer a contrast...
    1. Me too! Nevertheless...
    2. Me as well! But...

Week 2, Day 4 (synchronous)

Students have read an authentic article on the topic of cardiovascular disease prior to class (https://www.eluniverso.com/noticias/2020/09/28/nota/7993780/como-reconocer-enfermedades-cardiovasculares). The teacher begins class by highlighting parts of the reading and guides students in making contrasts using two sentence frames, shown in Figure 8.13.

= sin embargo

Los problemas cardiovasculares son muy comunes. No obstante, se pueden prevenir.

A pesar de que los problemas cardiovasculares son muy comunes, se pueden prevenir.

FIGURE 8.13.
Sentence Frames for Making Contrasts

Translation
Contrast
Cardiovascular problems are very common. Nevertheless, they can be prevented.
Despite the fact that cardiovascular problems are very common, they can be prevented.

Students are then placed in groups to investigate the reading more deeply and collect information on important aspects of cardiovascular disease. Students record their information on a Google Jamboard (shown in Figure 8.14), and then present their findings to the whole class.

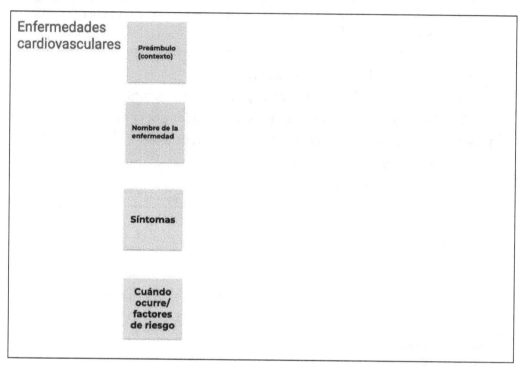

FIGURE 8.14.
Google Jamboard for Recording Information on Cardiovascular Disease

Translation
Cardiovascular illnesses
- *Preamble (context)*
- *Name of the illness*
- *Symptoms*
- *When it occurs/risk factors*

Week 2, Day 5 (synchronous)

Prior to class, students have read another article (https://medicoplus.com/neurologia/enfermedades-neurologicas-mas-comunes), this time focusing on common neurological diseases. The teacher uses class time to discuss the assigned reading and present new data on cause of death and neurological diseases. The teacher asks students questions such as:

- *¿Qué enfermedades del artículo ya conocías?* [What illnesses from the article did you already know?]

- *¿Qué puedes decir de ella?* [What can you say about them?]

- *¿Piensas que hablamos suficientemente de las enfermedades neurodegenerativas?* [Do you think that we talk enough about neurological diseases?]

Students then work in small groups to discuss the information from the reading and determine cause and effect of certain neurological diseases. The teacher has created a Google Jamboard for students to record their work and provides both a model and a word bank to serve as scaffolds for their work (Figure 8.15). Students present their findings to the whole class for discussion.

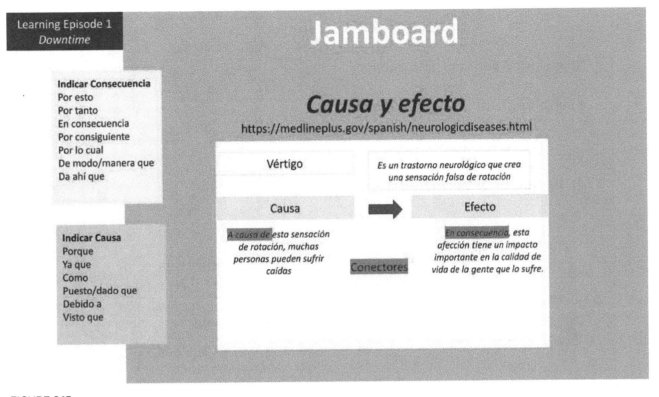

FIGURE 8.15.
Google Jamboard for Recording Information on Neurological Diseases

Translation
(Left-Hand Column)
To Indicate Consequences
- *For this*
- *Therefore*
- *Consequently*
- *Therefore*
- *Whereby*
- *So that*
- *Hence*

To Indicate Cause
- *Because*
- *As*
- *What*
- *Since*
- *Due to*
- *Since*

(Middle)
Cause and effect
Vertigo = It's a neurological disorder that creates a false sensation of rotation.
Cause: Because of this feeling of rotation, many people can suffer falls.
Effect: Consequently, this condition has an important impact on the quality of life for people who suffer from it.

Week 2, Day 6 (asynchronous)

For this last day of the learning sequence, students are assigned to work in groups. Class does not meet, so students must schedule time to work together on their own. Each group is given a different disease to focus on, such as anxiety, schizophrenia, or depression. Students must complete two parts for the assignment. First, they categorize basic information on the disease using Google Jamboard. Next, they record a conversation in which they discuss the disease and compare how it is treated in their community and in a Spanish-speaking community (Figure 8.16).

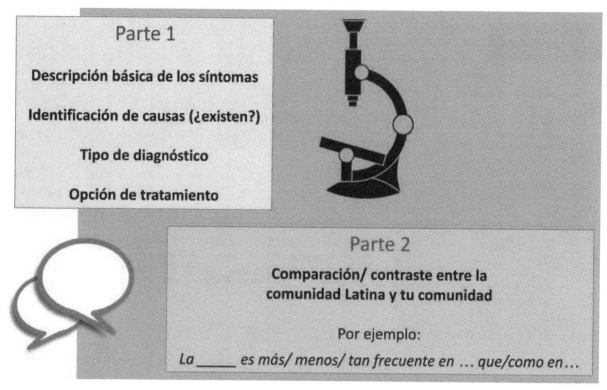

FIGURE 8.16.
Asynchronous Group Assignment

Translation
Part 1
Basic description of the symptoms
Identification of causes (do they exist?)
Diagnostic type
Treatment options

Part 2
Comparison/contrast between a Latino community and your community
For example: The ___ is more/less/as frequent in ... as in...

Reflection and Next Steps

In this chapter, we have looked at the Integrated Performance Assessment (IPA) and considered how it can be used as a framework for designing learning sequences. The IPA connects learning across the three modes: interpretive (input), interpersonal (interaction), and presentational (output). It outlines a learning sequence that begins intentionally with a strong focus on interpretive communication. Students receive significant input through the teacher's use of target language and authentic resources. The sequence then shifts to interpersonal communication after students have received sufficient input and culminates in a focus on presentational communication where students create an edited and polished product that draws from their learning during the interpretive and interpersonal phases. Alternatively, interpersonal communication may be placed as the final step in the sequence and presentational used as the middle stage. Using this framework does not mean that teachers *only* focus on one mode of communication at a time, but rather that teachers deliberately place a heavier emphasis on a particular mode to support students in moving from input to interaction. Finally, we looked at two classroom examples, one from the elementary level and one from the university level, that showed how two different teachers approached sequencing their learning.

Before moving on, take some time to reflect and assess your own practice. Consider how you are applying or would like to apply the framework discussed in this chapter.

Where are your strengths? Where would you like to grow your practice? What actions will you take to move forward? This one-point rubric is designed to help you reflect and assess your own learning sequence designs.

One-Point Rubric: Designing Learning Sequences

GLOW *Where are my strengths related to this practice?*	CRITERIA *What should I be looking for in my own teaching?*	GROW *Where do I need to grow or expand my practice?*	TAKE ACTION *What steps will I take to move my practice forward?*
	I begin learning sequences with a heavy emphasis on interpretive communication (input).		
	After providing sufficient input, I shift the focus of the learning sequence to a heavy emphasis on interpersonal communication (interaction).		
	As the culminating component of a learning sequence, I engage students in presentational communication (output).		
	Throughout the learning sequence, there is a connection whereby students use what they have learned from interpretive reading and listening activities to engage in interpersonal discussions and show their learning through a presentational product.		
	While my learning sequence may focus more heavily on one mode of communication, any given lesson will engage students in more than one mode.		
	I use a communicative learning outcome, which is shared with students. All activities used reflect steps towards attainment of the student learning outcome.		

Level Up Your Learning

- **Adair-Hauck, B., Glisan, E. W., & Troyan, F. (2013).** *Implementing integrated performance assessment.* **ACTFL.**
  If you would like to learn more about the Integrated Performance Assessment (IPA), this book provides detailed information on its history and theoretical framework, as well as specific directions for developing your own IPAs. Furthermore, numerous examples of IPAs are included in a range of languages and levels.

- **Clementi, D., & Terrill, L. (2017).** *The keys to planning: Effective curriculum, lesson, and unit design* **(2nd ed.). ACTFL.**
  To learn more about unit and lesson design, this book provides an excellent foundation along with templates and samples.

- **CLASSRoad. (n.d.) Create: Lesson plan author. Online at https://startalkcreate.org.**
  This free resource provides an online template for designing lessons for world languages. You can also search for lessons created by other teachers to use as models.

Final Thoughts

Are you ready to teach for proficiency with a focus on input and interaction? We hope that the numerous strategies, models, and real classroom examples presented in this book will equip you with the tools you need to make proficiency-based instruction a reality in your classroom. Our own experience—echoed by many who teach for proficiency—is that your students will thank you! Providing extensive target-language input and regularly engaging students in meaningful interaction transforms world language classrooms into spaces for genuine communication on topics of relevance and importance to learners. Students are more engaged in classes and are able to communicate more effectively and more fluently in the language. We wish you well on your teaching for proficiency journey!

Chapter 8 References

Adair-Hauck, B., Glisan, E. W., & Troyan, F. (2013). *Implementing integrated performance assessment.* ACTFL.

CLASSRoad. (n.d.) Create: Lesson plan author. https://startalkcreate.org

Clementi, D., & Terrill, L. (2017). *The keys to planning: Effective curriculum, lesson, and unit design* (2nd ed.). ACTFL.

National Institute of Mental Health. (n.d.) Recursos para compartir sobre la salud mental (en español). Retrieved from https://www.nimh.nih.gov/health/education-awareness/espanol/recursos-para-compartir-sobre-la-salud-mental-en-espa-ol.shtml

CATHERINE RITZ   CHRISTINA TORO

About the Authors

Catherine Ritz is a world language teacher and teacher educator. She taught French and Spanish at the middle and high school levels for many years—obtaining National Board Certification in teaching French—before becoming the director of world languages in a public school district close to Boston. Catherine is now a clinical assistant professor and program director for World Language Education and Curriculum & Teaching at the Boston University Wheelock College of Education & Human Development. Catherine serves on the Board of Directors for the Massachusetts Foreign Language Association (MaFLA), and the Northeast Conference on the Teaching of Foreign Languages (NECTFL) and on the Executive Board of the American Association of Teachers of French (AATF) as vice president. She is the author of *Leading Your World Language Program: Strategies for Design and Supervision, Even If You Don't Speak the Language!* (Routledge, 2021). Catherine is the mother of three wonderful (and bilingual) children—Adrien, Emma, and Mae—and lives with them and her husband in Massachusetts.

Christina Toro is a Spanish teacher and has taught at the high school level for 15 years in both private and public schools. Since 2012, she has been a Spanish teacher at Arlington High School in Massachusetts. Christina is an AP Reader for the Spanish Language and Culture Exam. In addition to teaching, she has presented workshops at the state, regional, and national levels. Her interests are curriculum and teaching, Colombia, virtual reality, and autism. Christina won a scholarship to participate in the 2012 U.S.-Uruguay Teacher Exchange Program sponsored by the U.S. State Department, the American Councils for International Education, and the Fulbright Commission in Uruguay. She is currently a candidate to become a National Board Certified Teacher. Christina is the mother of four Colombian-Irish children—Samuel, Alexander, Benjamin, and Kathleen—and lives with them and her husband in Massachusetts.

Appendix A.
The NCSSFL-ACTFL Can-Do Proficiency Benchmarks

NCSSFL-ACTFL CAN-DO STATEMENTS
PROFICIENCY BENCHMARKS

	NOVICE PROFICIENCY BENCHMARK	**INTERMEDIATE** PROFICIENCY BENCHMARK
COMMUNICATION		
INTERPRETIVE	*I can* identify the general topic and some basic information in both very familiar and everyday contexts by recognizing practiced or memorized words, phrases, and simple sentences in texts that are spoken, written, or signed.	*I can* understand the main idea and some pieces of information on familiar topics from sentences and series of connected sentences within texts that are spoken, written, or signed.
INTERPERSONAL	*I can* communicate in spontaneous spoken, written, or signed conversations on both very familiar and everyday topics, using a variety of practiced or memorized words, phrases, simple sentences, and questions.	*I can* participate in spontaneous spoken, written, or signed conversations on familiar topics, creating sentences and series of sentences to ask and answer a variety of questions.
PRESENTATIONAL	*I can* present information on both very familiar and everyday topics using a variety of practiced or memorized words, phrases, and simple sentences through spoken, written, or signed language.	*I can* communicate information, make presentations, and express my thoughts about familiar topics, using sentences and series of connected sentences through spoken, written, or signed language.
INTERCULTURAL COMMUNICATION		
INVESTIGATE	In my own and other cultures *I can* identify products and practices to help me understand perspectives.	In my own and other cultures *I can* make comparisons between products and practices to help me understand perspectives.
INTERACT	*I can* interact at a survival level in some familiar everyday contexts.	*I can* interact at a functional level in some familiar contexts.

NCSSFL-ACTFL CAN-DO STATEMENTS: PERFORMANCE INDICATORS FOR LANGUAGE LEARNERS © 2017

NCSSFL-ACTFL CAN-DO STATEMENTS
PROFICIENCY BENCHMARKS

ADVANCED PROFICIENCY BENCHMARK	SUPERIOR PROFICIENCY BENCHMARK	DISTINGUISHED PROFICIENCY BENCHMARK	
COMMUNICATION			
I can understand the main message and supporting details on a wide variety of familiar and general interest topics across various time frames from complex, organized texts that are spoken, written, or signed.	*I can* interpret and infer meaning from complex, academic and professional texts on a range of unfamiliar, abstract, and specialized issues that are spoken, written, or signed.	*I can* interpret and infer meaning from dense, structurally sophisticated texts on a wide range of global issues and highly abstract concepts, with deeply embedded cultural references and colloquialisms and dialects that are spoken, written, or signed.	INTERPRETIVE
I can maintain spontaneous spoken, written, or signed conversations and discussions across various time frames on familiar, as well as unfamiliar, concrete topics, using series of connected sentences and probing questions.	*I can* participate fully and effectively in spontaneous spoken, written, or signed discussions and debates on issues and ideas ranging from broad general interests to my areas of specialized expertise, including supporting arguments and exploring hypotheses.	*I can* interact, negotiate, and debate on a wide range of global issues and highly abstract concepts, fully adapting to the cultural context of the conversation, using spoken, written, or signed language.	INTERPERSONAL
I can deliver detailed and organized presentations on familiar as well as unfamiliar concrete topics, in paragraphs and using various time frames through spoken, written, or signed language.	*I can* deliver extended presentations on abstract or hypothetical issues and ideas ranging from broad general interests to my areas of specialized expertise, with precision of expression and to a wide variety of audiences, using spoken, written, or signed language.	*I can* deliver sophisticated and articulate presentations on a wide range of global issues and highly abstract concepts, fully adapting to the cultural context of the audience, using spoken, written, or signed language.	PRESENTATIONAL
INTERCULTURAL COMMUNICATION			
In my own and other cultures *I can* explain some diversity among products and practices and how it relates to perspectives.	In my own and other cultures *I can* suspend judgment while critically examining products, practices, and perspectives.	In my own and other cultures *I can* objectively evaluate products and practices and mediate perspectives.	INVESTIGATE
I can interact at a competent level in familiar and some unfamiliar contexts.	*I can* interact in complex situations to ensure a shared understanding of culture.	*I can* engage with complexity and pluricultural identities and serve as a mediator between and among cultures.	INTERACT

Appendix B. Lesson Plan Template

This lesson plan template was adapted from a STARTALK Learning Plan Template, available online at https://startalk.info/about/.

COURSE OVERVIEW	
Course Name	
Course Proficiency Target	
LESSON OVERVIEW	
Unit Theme	
Lesson Learning Outcome *I can + language function + context*	
Core Vocabulary and Forms	
Materials and Resources	
Lesson Length	

LEARNING SEQUENCE	
Focus of Learning *A brief bell-ringer to focus students' attention and begin to engage with the day's learning*	*Time:*
Preview of Learning *Reviewing the day's learning outcome and agenda*	*Time:*
Learning Episode 1	
Primetime 1 *Providing students with new input, information, or skills (often whole class)*	*Time:*
Downtime *Students work to apply new input, information, or skills (often pair/ group work)*	*Time:*

Primetime 2 *Providing students with additional input, information, or skills OR Students demonstrating their learning of new input, information, or skills (often whole class or group work)*	*Time:*
Brain Break *A 1–2 minute activity to allow students to rest and recharge*	*Time:*

Learning Episode 2
Optional: Depending on length of class, 1, 2, or 3 learning episodes may be included.

Primetime 1 *Providing students with new input, information, or skills (often whole class)*	*Time:*
Downtime *Students work to apply new input, information, or skills (often pair/group work)*	*Time:*
Primetime 2 *Providing students with additional input, information, or skills OR Students demonstrating their learning of new input, information, or skills (often whole class or group work)*	*Time:*
Check for Learning *A brief formative assessment to determine whether students have achieved the learning outcome.*	*Time:*
Celebration of Learning *Returning students' attention to the learning outcome.*	*Time:*

Check out more essential publications to add to your classroom teaching!

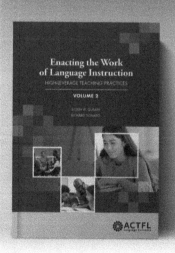

Go to: https://tinyurl.com/actflbooks